THE BIG HISTORY OF CIVILIZATIONS

Craig G. Benjamin, Ph.D.

THE
GREAT
COURSES®

PUBLISHED BY:

THE GREAT COURSES
Corporate Headquarters
4840 Westfields Boulevard, Suite 500
Chantilly, Virginia 20151-2299
Phone: 1-800-832-2412
Fax: 703-378-3819
www.thegreatcourses.com

FSC
www.fsc.org

MIX
Paper from
responsible sources
FSC® C011935

RAINFOREST ALLIANCE
CERTIFIED

CRAIG G. BENJAMIN, PH.D.

PROFESSOR OF HISTORY
GRAND VALLEY STATE
UNIVERSITY

Craig G. Benjamin is a Professor of History in the Frederik Meijer Honors College at Grand Valley State University (GVSU), where he teaches big history, East Asian civilization, ancient inner Eurasian history, and the historiography of world history to students at all levels. Professor Benjamin received his undergraduate education at the Australian National University in Canberra and Macquarie University in Sydney. In 2003, he was awarded his Ph.D. in Ancient History from Macquarie University for his dissertation on the migration of the Yuezhi, an ancient Central Asian nomadic confederation, and its impact on the establishment of the Kushan empire and the Silk Roads. In that same year, Professor Benjamin moved to the United States to take a position at GVSU in Michigan, where he has taught ever since.

Professor Benjamin is a pioneer in the teaching and research of big history, a rapidly expanding field that examines the past on the largest possible timescale, from the origins of the universe to the present and future. For the past 21 years, he has taught a university course on big history in Australia and the United States every year.

At GVSU, Professor Benjamin has received several awards for teaching, including the 2015 Glenn A. Niemeyer Outstanding Faculty Award; the 2012 Faculty of Distinction Award from Omicron Delta Kappa, a national leadership honor society; the 2009 Student Award for Faculty Excellence from the Student Senate; and the 2007 Inspirational Professor of the Year Award. In 2013, Professor Benjamin was nominated for the U.S. Professor of the Year Award, administered by the Carnegie Foundation and the Council for Advancement and Support of Education. In 2015, he was inducted as an honorary international faculty member of the Global Studies department at Moscow State University in Russia.

Professor Benjamin's primary research interest is in ancient Central Asia, specifically the relationship between the great nomadic confederations, such as the Scythians/Saka, Yuezhi, and Xiongnu, and the major civilizations of the period, including Han China and the Roman Empire.

Professor Benjamin is the author of more than 35 published scholarly papers, articles, and chapters. He is also the author or editor of several books, including *The Yuezhi: Origin, Migration and the Conquest of Northern Bactria*; *The Cambridge World History: Volume 4—A World with States, Empires, and Networks, 1200 BCE–900 CE*; and *The Routledge Handbook of Big History*. In addition, Professor Benjamin is a coauthor (with David Christian and Cynthia Stokes Brown) of the first big history textbook, *Big History: Between Nothing and Everything*.

Professor Benjamin is the immediate past president of the World History Association and the vice president of the International Big History Association, where he previously served as treasurer since the organization's inception. He is also a consultant for The College Board, a chair of the SAT* World History Subject Committee, and a cochair of the Advanced Placement World History Development Committee.

In addition to his many professional activities, Professor Benjamin has been featured in several big history programs on HISTORY and the Discovery Channel, has produced lectures and other material for the Big History Project, and has lectured for *Scientific American* and *New York Times* cruises as well as for Archaeological Tours. Before taking up an academic career, he was a professional musician and jazz educator for 25 years in Australia, playing flute and saxophone. In addition to pursuing his academic and musical interests, Professor Benjamin has spent much of his life hiking and climbing in the great mountain ranges of the world.

Professor Benjamin's other Great Course is *Foundations of Eastern Civilization*. ∎

TABLE OF CONTENTS

THE BIG HISTORY OF CIVILIZATIONS

SCOPE

What are the developments, inventions, and innovations that have forever changed civilization? And what role has the environment played in triggering these critical developments? This course provides a unique big history perspective on the rise and fall of civilizations. It explores how big historians view the rise of civilizations since the end of the last ice age, approximately 13,000 years ago. What were the geographic factors underlying the Fertile Crescent that encouraged the development of agriculture, and what did that development of agriculture mean for the civilizations located there? What factors related to land, flora, fauna, and climate more easily accommodated advancing civilizations in some areas than others, which remained more suited for hunting and gathering? This course explores the major developments in practically every aspect of civilization: the appearance of writing and communication, commerce, religion, transportation, agriculture, medicine, art, warfare, human organization, and more. Scholarly, grounded in evidence, and thoroughly thought provoking, this course offers nothing short of a new way of studying and understanding world history—and its future.

The course begins with an investigation of the history of the city of Jericho, the longest continuously settled urban space on the planet, and considers this 14,000-year history in the context of the physical environment that has sustained it. The next group of lectures (lectures 2–5) examines the big history of the human species, identifying the unique defining traits and abilities of *Homo sapiens*, before following the evolution of early human societies from the appearance of our species 250,000 years ago through the long Paleolithic era to the emergence of agriculture around 10,000 years ago. This section concludes with a discussion of the early agrarian era and how human lifeways were then transformed by the emergence of genuine power structures associated with the appearance of the first cities and states on our planet.

The heart of the course (lectures 6–31) is a sweeping consideration of the political, military, economic, cultural, and environmental history of all of the important cultures and agrarian civilizations of the ancient world, including those that appeared in Mesopotamia; Egypt; the Mediterranean region; central, South, and East Asia; sub-Saharan Africa; the Americas; Australasia; and the vast Pacific world zone. The focus is on the key developments in all of these civilizations and cultures: writing and communication, trade and commerce, religion and ideology, land and maritime transportation, innovations in agriculture and manufacturing, the evolution of science and its application to medicine, new forms of art and architecture, the continuing evolution of warfare, new mechanisms of governance and social organization (including changing ideas about gender and the role of women), and the role of the environment in continuously shaping the expansion and contraction of all these structures.

The final lectures of the course (lectures 32–36) are focused on modern civilization, from its gradual emergence through the 2ⁿᵈ millennium C.E., including the conquest of much of the world by European imperialists, to the Industrial Revolution and the intensification of human impacts on the environment that occurred during the 20ᵗʰ century. At the very end of the course, you will consider the lessons learned from this big history overview of the past and wonder how these trends and developments will play out in the future—a century from now, millennia from now, and billions of years from now to the ultimate end of the universe. This is history on the grandest scale—the big history of human civilization—and it reminds us that ultimately the future of our planet and our species is in the hands of every human alive today. ■

A TALE OF TWO ANCIENT CITIES

B ig history is an exciting way of studying the past over great spans of time so that important themes, trends, and developments reveal themselves in ways they otherwise wouldn't—yielding a deeper understanding of why events occurred as they did. In pursuit of that understanding, big history embraces all the disciplines of knowledge that humans have constructed to date and uses them as a multidisciplinary tool kit to unlock the secrets of the past. In this lecture, you will consider two ancient cities in the context of big history.

TWO ANCIENT CITIES

- The ancient city of Jericho is best known for its destruction at the hands of the Israelites, as described in the Bible's Book of Joshua. But Jericho might better be remembered for its longevity and its contributions to civilization. Archaeological evidence indicates that its site was first inhabited about 14,000 years ago—and today, you can still find a bustling community there. As far as we know, it's the oldest continually occupied city on Earth.

- In considering the roots of civilization—which can be defined as the advanced level of human social development and collective learning that could arise only once cities were established—it's instructive to compare Jericho to another ancient city, Anau.

- Anau is located in modern-day Turkmenistan across the Kopet-Dag mountains from Iran. Like Jericho, Anau is one of the world's earliest large human settlements, although it dates only to the 5th millennium B.C.E. But today it's deserted.

■ Why did Jericho endure, while Anau perished? Why did early peoples decide to settle down in these two arid environments and establish communities, and how did they sustain themselves? Answers to these questions and many more become clear through the lens of big history.

■ Jericho and Anau have a great deal to tell us about the origins and nature of civilization—and quite possibly about the future of our own.

■ When we consider civilization today, it's easy for us to take for granted something as commonplace as a city or town, because humans have been living in them for so long. But they haven't been around forever.

■ When archaeologists examine the oldest artifacts from Jericho, it's clear that it started as something closer to a temporary encampment, where the occupants stayed for extended periods of time but foraged for food in the surrounding countryside rather than growing crops to sustain themselves.

■ In fact, there was a time when all of humanity was nomadic and foraged for food—not because we lacked the intelligence to do anything else, but because the world was too cold and food was too scarce to make anything else possible.

■ For most of our first 100,000 years on Earth, the planet was beset by an ice age. Millennia of temperature fluctuations followed, but around 14,000 years ago, the planet began to enter a consistent warming phase.

■ Over the next few thousand years, this so transformed landscapes that the large grazing animals—such as mammoths, that humans had hunted for tens of thousands of years—migrated northward, clearing the way for smaller animals, such as boar, deer, and rabbit to thrive, along with new root and seed plants.

- These changes were especially notable in the Fertile Crescent, an arc of high ground that stretches north up the coast of the eastern Mediterranean, then east through the mountains of Turkey and northern Iraq, and south along the territory between Iraq and Iran.

- All across the Fertile Crescent, the change in climate encouraged the spread of small game and warmth-loving cereal grasses. Abundance was particularly great in regions where there were good supplies of water, and these locations were naturally especially attractive to wandering humans.

- Jericho was one such spot. About 8,000 years later, as our planet continued to warm, Anau became another.

JERICHO

- According to the Bible, Jericho presented quite a challenge to the Israelites when their leader, Joshua, led them to it upon their entry into the Land of Canaan. It was surrounded by huge, intimidating walls.

- However, it's the natural walls surrounding Jericho—great mountains to its east and west—that are of even greater importance in the story of this ancient city. These geological walls of Jericho gave its occupiers a significant advantage in times of military strife, well before they built new walls of their own, and help explain why nomads would have found the location appealing.

- Because of the mountains that protect it, Jericho's location was ideal for the control of trade and migration routes that pass up and down this natural valley. Throughout the city's long history, these strategic advantages have made it a coveted possession for a long series of invaders, including, according to the Bible, the Israelites.

- Another environmental factor seems to argue against establishing a settlement at Jericho's location. The Jordan River, the region's primary

Jericho, the oldest city in the world

source of freshwater, is about 43 miles away. Why would wandering peoples have chosen a spot so far from such a critical resource?

- The reason is that Jericho had ready access to its own reliable supply of water, one that enabled its residents to live comfortably even in its harsh desert environment.

- The city is located in an oasis, which is sustained by a reliable underground water supply known as the Ein as-Sultan, a spring that has not dried up during the entire 14,000-year period that various peoples have lived at Jericho.

ANAU

- About 2,500 miles northwest of Jericho, situated on an arid plain at the edge of the Karakum Desert, Anau seems today like a poor place to take up residence—neither readily defendable nor close to a good source of water.

■ Like Jericho, however, Anau was once sustained by an oasis, which in turn was fed by water that flowed down the nearby Kopet-Dag mountains. Unfortunately, it seems that Anau's residents had to search for new water repeatedly, because the source they relied on kept moving or drying up as climatic conditions in the region changed.

■ First excavated in a serious way by American archaeologist Raphael Pumpelly in 1904, the site of Anau consists of three mounds, each containing ruins from different periods: It was an agricultural settlement dating from 4500 B.C.E. through to the mid-3rd millennium, a well-planned town during the Bronze Age, and an impressive walled city during the classical period.

■ Ultimately, the site was abandoned altogether.

■ At the most basic level, it's easy to see why Jericho survived and Anau didn't: Jericho's residents had water, and Anau ran out of it. Consider also, though, the tremendous difference that the presence or absence of this basic resource made for these two cities.

■ In spite of repeated, large-scale relocations that suggest tremendous expenditures of effort, energy, and resources, the residents of Anau couldn't keep themselves or their city functioning without an adequate supply of water to meet their needs. Human will and ingenuity weren't enough to solve the problem.

■ In contrast, Jericho's supply of water was so abundant that the greatest challenge residents of the site faced seems to have been defending it. The Israelites were just one in a long series of invaders over the centuries who coveted Jericho for its precious resources and strategic location. And each people who took up occupancy there found the site hospitable.

- Jericho and Anau offer us a bracing lesson in the importance of conserving and protecting our most basic natural resources, and a worrisome reminder of how readily and predictably human conflict arises when those resources are scarce.

- But these cities reveal much more about humanity and the rise of civilization, because they also represent a tremendously important threshold in human lifeways—a transition that made a vast number of subsequent advances possible.

THE RISE OF AGRICULTURE

- The people who first settled Jericho are called the Natufians, and starting around 14,000 years ago, as the Earth's climate warmed up, they found places of natural abundance in Israel, Jordan, Lebanon, and Syria. They are called affluent foragers because, for the first time, they had access to enough resources that they could continue to live as foragers while settling down and staying in one place.

- It turns out that it wasn't only abundant water and defendability that Jericho offered the Natufians. The site and its surrounding lands also boasted rich alluvial soil and plenty of sunshine. These produced the plentiful wild plants and game with which the Natufians sustained themselves.

- Over time, however, these inviting qualities of Jericho presented the Natufians with a dilemma. The foraging lifeway that the Natufians had previously led had required near-constant migration in pursuit of food. The need for mobility and the scarcity of food had limited the size of their population. This, in turn, limited human progress.

- The evidence from Natufian settlements in the Fertile Crescent reveals, however, that once they became more sedentary and adopted a lifeway of affluent foraging, their populations began to grow.

The Big History of Civilizations

- Over time, they were forced to operate in smaller and more crowded territories, and feeding their rising numbers became more and more of a challenge. This is known as the trap of sedentism. It produced a crisis, and it appears that the crisis in turn produced a human breakthrough: the development of agriculture.

- Archaeological evidence from Jericho reveals that early farmers there somehow learned to domesticate emmer wheat and barley. And from this point forward, progress accelerates markedly.

- By 7300 B.C.E., the village the Natufians had initially established had evolved into a town that was home to 3,000 farmers living in mud-brick houses. All manner of implements have been discovered in the layers of soil from this period, including stone tools and eating vessels. By 5800 B.C.E., the residents had domesticated sheep.

- Jericho reached its most impressive size in the Middle Bronze Age, roughly the 18th and 17th centuries B.C.E., when chariot-riding elites defended the city during an age of widespread conflict across much of Palestine.

- The defenses were based on a massive stone wall, but even this was not strong enough to prevent disaster, because around 1550 B.C.E., the city of Jericho was destroyed.

- But Jericho's natural advantages ensured that it would not go uninhabited for long. It returned to such prominence that it was coveted and conquered by the Assyrians, and after them by the Babylonian king Nebuchadnezzar. During the Persian empire, Jericho served as an administrative center and was later an important agricultural center during the reign of the Hebrew king Herod.

- At Anau, about 8 millennia later, we again see natural conditions that made agriculture possible. In its oldest layers, Raphael Pumpelly discovered evidence of a planned farming settlement. A much later expedition led by archaeologist and explorer Frederik Hiebert was able to date the earliest evidence of wheat farming there to 6,500 years ago.

■ The houses were made of raw brick, and traces of paintings were discovered on the walls, along with copper ornaments and vessels with geometric designs. In subsequent layers, archaeologists found ceramics with paintings in different colors.

■ Most of the material found at Anau was manufactured within the settlement, but other artifacts had come from much farther afield, demonstrating Anau's important role in an extensive trade and exchange network extending as far as Mesopotamia and the Indus valley.

■ Iron tools were found in the later layers, demonstrating that, like Jericho, the residents of Anau eventually were able to intensify their agricultural practices over time. There is even some evidence that the residents of Anau might have developed writing, although this is ambiguous.

■ Anau struggled in the face of climate change and ultimately failed to meet the eternal challenge of human civilization: sustainability. But natural resources and human determination enabled it to rise to the level of a thriving walled city and to survive for thousands of years.

■ Together, Jericho and Anau show us how early peoples made the transition from nomadic hunting and gathering to agriculture and how agriculture led to the rise of towns and cities, where what we think of as civilization could develop.

■ But cities were not a uniform response to oases or farming. The cities that did emerge were limited to those regions that possessed enough favorable factors to sustain large communities. Rather than thinking of the emergence of cities as an inevitable outcome, we need to consider it a rare and precious occurrence.

The Big History of Civilizations

- Where such a unique collection of conditions comes together, civilization becomes capable of advancing across a threshold to a new level of complexity and possibility—one in which an entirely new range of opportunities for progress becomes available. What's especially fascinating is that, as rare as they are, we find such unique factors and thresholds throughout the history of the universe.

SUGGESTED READING

Benjamin, C. "The Little Big History of Jericho."

Kenyon, *Digging up Jericho.*

Wright, "Social Differentiation in the Early Natufian."

QUESTIONS TO CONSIDER

1. Compare the big history account to other creation stories that humans have devised. What is similar? What is different?

2. In what ways are the histories of Jericho and Anau quintessential examples of the role of the environment in human history?

THE RISE OF
HUMANITY

The appearance of humans marks a fundamental turning point in the history of our planet and all life on it—the crossing of a genuine threshold of complexity, after which nothing on earth would ever be the same again. To understand the roots, rise, and true nature of civilization, we need to understand the origins of the beings who created it: humans. And to understand our origins, we need to study the origin of humans from the perspective of big history. In this lecture, you will discover what fields such as archaeology, anthropology, paleontology, and linguistics can tell us about the origins of humanity.

THE EVOLUTION OF HUMANS
- The modern scientific explanation of the evolution of humans starts with Charles Darwin, because we are products of natural selection like all other animals. Our species fits well into the modern biological taxonomy, and our place in that taxonomy provides a sense of just how much life had to evolve before we came on the scene.

- We are multicelled organisms belonging to the super kingdom of Eukaryota (organisms with eukaryotic cells, which have a nucleus and DNA in the form of chromosomes); the kingdom of Animalia (animals, not fungi or plants); the phylum of Chordata (animals with backbones); the class of Mammalia (mammals); the order of primates (which includes lemurs and monkeys); the family of Hominidae (which includes humans, chimpanzees, and gorillas); the subfamily of Homininae (bipedal apes); the tribe of Hominini (which contains humans and our close extinct relatives); the genus of *Homo* (or "man"); and the species of *Homo sapiens* (or "wise man").

- The first hominines evolved about 7 million years ago, and there have been at least 30 or more different species, with new ones being discovered seemingly every year. But only one of these hominine species is still around today: human beings.

- Evidence gathered from different fields, including paleoarchaeology (the study of fossil bones and stone tools), primatology (the study of modern primates), and genetics (the study of genes), has allowed specialists to construct a reasonably coherent account of the history of our hominine ancestors.

- For most of the period that specialists have been investigating hominines, the most important type of evidence has been bones

Charles Darwin
(February 12, 1809–April 19, 1882)

and associated remains. Skulls and skull fragments tell us how large hominine brains were and even if there are notches in the skull where critical brain developments may have been located. And many skull fragments still have teeth in them, which can tell us a lot about what an animal ate and therefore how it lived.

■ Stone tools, found with bones or in isolation, were manufactured by all later hominines, such as *Homo habilis*, *Homo erectus*, and the Neanderthals, and these offer all kinds of clues about how these hominines thought. Like hominine teeth, microscopic studies of edges of these tools can tell us what hominines ate and how they lived.

■ Another form of evidence comes from studies of modern primates, such as orangutans and gorillas, which have the potential to tell us something about the social behaviors and abilities of our closest primates.

■ An increasingly important avenue of more recent research comes from genetics. When two species separate from each other, neutral mutations—which are changes in the noncoding DNA of a gene—accumulate in each line.

■ Because the rate of accumulation of these mutations is constant, the number of mutations can tell us how old the species is and when the two lines diverged from a common ancestor.

■ DNA evidence shows us that 98.4 percent of our genetic material is identical to that of chimps, and researchers have been able to show that it would have taken around 7 million years for such a difference to evolve.

THE ROLE OF THE ENVIRONMENT

■ These various forms of evidence tell an extraordinary story of increasing complexity: Over 7 million years of hominid evolution, our ancestors' spines became straighter, their pelvises became narrower, their brains became bigger, their arms became shorter, pairs bonded to form social and sexual relationships, communication and cooperation increased, fires got built, and hand axes got shaped.

■ Given that the role of the environment in shaping human history is one of the key themes that big history identifies, it is not surprising that all of these adaptations occurred in the context of significant global climate change.

■ Often, this change was so severe that many individuals would have died before they could make the necessary biological and social adaptations.

■ Between 6.5 and 5 million years ago, the climate became significantly cooler and drier, causing the equatorial forests in Africa to shrink and, in many cases, turn into open woodlands.

■ In this new environment, bipedalism, which is upright walking on two legs, would have become an advantage, although climate change is just one theory explaining the emergence of bipedalism. Along with bipedalism came the gradual loss of body hair to help keep cool on the savanna.

■ After the significant cooling 5 million years ago, the climate stabilized until another period of dramatic cooling began about 2.5 million years ago. This renewed climate change may have triggered the appearance of the genus *Homo*—hominines with larger brains, shorter arms, and guts and teeth adapted for eating more meat and less vegetation.

■ Early *Homo* species were still rather apelike, but *Homo habilis* is found with the earliest stone tools. The discovery of these tools led paleontologists at the time to suggest that they had discovered the first humans, but today *Homo habilis* is regarded as being closer to apes than humans.

■ By two million years ago, australopithecines and various *Homo* species were coexisting in open landscapes in larger groups. Their brains were larger, and they were using their tools to eat scavenged meat and possibly using fire to frighten off predators. The vocalizations early hominids made were probably similar to those of apes.

- Around 1.8 million years ago, the new species *Homo erectus* appeared, with decidedly more humanlike abilities. They were almost as tall as humans, and their brains were about 70 percent the size of ours. They were fully bipedal, with shorter arms because they no longer needed to climb into trees.

- *Erectus* had also evolved the three semicircular canals of the inner ear that provide balance for jumping, running, and dancing. And the pelvis had considerably narrowed and flattened, making full standing and running easier but childbirth more difficult. This meant that babies had to be born earlier, to get them out before their heads grew too large.

- These helpless babies required longer care, and mothers needed male assistance to feed infants and protect the family from predators. This, in turn, led to pair bonding between parents and the emergence of patterns of cooperation and mutual assistance.

- Evidence indicates that *Homo erectus* also used fire for cooking, and this may be one of the most significant adaptations made by our hominid ancestors. The use of fire distinguishes us from all other animals, and the social scene that developed around fires may have contributed to enhanced language and tool-making abilities.

- Fire allowed us to stay warm, venture into colder climates, ward off predators, and cook our food. Cooking enabled us to derive more calories from our food, so that we could spend less of our time hunting and eating and more of it on other activities.

- *Homo erectus*, or its close relation *Homo ergaster*, was also the first hominine to move out of the African continent, perhaps as early as 1.7 million years ago. This is another example of one of the key themes in human history: the role of the environment and climate change in necessitating migration.

- In a series of migrations probably motivated by population pressure in their African homeland, or because they were following migrating animals that they had become dependent on, *erectus* undertook extraordinary migrations that took them all the way to China by 1.6 million years ago.

- *Erectus* probably spoke a protolanguage, and those that migrated into colder environments evolved to be lighter skinned to help them synthesize enough vitamin D in environments with less sunshine.

ADAPTATION

- Hominines became more and more like us over time, but none have the creativity of our species, and natural selection still seemed to rule their behavior. In contrast, we have a significantly enhanced ability to adapt—not biologically through natural selection, but culturally and technologically, using our creativity to change the environment to suit ourselves.

- This adaptation is a product of learning, something that many other animal species can do, although learning is not as important as natural selection for most species. And even those animals that learn something well generally cannot share in any sort of detail what they have learned with other members of their species; this knowledge is lost when they die, and each individual has to start from scratch.

- A third way of adapting depends on symbolic language, and humans alone seem to have this ability. The words we use when we speak or write are symbols that can convey an extraordinary amount of information about something very concrete or something completely abstract or hypothetical. This symbolic language ability allows us to learn with other humans, and learn in detail, with precision.

- Perhaps the most important outcome of symbolic language ability is that whatever we learn as individuals can be shared, pooled, and passed on from generation to generation. It is this sharing and pooling of knowledge that explains why our species has adapted more successfully than any other large animal on earth. It has given us the ability to collaborate through collective learning, an ability that clearly marks the crossing of another threshold of complexity by our extraordinary species.

■ Although large brains appear to be crucial for the acquisition of symbolic language ability, the way the brain is organized also matters in the acquisition of language. Tiny evolutionary changes in the wiring of the brain have made all the difference, particularly the evolution of a node known as Broca's area that facilitates speech and the appearance of specialized genes that permit language.

■ Human ecological, technological, and artistic creativity explains why we alone have a history of long-term cultural change and increasing control over our environment. The source of this creativity appears to be the efficiency of human language and the fact that we can share ideas so well that they get locked within the collective memory and begin to accumulate.

■ In each human community, the available knowledge increases from generation to generation, with the result that humans can collaborate more effectively than any other animal species we know of.

SUGGESTED READING

Klein, *The Dawn of Human Culture.*

Lewin, *Human Evolution.*

Wade, *Before the Dawn.*

QUESTIONS TO CONSIDER

1. What do we know about the defining abilities, beliefs, and lifeways of our hominine ancestors? When do we see them become more humanlike?

2. What qualities make humans unique and separate us from even our closest hominid relatives?

FORAGING IN THE OLD STONE AGE

This lecture is focused on the Stone Age—more specifically, the Paleolithic era, or Old Stone Age—which lasted from roughly 200,000 to 11,000 years ago. During the Paleolithic, a period of human history in which technologies were dominated by stone tools, humans first demonstrated the remarkable abilities and characteristics that make us who we are. Two crucial large-scale themes stand out from the Paleolithic: Humans began to apply their unique collective learning ability to cope with massive global climate changes, and humans spread all around the world using new technologies they invented to adapt to a range of different environments.

CLIMATE CHANGE

- During the Paleolithic era, humans left Africa and peopled the earth, despite the ravages of the Ice Age, which, remarkably, corresponds with these great global migrations. The last ice age began about 100,000 years ago. By 90,000 years ago, humans had left Africa and were settling in Southwest Asia; by 60,000 years ago, we were living in Australia. By 35,000 years ago, in the face of bitterly cold conditions, humans were living in Siberia, and by at least 15,000 years ago, we had migrated to the Americas.

- The idea that the earth has been subject to regular cycles of cooling is a relatively recent one. In 1821, Swiss engineer Ignaz Venetz argued that glaciers had once been much larger and active at long distances from their current locations. By the early 20th century, geologists were able to accurately map the extent of Ice Age glaciation and also show that there had been many ice ages.

■ Despite extensive investigation, geologists are still unsure of what causes ice ages and the complicated cycles of freezing and warming that occur within them.

■ The best we can say is that ice ages are triggered by the dynamic interplay of several conditions, including the levels of solar energy, the distance of the earth from the sun, the changing position of the continents driven by plate tectonics, the pattern of currents in the ocean, and just the right mix of gasses in the atmosphere.

■ Some geologists argue that the last ice age has not ended and that we are simply in the midst of a warming cycle within the larger context of an ice age.

■ Humans living in the Paleolithic had to deal with at least two periods of major cooling, which means that our lifeways and belief systems evolved under ice age conditions.

■ Around 200,000 years ago, when our species first emerged, the climate was relatively mild. But from 195,000 years ago, conditions began to deteriorate as the planet entered a long glacial stage that lasted until about 123,000 years ago. Then, a second period of cooling began roughly 110,000 years ago, which lasted until the beginning of the most recent warming trend about 11,500 years ago.

■ Between 123,000 and 110,000 years ago, earth's temperatures were similar to those of today, but from around 110,000 years ago, evidence shows the onset of a long-term shift to considerably colder climates. Forests fragmented and retreated, winters grew longer and colder, and great ice sheets began to spread across the landscape in high latitudes.

■ Geologists now estimate that during this frigid period, glacial ice covered 30 percent of earth's land area, including 10 million square kilometers of North America. Even in those regions of the globe not directly affected by ice, the cold caused earth's climate to become dryer.

- Forests died out, to be replaced by dry grasslands that turned into widespread cold deserts by about 70,000 years ago. Temperatures warmed up again after 60,000 years ago.

- But around 30,000 years ago, earth was once again plunged into the grip of an intense, dry cold that reached its most extreme temperatures between 21,000 and 17,000 years ago.

- Then, around 14,000 years ago, earth experienced a rapid global warming and moistening. The ice sheets began to retreat, and the forests began to grow back.

- After a couple of thousand years of recovery, the planet was once again plunged into a new, though short-lived, glacial event known as the Younger Dryas. This may have come on over a period as brief as 100 years, before disappearing again even more quickly in just a few decades.

- Finally, from 11,500 years ago, earth became warmer and wetter, the ice sheets gradually melted, and vegetation spread over much of Afro-Eurasia.

- Geologists call the period between 9,000 and 5,000 years ago the Holocene Optimum, and it was in this period that many human communities made the transition to agriculture.

EXTENSIFICATION

- The second key development of the Paleolithic, extensification, allowed humans to spread across the planet using new techniques devised through collective learning. But there was no parallel increase in the size or density of human communities and therefore little increase in the complexity of human societies as a result of extensification.

- Correlating the dates of human migration with the chronology of climate change not only offers stunning evidence of human adaptability, but it also suggests possible explanations for these migrations.

- Recent DNA studies have suggested that a severe and long-lasting drought in Africa may have been a motivating factor. It forced humans to live in smaller and more isolated communities that were constantly threatened with extinction, so when the drought began to recede, the survivors joined forces and began to emigrate out of Africa.

- The actual route taken might have been facilitated by cold snaps that lowered sea levels and opened up land bridges, such as one across the southern straits of the Red Sea. The migrants then used collective learning to invent new technologies that allowed them to prosper in new lands, thus ensuring the survival of the entire species.

FORAGING

- Based on the available archaeological evidence, all Paleolithic human communities, wherever they were located, employed the strategy of foraging, which involves the gathering of foodstuffs and other needed materials from the environment, to survive.

- Foragers need a large territory to support themselves, so foraging populations are inevitably small; most foragers lived in small family-sized groups numbering somewhere between 10 and 50 people. These communities would split into smaller groups again to complete specialized tasks.

- Living in small groups meant that this was a do-it-yourself lifestyle. There was no government, so every task—justice, education, eating, ceremonies—had to be taken care of within the family.

- The practice of gift-giving emerged during the Paleolithic era as a mechanism for holding groups together, because it established a reciprocal relationship between members. Ceremonies were also part of communal life; contacts with neighboring groups were made at regular meetings and rituals, where gifts, information, and marriage partners were swapped.

- To modern eyes, such foraging strategies might appear primitive, but they required a great deal of ingenuity. To survive, Paleolithic humans invented sophisticated tool kits of hunting, fishing, digging, and carrying equipment. They also acquired an immensely detailed knowledge of the environment and a wide range of skills to exploit it.

BELIEF SYSTEMS

- The scarcity and ambiguous nature of evidence about Paleolithic lifeways means that anything we say about their belief systems is highly speculative.

- Studies of modern small-scale societies suggest that foragers probably thought of themselves as part of the natural world and believed that their spirits would return in the form of other animals or natural features of the landscape after they died.

- So, the first religious ideas devised by our species were shamanistic: a world full of spirits of many different kinds that humans could interact with under certain conditions. But the spirits were specific and localized, or tied to particular places, so there was no sense yet of a belief in universal divinities.

- About 15,000 rock art sites of the San Bushmen have been discovered in South Africa, the oldest dated to 70,000 years ago. San art has powerful ritual significance associated with their shamanistic religious practices.

- The shamans, often in a drug-induced altered state of consciousness, would enter the spirit world by somehow activating a supernatural force in the animals of the region and would later depict these experiences in cave paintings. Not all San art is supernatural or magical in character; much of it depicts daily life and the skills needed to cope with survival in the harsh environment.

- There is an ongoing debate among prehistorians concerning the standards of physical and mental health enjoyed by Paleolithic foragers.

San Bushmen rock
painting

Until the 1960s, the modern conception of early humans was that these
"Stone Age cavemen" lived lives that were "nasty, brutish, and short."

■ But fieldwork done in the 1960s among the San, who were at the time
   seen as a relatively pristine foraging people, caused anthropologists to
   revise this view substantially. A new conception emerged of foragers
   enjoying an almost idyllic lifeway with plenty of free time for interests
   beyond food gathering and a diet that ensured good nutritional health.

■ Since the 1980s, this view has been increasingly challenged. A new
   generation of anthropologists working in the Kalahari Desert have noted
   that the San often lived on the verge of starvation and that they did not
   choose to continue pursuing this lifeway but had no other option.

■ In addition, none of the so-called pristine societies studied by
   anthropologists had in fact been untouched by the modern world,

so their activities can't necessarily be considered accurate examples of Paleolithic lifeways.

HUMANS AND THE ENVIRONMENT

■ A very contentious aspect of the Paleolithic era is the impact of humans on the environment. The traditional view is that Paleolithic communities lived in harmony with nature, but modern evidence suggests that they had a considerable environmental impact through two habits in particular: fire-stick farming and the extermination of entire species by hunting them to extinction.

■ For tens of thousands of years, Australian aborigines set fire to huge tracts of bushland, both to drive game out for hunting and to promote the growth of new vegetation for gathering and to attract game.

■ Archaeologist Rhys Jones coined the term "fire-stick farming" in 1969 to describe this practice, which had the long-term effect of turning scrubland into grassland and suppressing the growth of certain species. In many areas, the practice dramatically impacted natural ecosystems by altering the vegetation to maximize food productivity for aboriginal communities.

■ Fire-stick farming was also practiced in parts of Eurasia, New Zealand, and North America and has been implicated in the other significant impact of Paleolithic humans on the environment: the extinction of large animal species.

■ As early humans spread across the globe, they entered continents that had no experience of earlier hominine colonization, particularly Australia and the Americas. Since the 1960s, paleontologists have amassed considerable evidence of the dramatic impact of these migrations.

■ Humans demonstrated their adaptive abilities and technological prowess by unintentionally initiating a wave of extinctions among

As early humans spread across the globe, they unintentionally initiated a wave of extinctions. The largest species, such as mammoths, were the most threatened, because they moved and reproduced very slowly.

the megafaunal inhabitants of these continents, who had no previous experience with this new predator.

■ The largest species were the most threatened, because they moved and reproduced very slowly. The mammoth, woolly rhinoceros, and giant elk disappeared in Eurasia; the prehistoric horse, elephant, giant armadillo, and sloth vanished in North America. In Australia, dozens of large marsupial species disappeared soon after the arrival of humans.

- These extinctions were destined to have a dramatic impact on the course of human history, forcing some communities to abandon foraging and take up farming and depriving others of incredibly useful animals like horses.

Suggested Reading

Brantingham, Kuhn, and Kerry, *The Early Upper Paleolithic beyond Western Europe.*

McBrearty and Brooks, "The Revolution That Wasn't."

Ristvet, *In the Beginning.*

Schick and Toth, *Making Silent Stones Speak.*

Questions to Consider

1. How did humans utilize the advantages of collective learning to migrate out of Africa and occupy every continent on earth, with the exception of Antarctica?

2. What does the evidence of archaeology and anthropology tell us about the belief systems of Paleolithic humans?

ORIGINS OF AGRICULTURE

I n this lecture, you will explore perhaps the most important revolution in the history of humanity, and even of our planet: the transition from foraging to agriculture. Anthropologists and archaeologists have struggled to answer the following three questions for more than a century: Why would humans give up foraging, a lifeway that had successfully sustained them for almost 200,000 years, and adopt agriculture? Did this happen all over the world at the same time, or did some humans in just a few places adopt farming and many others not? What has been the impact of the agricultural revolution on human lifeways and the biosphere?

THE SHIFT TO AGRICULTURE

- Around 12,000 years ago, humans were living on all of earth's continents except Antarctica. Wherever they lived, humans survived through foraging, by using collective learning to invent a range of technologies perfectly adapted to different environments, from the icy world of the Arctic to the deserts of Australia.

- Collective learning and technological innovation were going on, but the small size of human communities in the Old Stone Age, and the limited exchanges between them, meant that the pace of change had been slow for close to 200 millennia. But then something changed, and it changed quickly.

- By 11,500 years ago, new subsistence technologies were beginning to appear in certain regions of the planet—technologies that, by enabling humans to cultivate their own sources of food, over time gave humans access to more energy and resources.

- This meant that not only did human populations begin to increase globally, but in the new agricultural zones, humans were living in larger and denser concentrations in new types of communities, such as villages and towns.

- Increased densities like this were frankly impossible during the Paleolithic, because foragers needed a huge range of territory to support themselves. But farming can support many more people in the same area.

- Where agriculture was adopted, denser populations appeared and the pace of historical change began to speed up, putting humans onto a new historical pathway that led directly toward the astonishing world of complex states and civilizations.

- But where foraging remained the dominant lifeway and populations remained small and scattered, change was slower. This meant that, for the first time in human history, the pace of change began to vary from region to region.

- The transition to agriculture was thus of such profound significance that it marks the crossing of another threshold of complexity by our species—and indeed by planet earth.

- The timing of the transition was critical: Agriculture was adopted early in parts of Afro-Eurasia, much later in the Americas and the Pacific, and hardly at all in most of Australasia, and this had significant implications for the appearance of civilizations.

FORAGING VERSUS FARMING
- To understand why and where agriculture appeared when it did, let's consider how foraging and farming differ.

■ Foragers are very good at finding new sources of energy by spreading into new environmental niches, a process called extensification. In contrast, farmers largely stay in one place, so they have to find ways to extract more energy from the area of land they have available, a process called intensification.

■ Foragers live off a wide variety of animal and plant species that are products of natural selection. Farmers, on the other hand, depend on a much smaller number of species and have learned to increase their output through artificial selection.

■ Successful farming also depends on the establishment of a strong relationship among plants, animals, and the human farmer, an interaction that evolves into a form of symbiosis, or species codependence. Symbiosis is common in the natural world, where different species have evolved to rely on each other for food or protection, often becoming so dependent that they can no longer survive alone.

■ Humans have learned over the course of 11,000 years to herd and manipulate useful species, such as corn and cattle, and how to increase production of our "domesticates" to support more of our own species. Humans benefit from this symbiotic relationship, but so do our domesticated species, which we protect from predators and help reproduce, ensuring their success as a species.

■ Note, though, that the impact of this relationship has been different for each partner. Humans have changed culturally because of domestication, leading to the invention of new technologies and lifeways and the evolution of our communities from small foraging bands to complex, interdependent cities, states, and civilizations. Our domesticates have changed genetically, often evolving into an entirely new species.

THE ORIGINS OF AGRICULTURE

- It appears that the transition to agriculture was not an abrupt change; the road from gathering plants in the wild, then cultivating and finally domesticating them, was long and convoluted.

- Geneticists working on plant genomes have been crucial in unlocking the nuances of this transition, as they look for genetic evidence of physical changes in species as a product of domestication. Plant genomes show us that humans were harvesting and eating wild cereals for thousands of years before actual domestication began.

- The earliest sites and dates for actual species domestication are difficult to determine. But there is little doubt that the first successful attempt at domesticating a species was undertaken by Paleolithic foragers, and that was the domestication of the dog. The oldest actual remains of a domesticated dog have been dated to around 15,000 years ago.

- The domestication of other species by early farmers occurred gradually around the world over long time periods. This began in Southwest Asia

Successful farming depends on the establishment of a strong relationship among plants, animals, and the human farmer.

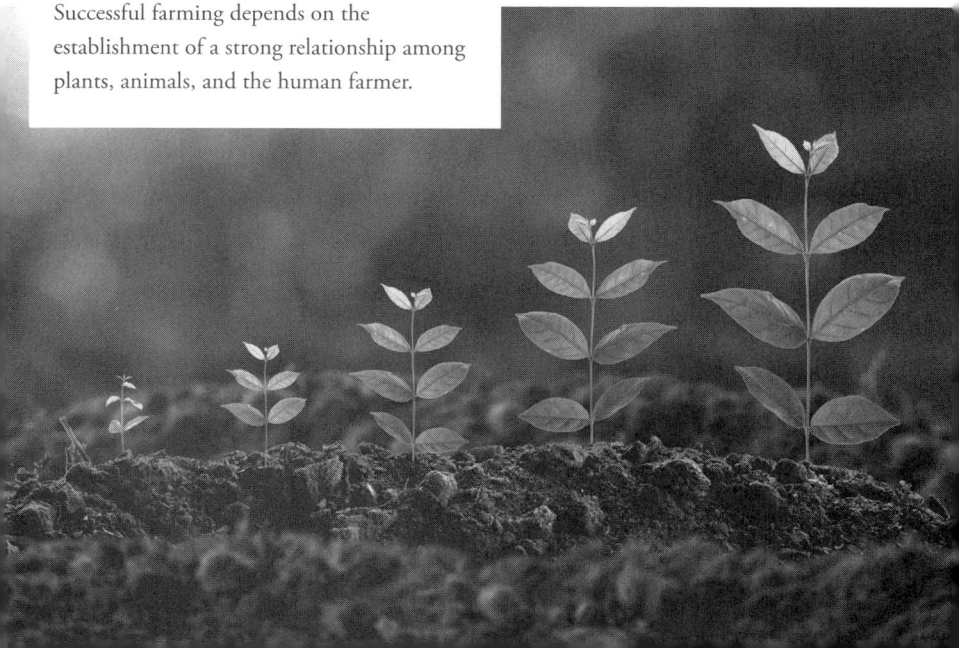

around 11,500 years ago, then in northeast Africa perhaps a thousand years later, in East Asia at least 9,000 years ago, and eventually in New Guinea, sub-Saharan Africa, South Asia, and the Americas in the millennia that followed.

- The agricultural revolution can be explained as a step-by-step process in which conscious human decision making may have played only a limited role. Critical to the "evolutionary not revolutionary" model is climate change and the emergence of environmental conditions that facilitated the transition, coupled with demographic pressure as a result of increasing population densities in some regions.

- The last cycle of the most recent ice age began around 110,000 years ago, and global temperatures plunged to their coldest level between 21,000 and 17,000 years ago. Conditions were so cold that forest disappeared and frigid tundra covered much of the planet.

- Under these conditions, foraging was the only survival strategy possible for humans, and this remained the situation until the beginning of the Holocene epoch around 11,700 years ago, when the earth experienced a rapid global warming at the end of the last ice age.

- The Holocene was not only warmer and wetter, but also more climatically stable, and as different groups experimented with domestication, they increased in size relative to foraging bands. Researcher Peter Richerson argues that this increase in group size led to intergroup competition, and this more or less forced communities to adopt farming.

- Building on the work of Richerson and other specialists, big history offers a five-step model to try to explain the origins of agriculture.
    1. Humans already had a lot of the necessary knowledge and skills for farming. For almost 200,000 years, humans had been endlessly manipulating other species and landscapes to enhance our food supply and reduce our exposure to predators. So, our foraging ancestors were already preadapted culturally to manipulate the natural environment.

2. Some animal and plant species were also essentially preadapted as potential domesticates. This means that some animals and plants had evolved in a way that made them more suitable for domestication than others. Potential animal domesticates have to meet some demanding criteria, including rapid growth, regular birth rates, a herd mentality, and a good disposition.

3. Humans in certain key regions of the globe were already adopting less nomadic lifestyles and becoming at least part-time sedentary. Sedentism began to increase in some parts of the world from about 11,000 years ago. The two main reasons for this were climate change and population pressure. As climates became warmer and wetter at the end of the last ice age, in some areas there appeared regions of natural abundance, where large numbers of humans settled, and increased sedentism eventually led to overpopulation.

4. Because of affluent foraging, population pressures resulting from sedentism and continuing migration forced human communities into smaller and smaller territories. By 13,000 Before Present, foragers were occupying a wide range of environmental niches all over the planet, and in some cases these niches could not support increased populations. These groups were forced to try to feed themselves off rapidly diminishing parcels of land, and with further migration not really an option, they found themselves caught in the "trap of sedentism."

5. Faced with increasing populations, many communities were left with few alternative survival strategies. Because of continuing climate change and the resulting lack of space, a return to a nomadic, foraging lifeway was impossible. The only viable option available for affluent foragers faced with overpopulation pressure and climate change was to intensify cultivation and adopt farming. And that's exactly what appears to have happened at sites that could support large populations.

SUGGESTED READING

Bellwood, *First Farmers.*

Diamond, *Guns, Germs, and Steel.*

Ruddiman, *Plows, Plagues, and Petroleum.*

QUESTIONS TO CONSIDER

1. Why do big historians view the transition to agriculture as perhaps the most important revolution in all of human history?

2. Does the five-step model explain the appearance of agriculture in all regions?

The Big History of Civilizations

POWER, CITIES, AND STATES

Once humans had made the transition from foraging to agriculture, the process of creating cities and states took millennia to complete, and it represents a distinctive turning point in the history of civilization. To understand why cities and states took so long to appear, you will learn what the earliest farming communities were like: How did people live, and what were their beliefs? Then, you will consider the appearance and evolution of power, a process closely tied to the appearance of the first cities and states on the planet, which marks the crossing of a major threshold of complexity by the human species.

THE EARLIEST FARMING COMMUNITIES

- During the early agrarian period, which occupied the first 5,000 of the last 10,000 years, there existed many societies based on agriculture, but there were not yet any cities or states. The earliest farming communities were essentially self-sustaining villages whose size meant it was unnecessary to adopt any complex mechanisms of government.

- Early farmers were faced with several serious constraints that limited the amount of food they could produce, particularly shortages of energy and labor, fertilizer, and water.

- Early-agrarian-era farmers practiced three basic forms of agriculture, each well adapted to specific environments: horticulture, slash-and-burn agriculture (also known as swidden), and chinampa agriculture (in Mesoamerica in particular).

- As ingenious as these early farming practices were, they were not particularly productive, so populations grew slowly. But even slow and steady population growth meant that eventually there were too many mouths to feed in a village, so families had to move on periodically and clear new land.

- Gradually over the millennia, the number of farming communities in a region increased until, by about 5,000 years ago, most people on earth were farming for a living.

- Using archaeological and genetic evidence, and also comparisons with modern but perhaps similar agrarian societies, we are able to determine how people lived in the early agrarian era. Farm life in this era was essentially sedentary. Farmers were living in permanent dwellings in villages ranging in size from a few dozen to perhaps a hundred dwellings.

- The village was these peoples' world, but the nature of this world varied depending on the resources that were available where it was located, demonstrating how the environment persistently put human ingenuity to the test.

- In the area that is today New Mexico and Colorado, for example, ancient farmers lived in stone structures built into preexisting caves in the cliffs. They created a thriving populous civilization that eventually raised towers and built complex settlements into the cliffs of Mesa Verde, one of North America's richest archaeological areas.

- By comparison, the Neolithic village of Skara Brae, dated to around 3200 B.C.E., was constructed in an entirely different environment—on the shores of a wild and windswept bay in the Orkney Islands of Britain. Because there are no caves and almost no trees there, other construction materials had to be used, particularly stone. Not only were the dwellings all made of stone, but there were stone beds, dressers, fireplaces, and utensils.

- Over the millennia, some villages grew especially large, perhaps because they had some important spiritual significance, or because they had a reliable resource like water, or because they became centers for the trade of valuable merchandise.

- Despite the size of some early settlements, there is little evidence of power structures, or even of serious social hierarchies, in any Neolithic communities. There were no states, jails, police, or armies. Although there is evidence of occasional conflict, the lack of fortifications in most villages suggest that warfare was very limited.

- Most people lived at about the same economic level, and we can tell this because the size of houses and the wealth in them does not vary much. It also appears that men and women had roughly the same amount of power and responsibility within the community. This is a noteworthy contrast from life among foraging groups, in which female children often had to be killed to manage population growth.

- Eventually, however, living in a sedentary world did change the relative positions of men and women, a major development in one of the key themes this course pursues: gender relations.

- One reason for this could be that sedentism confined women to the relative isolation of the home, where their real job was to be pregnant or rear children. This freed up the men to play at more public roles, such as cattle herding and "politics."

- For some reason, this also meant that women's jobs, such as drawing water from the well and other household chores, were eventually designated as being of lower status.

THE APPEARANCE AND EVOLUTION OF POWER

- The appearance of power that can be defined as "the concentration in the hands of a few, of substantial control over considerable human and material resources," marks another fundamental transition in human history and in the evolution of governance.

- This definition suggests that power can only emerge in a society that is producing "considerable" resources, which means that for most of human history, power was relatively unimportant.

- In Paleolithic and early Neolithic societies, there were few people and resources, so if an individual tried to obtain power, it would only have been over a few people. Most activities took place without the need for political or military leaders; matters were sorted out within and between families in these small villages.

- But from about 5,000 years ago, the archaeological record provides stunning evidence of the appearance of power structures and the first cities and states. These cities and states appeared only in specific regions within two zones of the world: Afro-Eurasia and the Americas.

- No cities or states—no power structures, appeared in Australasia— apparently because there were never enough resources available to sustain them. But in the Americas and Afro-Eurasia, the appearance of hierarchies and power structures is demonstrated through differences in the size and wealth of tombs, in the amount of possessions different households had, and in the appearance of monumental architecture.

- We have plenty of evidence of when and where powerful rulers emerged, but our understanding of why humans allowed a few people within their society to gain this sort of power is less clear.

- Anthropologists distinguish two types of power: consensual and coercive. Power based on consent is power conferred from below—from the people who willingly give power to certain individuals. Coercive power comes from above; somehow leaders gain the ability to control people and resources, by force if necessary.

- Power is actually a relationship that is both top-down and bottom-up. Both sides gain something, so it is usually supported from below, but one side gains more than the other, which means that those at the top sometimes have to use force to maintain their power.

- When we apply this principal to history, it seems that we need a two-part explanation for the origins of power in early human societies. It may be that, in the first stage, people began to need leaders for various reasons, so they were appointed from below. But in the second stage, these leaders gained sufficient control over resources to put them in a position to impose their rule from above.

- A small village can sort out its own problems and coordinate its activities face-to-face, but a village of 50 to 100 families can't do this without a chief.

- As populations and productivity continued to increase, so did the power of leaders, and we have excellent evidence to show that toward the end of the early agrarian era, farming was becoming more productive, particularly through the use of increasingly elaborate and efficient irrigation systems.

- Thousands of years ago, and still today, irrigation makes it possible to feed millions of people in arid zones where agriculture would be otherwise impossible. At the same time, humans were also learning how to better exploit their domestic animals, a process English archaeologist Andrew Sherratt termed the "secondary products revolution."

- From about 6,000 years ago, Sherratt pointed out, humans began to use their animals not just for their meat and hides, but also for the "secondary products" they yielded while still alive, such as wool, milk, blood, and traction power to haul plows, carts, and chariots. Essentially, this gave humans a more efficient way of turning grass into energy, making available new forms of traction and haulage.

- This also allowed some human communities to follow a new lifeway—that of pastoralism, or nomadic livestock herding, a lifeway that would eventually play an important role in connecting the various civilizations of ancient Eurasia together.

- But the impact within farming communities was equally profound. The advent of a plough pulled by animals significantly increased agricultural productivity because it made it possible to farm lands that were too tough to plough by hand.

- As part of this revolution, farmers also discovered the fertilizing potential of animal excrement, which allowed agriculture to spread even more widely.

- It was these innovations that allowed agricultural resources and human populations to increase enormously, culminating in the appearance of the first cities and states—and power structures with sufficient wherewithal to rule them.

CITIES AND STATES

- States are large-scale political structures that wield power based on coercion. The leaders of states—whether they are pharaohs, lugals, kings, emperors, prime ministers, or presidents—can essentially impose their will on thousands or millions of people by force.

- States became possible when the rulers of cities amassed enough wealth and power to exert their will on other cities and communities around them. The appearance of cities and states marks the crossing of a significant threshold of complexity, the transition from the early agrarian era to the long era of agrarian civilizations.

- Mesopotamia, and particularly Sumer, in Southwest Asia, is the region in which the first cities and states appeared. Mesopotamia—meaning "the land between rivers" in ancient Greek—consists of the flat lands

Mesopotamia—meaning "the land between rivers" in ancient Greek—is where agriculture first appeared.

between the great rivers of the Tigris and Euphrates. This region, at the center of the Fertile Crescent, is where agriculture first appeared.

- Archaeology shows us that after around 5,000 B.C.E., more and more villages were appearing in the arid lands of Mesopotamia. There was little rainfall here, but if farmers could obtain enough water through simple irrigation, crops grew well, and agricultural productivity gradually increased. Over time, irrigation systems became more sophisticated, leading to population growth and the appearance of large regional settlements that provided services for nearby villages—the first towns.

- Rulers also appeared in these towns, as archaeologists can tell from the appearance of large building projects.

- It was in Sumer, the delta region of the Tigris and Euphrates, that the first cities on the planet—such as Ur, Eridu, and Uruk—appeared as a product of better irrigation and productivity increases.

- With the appearance of cities, not everyone needed to be a farmer anymore (nor wanted to be, for that matter), so tradesmen and craftsmen started to appear in these early urban centers. Because they had had to depend on others for basic necessities, including food, urban populations became increasingly interdependent.

- Interdependence increased the need for organization, which required leadership. Once people agreed to be led, it was only a matter of time before ambitious individuals turned consensual into coercive power.

- This process was accelerated by climate change in Sumer, which from roughly 3500 B.C.E. became drier, necessitating the construction of larger and larger irrigation works. People were drawn to centers that had the more reliable sources of irrigation water, and by 3200 B.C.E., Sumerian towns had the densest populations in the world. Very quickly, some of these towns grew into a dozen or so independent city-states.

- All early city-states share common features: monumental architecture, taxation, more sophisticated forms of administration, writing, and large state armies. All of these developments pushed human history across a major threshold of complexity into the distinctly new era of agrarian civilizations—a period that would last for nearly 5,000 years.

SUGGESTED READING

Fernandez-Armesto, *Civilizations.*

Genet, *Humanity.*

Wolf, *Europe and the People without History.*

QUESTIONS TO CONSIDER

1. Why did some communities allow individuals to exercise power over them, and how did early forms of consensual power evolve into coercive power?

2. What political, cultural, and social features seem to appear in virtually all early city-states, and how do we explain these common features?

THE ERA OF AGRARIAN CIVILIZATIONS

T he vast era of agrarian civilizations stretches from roughly 3200 B.C.E. to around 1750 C.E., a mere 250 years ago. The era in which civilizations dominated the globe is marked by phenomenal advances in human society—as well as countless setbacks and tragedies, many inflicted by humanity itself. It's a complex story that unfolded in somewhat different ways and at different times around the world. Big history is an especially useful way of making sense of this 5,000-year period, because it brings multiple disciplines together to help us tease out large-scale trends and patterns.

TYPES OF COMMUNITIES

- Agrarian civilizations were a new type of human community, one that had never existed before. Small, family-sized communities of foragers were the only type of community that existed during the Paleolithic era, which represents 96 percent of human history. Even with the appearance of cities and states, these small foraging communities continued to survive in different parts of the world, although they have pretty well vanished today.

- As humans made the transition to agriculture, a new type of community appeared: the village. Some villages evolved into towns that required new forms of leadership to help coordinate activities.

- A third type of community is that established by the pastoralists. Because pastoralists traveled with their flocks and herds, they were normally nomadic and were mostly organized in family or tribal units.

- But sometimes, under charismatic leaders like Chinggis Khan or Attila the Hun, pastoral nomads created huge armies and organized themselves into vast communities, even empires. Still, compared with even the most extensive pastoralist communities, agrarian civilizations were on an entirely new level of complexity.

- At their most fundamental level, virtually all civilizations were rooted in cities, which are themselves incredibly interconnected and complicated. Despite the size and complexity of the cities and their urban lifeways, most people still farmed for a living, and the vast urban populations were utterly dependent on successful farming in the hinterlands.

- Agrarian civilizations were much larger and much more diverse than all previous human communities, linking hundreds of thousands, or even many millions, of farmers and pastoralists, priests and soldiers, merchants and potters, musicians and prostitutes, and rulers and scribes together into interdependent, coherent communities that shared new emergent properties.

- These new communities needed to generate much larger amounts of energy to sustain themselves. Keeping these massive, complex structures together took the efforts of millions of people, who learned to extract new forms of energy from the animals, plants, rivers, oceans, and winds provided by their environments.

DEFINING FEATURES OF AGRARIAN CIVILIZATIONS

- Let's consider the defining features of agrarian civilizations. The first, of course, is agriculture: All agrarian civilizations were based on the productivity of large numbers of farmers, and it was in towns and farming villages that most resources were generated.

- Peasant farmers, often working under powerful landlords in plantation-like conditions, provided the bulk of the foods and other produce used in the towns and cities.

- The environment played a critical and obvious role. Civilizations could only appear in geographical zones that favored large-scale farming, which meant fertile soil and ready access to water. So, it is hardly surprising that most ancient civilizations evolved in the valleys of great rivers like the Tigris and Euphrates, the Nile and Indus, and the Yangtze and Yellow Rivers.

- In spite of the centrality of farming for civilizational sustainability, the power and prestige of agrarian civilizations was firmly based in their cities, astonishing urban centers like Uruk in Mesopotamia, Chang'an in China, Pataliputra in South Asia, Tenochtitlán in Mesoamerica, and Rome in the Mediterranean Basin.

- These were places of high population density, which allowed for a myriad of specialized occupations, enhanced opportunities for collective learning, and great wealth accumulation.

- These cities were also the hubs of the coercive power structures we call states, which were ruled by elites. They contained important symbols of those power structures, such as enormous palaces, high walls, and beautiful temples to the city's gods.

- The most obvious example of the concentration of power in the hands of ruling elites and states was the creation of armies, large disciplined bodies of fighters who were used to both conquer neighbors and put down any internal rebellions.

- Every agrarian civilization also developed writing in some form, because writing allowed elites to control resources through accounting and to control ideas and behaviors through laws or religious pronouncements.

- Finally, the elites of all agrarian civilizations sustained themselves through the collection of tributes extracted from the population under the threat or reality of coercion. Tributes are essentially levies on resources—which could include goods, labor, cash, or even people—that are extracted by the state.

- In all tribute-taking societies, wealth was constantly flowing from the population at large to the elites who dominated the states. It was these energy flows that sustained the complex structures of agrarian civilizations.

- Some of these energy flows were commercial, taking the form of relatively equal exchanges of goods in markets. Whenever a peasant exchanged some wheat for some pottery, this was a form of market exchange. But tributes were much less equal. They were usually demanded by states as a matter of right but driven ultimately by the threat or reality of coercion, like modern taxes.

- Direct coercion, or at least the threat of direct coercion, was one of the main mechanisms elites used to control human behavior throughout this era, which is why virtually every agrarian civilization regarded slavery as normal. Yet even those members of the community who were technically "free" were subject to coercive pressure to ensure that they surrendered the resources used to support elite groups and the state itself.

LONG-TERM TRENDS OF THE ERA

- The first long-term trend of the era of agrarian civilizations is that, despite regular cycles of expansion and contraction within individual civilizations, on the scale of big history, we see overall a story of the relentless expansion and increasing size, power, and effectiveness of agrarian civilizations and their administrations over thousands of years.

- One way of measuring this is to think about the actual size of the geographical areas civilizations controlled as a percentage of the area of the globe under state control today, which is 100 percent. This includes the oceans, too.

■ At the beginning of the 3rd millennium B.C.E., the only agrarian civilization in the world was in Sumeri in Southwest Asia, essentially the delta region of the Tigris and Euphrates Rivers; it controlled only about 0.2 percent of the area controlled by modern states today.

■ By 4,000 years later, in circa 1000 C.E., agrarian civilizations controlled about 13 percent of the area controlled by modern states. And by 1300 C.E., the Mongol empire, the largest contiguous empire ever constructed, by itself controlled a whopping 25 percent of the area controlled by modern states.

■ This sort of geographical expansion was only possible because ruling elites got better and better at their jobs. Over time, rulers of individual city-states learned to become more skillful and more powerful until pharaohs, emperors, and kings were ruling enormous empires.

■ States also took on a wider range of functions, extracting more tribute, building larger armies, constructing roads and other infrastructure to facilitate the movement of armies and keep their empires together, and establishing law and order over large areas.

■ The second trend is the establishment of significant networks of exchange between all agrarian civilizations. By the 1st century C.E., most of Afro-Eurasia was linked by the Silk Roads—which led to increasing interconnections between civilizations and the establishment of vast transregional networks—into one huge zone of "collective learning," exchanging ideas, goods, people, technologies, and religions. The more interconnections there existed between different communities, the more knowledge accumulated, the more collective learning flourished, and the faster the pace of change.

■ A third trend is the increasing complexity and interdependence of social relations. Wherever we look during the era of agrarian civilizations, we see more rigid, hierarchical social structures being established, and these hierarchies were explicitly supported by secular and religious law codes.

- Bound up with this is the embedding of patriarchal structures in virtually all agrarian civilizations as a means of regulating gender relations, also clearly articulated and justified in state and religious law.

- Despite this trend toward expansion, the increasing trans-regional connections, and the more complex social interactions, when viewed on the scale of big history, the era of agrarian civilizations is actually characterized by its generally slow pace of change, certainly when we compare this to the pace of change in our modern era.

- However, compared to the eras of human history that preceded it, the early agrarian and Paleolithic, significant growth did occur during the era of agrarian civilizations, encouraged by innovation, trade, and the increased power of the state.

BARRIERS TO GROWTH

- There were also significant barriers to growth during the era of agrarian civilizations. The most significant barrier as the essentially militaristic, tribute-taking nature of most elites in premodern states.

- Ruling elites in agrarian civilizations were generally opposed to commercial and agricultural innovation, because investing resources in raising productivity and seeking out new trading opportunities was generally seen as unreliable, unrewarding, and politically useless. Governments survived by extracting tributes, and they were hostile to traders and stifled their activity.

- The business of government in the era of agrarian civilizations was waging war, looking after the interests of their own elite groups, and constructing monumental architecture. With expenditures like these, most ruling elites who wanted to increase their resources were forced to tackle the problem of growth through warfare.

■ Growth became a zero-sum game that necessitated taking what others had produced, rather than trying to increase productivity within the state. This helps explain the almost constant warfare and attempts at expansion through the conquest of one's neighbors that characterize the era.

■ Another barrier to growth was the fact that all ancient cities were unhealthy places with limited sanitation and large numbers of people crowded together, and this acted as a check on population growth. Diseases flourished because there were few means of removing sewage, and the drinking water and air were polluted. Premodern cities kept growing only because of migrations from the country, not because of internal population growth.

■ Military expeditions and the gradual expansion of trade between agrarian civilizations were also sources of disease. The result of these health and disease barriers was that the pace of population growth and innovation were both constantly being checked, which meant that innovation could rarely keep up with what population growth there was.

■ The led to another, more basic but crucial factor that limited population growth during the era of agrarian civilizations: the lack of food. With slow growth in agricultural output, because there was little technological innovation in the sector, populations were subject to periodic famines. The result was long-term cyclical patterns of population growth and decline.

■ These patterns were first highlighted in the work of English academic Thomas Malthus, who argued that, contrary to the then-prevailing view that society is always improving, historically population growth has always been checked by famine and disease. The cycles that Malthus detected affected not only population levels, but all aspects of society.

SUGGESTED READING

Benjamin, ed., *The Cambridge World History.*

Stearns, et al, *Documents in World History.*

Weisner-Hanks, *Gender in History.*

QUESTIONS TO CONSIDER

1. What are the defining features of all agrarian civilizations, and what key trends within these agrarian civilizations become clear when viewing them through the lens of big history?

2. Using specific examples, explain how Malthusian cycles help historians make sense of the decline and fall of civilizations over almost 5,000 years of human history.

INNOVATIONS OF MESOPOTAMIA

S ometime around 2750 B.C.E., a semilegendary king called Gilgamesh was ruling the Sumerian city of Uruk. Gilgamesh is the central figure in the first great piece of literature produced by humanity, the *Epic of Gilgamesh*, originally a series of oral tales that were written down somewhere between 2500 and 2000 B.C.E. Gilgamesh is a quintessential example of the rulers who emerged in the first city-states and civilizations in history, which began to appear soon after 3200 B.C.E. in Sumer, in the delta region of Mesopotamia, an area that is now part of the modern nation of Iraq.

THE SUMERIANS

- The great achievement of the Sumerians was that they were the first to construct an orderly, prosperous civilization that functioned very well, despite the lack of any precedents. The Sumerian model of governance then spread north along the Tigris and Euphrates valleys, west to the Mediterranean coast, and south into Egypt.

- Within a few centuries, much of Southwest Asia and northeast Africa found itself under the control of strong, coercive leaders like Gilgamesh who used their self-proclaimed relationship with the gods, exaggerated superhuman strength and courage, and perceived wisdom to guide and protect their communities.

- But midway through the *Epic of Gilgamesh*, the heroic king discovers that even he cannot escape death, the fate of every mortal being. It is the epic's exploration of this theme that gives us some deeper insight into the interests and concerns of the people who dwelt in the first civilizations.

■ Even as they organized themselves into successful societies, the fear of failure and death continued to haunt the Sumerians, as it has done to varying degrees for every society that has followed them, including all the nations of the world today.

■ Civilizations can be tremendously powerful, creative, and productive, but they always have vulnerabilities—and history demonstrates that, eventually, something brings them down.

SOCIAL ORGANIZATION

■ During the first period of Mesopotamian civilization—essentially the millennium between 3000 and 2000 B.C.E.—most of the population of Sumer was living in a dozen or so large cities like Uruk.

■ The population of these cities was made up of both native residents and of various alien Semitic-speaking groups that had migrated into the region, attracted by Sumerian agricultural riches. By circa 3000 B.C.E., the population of the region may have numbered as many as 100,000, by far the largest concentration of humans thus far seen in world history.

■ The term "Semitic" refers to a largely Middle Eastern family of languages spoken by some 250 million people today. By far the most widely spoken Semitic language today is Arabic, followed by Aramaic and Hebrew. Genetic analysis suggests that Semitic peoples share a common ancestry, despite important differences and contributions from other groups.

■ The proto-Semitic peoples probably originated in the Arabian Peninsula, and it was their migrations out of Arabia into Mesopotamia that added significant numbers to the population of Sumer.

- The cities occupied by Mesopotamian and Semitic-speaking peoples included many that, like Uruk, were later named in the Judeo-Christian Old Testament. Some of them are Eridu, Ur, Uruk, Nippur, Babylon, and Kish.

- These ancient cities utterly dominated their surroundings. The most powerful entities in their region, they were constantly drawing in ideas, goods, innovations, people, and energy, thus directly stimulating collective learning.

- It was in cities like Uruk, with their gleaming ramparts and rich surrounding farmlands, that humanity carried out its first political experiments to try to solve the problems of large-scale social organization.

- These experiments have left an excellent archaeological record that we can use to understand the early evolution of power and hierarchies in agrarian civilizations.

- The first form of government in these cities was a carryover from the way that earlier and much smaller human communities had been ruled—by assemblies of leading male citizens "elected" because of their seniority or status.

- However, during political, economic, or environmental times of crisis, the assemblies temporarily gave up their power to individuals who wielded absolute authority until the crisis had passed. It seems that eventually in each city, some of these individual rulers were able to usurp the authority of the assemblies and establish themselves as monarchs, called *lugals*, the Sumerian term for king.

- Even though the *lugals* had absolute power in theory, they still needed to rule in cooperation with local nobles in practice—nobles who functioned as military leaders upon whom the *lugals* depended. This arrangement is a feature of the *Epic of Gilgamesh*; and like Gilgamesh, the other *lugals*

A Sumerian artifact

and nobles of the Sumerian city-states had sufficient power to impose their will on hundreds of thousands, and later millions, of humans.

- The reliance of the *lugals* on military leaders is evidence that warfare had become endemic in Sumer by the 3rd millennium B.C.E., a situation that has barely changed all over the world during the subsequent 5,000 years.

- Constant warfare is another of the key features of all agrarian civilizations, warfare that usually arose over access to land and other precious resources, such as water. Evidence suggests that some form of warfare was probably present in Sumer even before 4000 B.C.E., before the appearance of the city-states.

- The constant military conflict in the region evidently served as justification for *lugals* and military leaders to increase their landholdings and domination of political life. These leaders then used their lucrative agricultural lands to finance the acquisition of military forces that could be deployed in support of the *lugal* when necessary.

■ At the beginning of the 3rd millennium, the *lugals* ruled over their own individual city-states only. But by as early as 2800 B.C.E., we have evidence of attempts by the rulers of the city of Kish to use their militaries to extend their rule over other regional cities.

■ Such attempts to create an empire came to a head during the reign of Sargon of Akkad, a city not far from Kish and Babylon, although it has never been discovered by archaeologists. A brilliant warrior and talented administrator, Sargon established the world's first empire. He spent much of his reign traveling from city to city with his army to reinforce his power through his physical presence.

■ But maintaining a huge army was expensive, so in addition to collecting vast amounts of tribute from his increasingly resentful subjects, he also monopolized all the high-value trade in the region, particularly in natural resources. Sargon was so successful that he and several generations of successors were able to maintain an empire that embraced almost all of Mesopotamia.

■ However, an imposing, charismatic leader like Sargon is almost inevitably followed by rulers of lesser ability, and gradually the empire collapsed around 2150 B.C.E. because of rebellion in the captive city-states and invasion by powerful nomadic peoples.

■ Climate change might also have played a role. Ever since the waning of the last ice age, Mesopotamia had become increasingly dryer and warmer. There is evidence that a devastating dry episode occurred in northeastern Syria around 2250 B.C.E. If this dry spell was felt widely throughout Sumer, it would undoubtedly have contributed to lower crop yields and social unrest in the city-states of the region.

ADVANCES IN SUMERIAN SOCIETY

■ Archaeologists and historians have been able to construct an understanding of how Sumerian cities and other communities were organized socially during the 3rd millennium B.C.E. The existence of kings, military aristocracies, and assemblies of nobility all indicate that a clearly delineated and hierarchical social structure had emerged early in Sumerian history.

■ The elite class consisted of powerful kings and a military, along with an increasingly influential group of priests associated with the great ziggurat temples that lay at the heart of all Sumerian cities. Both secular and religious elites owned huge tracts of land in the form of agricultural estates and workshops that were worked by both free and enslaved labor.

■ Lower down in the social hierarchy were subsistence farmers, and at the bottom were slaves. These were war captives, criminals, or heavily indebted citizens, who accounted for up to 50 percent of the population in some cities.

■ Women in agricultural societies were increasingly assigned to the activities of rearing children and housekeeping, and that trend intensified in Sumerian society. Women were now largely confined to the home and denied any significant public role, and their daily work was further devalued in status.

■ Sumerian society was thus patriarchal in nature, with public and private authority vested in the hands of men, who controlled both their families and all facets of public life. Yet some women were able to carve out other roles in the first cities, as scribes, priestesses, midwives, textile workers, shopkeepers, and even very occasionally as advisers to kings and governments.

■ But in the millennium that followed, all Mesopotamian states progressively tightened their control over women through the codification of more rigidly patriarchal secular and religious laws and by enforcing new social customs that spread throughout West and central Asia.

- Occupying a stratum somewhere between the elites and the farmers and slaves, a middle class also emerged during the early Mesopotamian period, as specialized labor and crafts became more important in the increasingly diverse economies of the region's city-states.

- It was in this atmosphere of intense craft specialization that Sumerian craftsmen made stunning advances in technology—advances that drove humanity across new thresholds of complexity.

- One example was bronze metallurgy, a discovery that some unknown metal workers made around 4000 B.C.E. after alloying copper with tin. The invention of bronze had an immediate impact on military affairs, as swords, spears, axes, shields, and armor could now be made from this strong and durable alloy, rather than wood and stone. Mesopotamian farmers also began to use bronze tools and plows, which increased agricultural production and thus also human populations.

- Another stunning invention that has been attributed to Sumerian craftsmen is the wheel, although it may actually have been invented simultaneously in Sumer, the Caucasus, and eastern Europe. The wheel had a dramatic impact on trade because it increased the volume of resources that could be hauled and made it easier to transport them over longer distances. The wheel rapidly spread throughout Eurasia and became a standard means of overland transportation.

- Living along the banks of two great rivers, Sumerians also made great advances in shipbuilding. By around 3500 B.C.E., Sumerian boatbuilders had constructed ships that were capable of leaving the rivers and venturing out into the Persian Gulf, the body of ocean into which the Tigris and Euphrates Rivers drain. A great motivation for these bold journeys was trade.

- Despite the extraordinary historical significance of bronze, the wheel, and maritime technology, perhaps the most important Sumerian invention was writing.

- The first writing appeared in Sumer around 3200 B.C.E.—not as a way of expressing humanity's deepest beliefs and yearnings, but for purposes of accounting. It began as a simple pictorial system used to record animals, agricultural products, and trade goods that were donated, or paid as tribute, to temple and civic authorities.

- And yet, over the course of a few centuries, it blossomed into a sophisticated and flexible system capable of producing a literary masterpiece like the *Epic of Gilgamesh*—and a tool for collective learning that has made possible most of the subsequent achievements of civilization.

A stunning invention that has been attributed to Sumerian craftsmen is the wheel, which had a dramatic impact on trade because it increased the volume of resources that could be hauled and made it easier to transport them over longer distances.

SUGGESTED READING

George, trans, *The Epic of Gilgamesh.*

Leick, *Mesopotamia.*

van de Mieroop, *A History of the Ancient Near East.*

QUESTIONS TO CONSIDER

1. What mechanisms of governance did early Sumerian rulers use to construct and maintain the first agrarian civilizations in world history?

2. What does the *Epic of Gilgamesh* tell us about Sumerian daily life and religious beliefs?

THE DOWNFALL OF SUMER

T he key drivers of civilizational contraction—ineffective leadership, resentment of imperial rule, and climate change—reoccurred time and time again over the course of the early history of civilization. Imperial leaders struggled to find ways to maintain effective control over vast regions, and large populations of often restive peoples demanded freedom and self-rule, often during times of environmental stress.

THE ELAMITES

- In Mesopotamia, after the collapse of the Akkadian empire, order was eventually restored by the *lugals* of one of the newly independent cities, the ancient city of Ur, which reestablished centralized administration in Sumer and in Sargon's old homeland of Akkad to the north.

- During this so-called neo-Sumerian period, the status of the *lugals* was further enhanced by the memory of the success of Sargon, Akkad's first imperial ruler, in that the reigning *lugal* was now regarded not just as a semidivine leader, but as an actual living god.

- With a divine *lugal* in power in Ur, the other city-states became part of a confederacy under the leadership of that *lugal* and were directly administered by governors appointed by the authorities in Ur.

- This arrangement lasted for the next 150 years, but sometime around 2000 B.C.E., invasions by Elamite peoples effectively destroyed the power of the Sumerian *lugals* and ended this chapter of Sumerian self-government.

- The Elamites came from the high country to the east of Sumeria, in what is today southwestern Iran. Their culture was destined to have a major influence on the great Achaemenid Persian empire that would emerge 1,500 years later.

- Following the Elamite invasion, the formerly orderly society of the Sumerians was fragmented and chaotic for almost the next two centuries.

- Some local city rulers were able to hold onto their power and pass sometimes impressive pieces of social legislation, but there were also periods of ineffective government in all the cities of the region.

- Although defeated militarily and politically by the Elamites, however, the sophisticated cultural achievements of the Sumerians were destined to powerfully influence all subsequent civilizations that established themselves in the region.

KING HAMMURABI

- In the early 18th century B.C.E., a group of Semitic-speaking Amorites gained power in the city of Babylon, restoring order and paving the way for the reign of one of the most extraordinary rulers in all of world history, King Hammurabi.

- Hammurabi ruled Babylon from 1792 to 1750 B.C.E., and during that period of more than two decades, his political and military power expanded until he had built a substantial empire that would last until about 1600 B.C.E., and that included most of Mesopotamia.

- Hammurabi maintained his empire in part by promulgating one of the first written law codes in human history, a law code that proved enormously influential.

- As an imperial ruler, Hammurabi was aware of, and able to learn from, his imperial predecessors. For example, he improved Sargon's administrative techniques by establishing a centralized bureaucracy and regular system of taxation. Through these measures, Hammurabi established an imperial administration that was more efficient and more predictable.

■ Despite his reputation as a very able administrator, King Hammurabi is most famous for his code of 300 laws, which he claimed in a prologue were aimed at protecting the poor from exploitation by the wealthy. Hammurabi borrowed liberally from earlier Sumerian precedents in codifying these laws.

■ These are not the first laws we are aware of in world history; that honor belongs to the code of Ur-Nammu, written about four centuries earlier. But the code of Hammurabi is undoubtedly the most systematic, comprehensive, and influential of all the codes produced in Mesopotamia during the 3rd and 2nd millennia B.C.E., and their promulgation marks the crossing of another threshold in political administration.

■ There are strong claims for equal treatment under Hammurabi's laws, but at the same time, the punishments differ considerably depending on the class or status of those involved. The laws explicitly recognize men as heads of their households. Some of the laws seem particularly harsh on women, but other laws seem to offer genuine protection for women.

■ The codification of laws was not the only extraordinary contribution King Hammurabi made to world history. During his reign, the Babylonians also made great advances in mathematics, and a thousand years later, the classical Greeks were tremendously impressed by Babylonian achievements in geometry.

■ Babylonian religious beliefs, probably expressing preexisting Sumerian views, explicitly stated that immortality is exclusively reserved for the gods. There was no concept of an afterlife as a reward for good behavior in Sumerian or Babylonian belief systems, a view that probably contributed to a pervasive sense of futility and pessimism that seems to characterize Mesopotamian society and ideology more broadly.

- Overall, the efforts by Hammurabi and his successors to administer the large imperial state of Babylonia were successful—further evidence that by getting better at their jobs, rulers and elites facilitated the expansion of early agrarian civilizations. But the downside of that success was that Mesopotamia became even more attractive to outsiders.

THE HITTITES

- After a few centuries of effective rule, the Babylonians crumbled in the face of invasions by a new group of militarized invaders, the Hittites, who in 1595 B.C.E. came sweeping from the north down the great river valleys of the Tigris and Euphrates, valleys that acted as virtual highways into the Mesopotamian heartland.

- The Hittites spoke the oldest known example of a family of languages: the Indo-European languages. The various branches of the family can be located over a great geographical area stretching from the Atlantic to central Asia but can all be traced back to an original prototype.

Hittite statue

Today, the Indo-European family includes an estimated 443 different languages and dialects spoken by roughly 50 percent of the people on the planet.

■ At its peak in the 14th century B.C.E., the Hittite empire included much of Syria, Mesopotamia, and Anatolia, which is modern Turkey. Despite the fact that they were clearly successful conquerors, the Hittites, like the Elamites, were in turn heavily influenced by the complex and sophisticated cultural and social innovations that the Sumerians had created over the preceding 2,000 years.

■ The key reasons for Hittite military dominance were their use of the chariot (the first time this war machine had been seen in world history) and also their skill as iron workers. The Hittites are the first people known to have manufactured and used iron weapons and tools, a metallurgical revolution that marks the crossing of another threshold of complexity by our species.

■ With their success, western Eurasia moved out of the Bronze Age and into the Iron Age sometime around 1300 B.C.E. as Hittite iron metallurgy spread throughout Anatolia and Mesopotamia. This rapid diffusion was partly because iron ore deposits are relatively abundant and much cheaper than copper and tin, the ingredients of bronze. Also, iron is much stronger than bronze.

■ Despite their sophisticated military innovations and their adoption of many Mesopotamian administrative techniques, the Hittites rarely had a unified political structure, and the kings often fought with their nobles, which effectively limited the power of the monarchy.

■ But when they did present a united front, their powerful army was able to conquer much of West Asia in a series of expansionary campaigns. Sometime around 1200 B.C.E., mysterious and dramatic changes began to occur throughout much of southwest Asia.

- Climate data shows that a severe drought in the eastern Mediterranean region came to a climax just around that time, at the end of a significant warming period. The deteriorating climate and potential subsistence crisis it engendered forced major population movements among many different peoples of the region. These movements, essentially forced and often violent migrations, were so severe and disruptive that this chaotic period is described by historians as a dark age.

- The chaotic migrations and invasions of the period meant that many organized sedentary ruling elites were displaced and many were states weakened, including Egypt, Mycenaean Greece, and the Hittite hegemony in Mesopotamia.

THE ASSYRIANS

- The Hittite empire collapsed around 1200 B.C.E., presenting an opportunity for another ambitious people. The next chapter in the history of civilization in southwest Asia was written by the Assyrians, a Semitic people who during the 19th century B.C.E. had created their own small but militarily powerful state in the upper Tigris River valley.

- The Assyrians used their military, which, like that of the Hittites, was based on the devastating effectiveness of horse-drawn chariots, to gradually extend their domain until they had created their own substantial empire.

- The first cities and states that had appeared in the Sumerian delta almost 2,000 years before now found themselves once again acting as small cogs in an enormous imperial machine that stretched from the Persian Gulf to the Mediterranean Sea.

- By the 8th century, the Assyrians were, along with the Egyptians, one of the two great powers of western Afro-Eurasia. The great Assyrian king Assurbanipal (who ruled from 668 to 627 B.C.E.) presided over a realm that included all of Mesopotamia, Syria, Palestine, parts of Anatolia, and most of Egypt.

Ancient relief of an Assyrian god

- Assyrian success was built on a powerful and intimidating army, in which troops were organized into standardized units under the command of professional officers, who were appointed to their commands because of their skill and bravery, rather than the nobility of their birth. The Assyrians used chariots brilliantly, placing archers on them so that they became fast-moving firing platforms.

- Defeated peoples and their cities and states were ruthlessly ruled through strong centralized bureaucratic administration. But despite their military prowess, like the Elamites and Hittites before them, the Assyrians were captivated by sophisticated Mesopotamian cultural inventions, including Hammurabi's laws and Sumer's superb literature.

- Assurbanipal's successors could not sustain an empire as large as the one that he had controlled however, because, despite the precedents established by Sargon and Hammurabi in maintaining smaller empires, political leaders had still not learned the necessary techniques for sustaining much larger imperial structures.

■ Given their ruthless tactics, Assyrian rule was extremely unpopular, and rebellions were almost constant. During the 7th century B.C.E., these revolts, along with internal disunity, significantly weakened the Assyrians. In 612 B.C.E., the Assyrian capital of Nineveh was destroyed by Medes and the Chaldeans, and the Assyrian empire, the largest the world had seen, crumbled quickly.

KING NEBUCHADNEZZAR

■ In the aftermath, the city-state of Babylon, one of the original dozen cities of Sumer, enjoyed a final, glorious half century of independence under King Nebuchadnezzar between 605 and 562 B.C.E.

■ Nebuchadnezzar turned Babylon into one of the wonders of the ancient world. Its massive walls were purportedly wide enough to turn a chariot on; the city covered more than 2,000 acres and featured 1,179 different temples. The king's famous hanging gardens spilled from terraces built one above the other behind the city's walls.

■ Nebuchadnezzar's 43-year reign marked the end of Mesopotamian self-rule forever. After his death in 562 B.C.E., his kingdom, and indeed all of Mesopotamia, was reduced to playing a small role in a series of much larger agrarian civilizations.

■ These civilizations were destined to be ruled by extraordinarily powerful rulers who mastered the technique of managing huge populations and vast transregional empires. But the methods worked out in Mesopotamia, of building and managing cities and states and organizing their people into productive social structures, deeply influenced all subsequent Afro-Eurasian civilizations.

SUGGESTED READING

Bryce, *The Kingdom of the Hittites.*

Nemet-Nejat, *Daily Life in Ancient Mesopotamia.*

Schmandt-Besserat, *How Writing Came About.*

QUESTIONS TO CONSIDER

1. What were some of the key cultural and political innovations of the Babylonian king Hammurabi, and why were these so influential on subsequent invaders who possessed much stronger militaries?

2. What evidence does ancient Mesopotamia provide of the problem of long-term environmental sustainability? Are there lessons to be drawn from this in the 21st century?

EGYPT: DIVINE RULE IN THE BLACK LAND

T he brief reign of the Egyptian boy-king Pharaoh Tutankhamen was anomalous in many ways. However, it was also profoundly representative of the very nature of agrarian civilizations. In this lecture, you will learn about the reign of King Tut as the course begins its investigation of the extraordinary civilization of the ancient Egyptians.

KING TUTANKHAMEN

■ Tutankhamen's father was the controversial Pharaoh Akhenaten, whose radical religious views led to political chaos in the Egyptian state. Upon his father's death, King Tut ascended to the throne at the tender age of 9, and then ruled for about 10 years between 1332 and 1323 B.C.E.

■ In the third year of his reign, probably on the advice of his powerful advisor Ay, Tutankhamen reversed the religious policy of his father. He restored the ancient and powerful god Amon to the position of supremacy that he had held before Akhenaten's reign.

■ To reinforce this return to pre-Akhenaten religious orthodoxy, Pharaoh Tutankhamen began the construction of new temples dedicated to Amon at Thebes and Karnak.

■ In foreign policy, the boy-king's administration was also remarkably active: It restored diplomatic relations with the Mitanni, a powerful imperial state then in control of much of modern Syria, and this freed up the resources needed to wage military campaigns far to the south, against the Nubians.

- These initiatives suggest a very promising reign for Pharaoh Tutankhamen. But the young ruler was also dealing with serious health problems, most of which stemmed from the fact that he was a product of inbreeding between his father and his father's sister.

- With Pharaoh Tutankhamen's death at age 19 in 1323 B.C.E., his royal lineage—that of the Thutmosid family—came to an end. After Tut's death, his advisor Ay seized the throne, to be succeeded in turn by the usurper Horemheb.

- Horemheb was succeeded by Ramses I, who had served as Horemheb's co-regent and who established Egypt's 19th dynasty. He was to become one of the most powerful pharaohs.

Tutankhamen's funerary mask

SUCCESSFUL AGRICULTURE: THE NILE RIVER

- Tutankhamen, despite his numerous debilitating health problems and brief reign, is actually a quintessential example of the absolute, semidivine rulers who were presiding over vast states and civilizations all over Eurasia by the 14th century B.C.E.

- These rulers owed their power and prestige to the administrative templates established by their regional predecessors, by Sargon of Akkad, by Hammurabi of Ur, and by the many great pharaohs of Egypt that had preceded Tutankhamen.

- In every region of Eurasia where leaders like this were flourishing during the 14th century B.C.E.—Mesopotamia, Egypt, the Mediterranean, the Indus valley, East Asia—these rulers and their elite class owed their wealth and success to farming.

- The reason why the Egyptian state was able to achieve such heights of military power, and to create such great wealth, is successful agriculture. This in turn was dependent on the exploitation of the particular environmental circumstances these states were located in.

- If the environment had not favored successful agriculture, and if local farmers had not been able to exploit these conditions, the great civilizations of the ancient world would never have appeared or been able to sustain themselves.

- As was the case in Mesopotamia, river valley–based irrigation agriculture explains the success, prosperity, and longevity of Egyptian civilization. At the heart of Egyptian civilization was the Nile, which created a valley that was—and still is—rich with alluvial soils and provided water for irrigation.

- The predictable annual flooding of the Nile sustained Egyptian civilization for millennia. Archaeology shows us that by 5000 B.C.E., the beginning of the so-called Predynastic period, farmers had learned to plant their crops in the floodplain in late summer, after the recession of the annual flood. The crops matured during the cooler months of the year and were then harvested late in the winter or early in the spring.

- The system worked so well that substantial agricultural resources were accumulated, leading to increased populations that gathered together in villages along the river valley, all of them practicing intensive irrigation agriculture.

- By 4000 B.C.E., there were many such villages along the Nile's shores, stretching hundreds of miles. As had been the case in Mesopotamia, denser concentrations of people increased the need for formal organization, and in what is today Sudan, several small farming communities evolved into independent kingdoms.

- This led inevitably to competition between the kingdoms, and as a result, some became larger and more powerful, such as Ta-Seti, a Nubian kingdom that flourished between 3400 and 3200 B.C.E. and that extended its rule down into the Nile Valley of Upper Egypt.

- Tradition, somewhat substantiated by historical evidence, suggests that unified rule came to Egypt later in the 4th millennium as a result of the efforts of a semilegendary conqueror named either Menes or Narmer.

- By circa 3100, Menes had succeeded in uniting all of Upper Egypt (the upper or southern Nile Valley), after which he began to incorporate all the villages of Lower Egypt (the delta region) into an expansive state.

- To facilitate this, he founded the first city of Egyptian civilization, Memphis, near modern Cairo, strategically located at the junction of Upper and Lower Egypt. Memphis became the political and cultural center of early Egypt, and Menes and his successors were eventually able to unite all the territory between the Nile delta and the first cataract into a single, powerful kingdom.

FROM THE OLD KINGDOM TO THE NEW KINGDOM

- During the next period in Egyptian history, known as the Old Kingdom and lasting between 2686 and 2180 B.C.E., rulers of the 3rd through 6th dynasties established order and stable administration throughout Egypt.

- These powerful Old Kingdom rulers saw themselves as both divine and human, and they adopted the name "pharaoh," meaning "great house." To finance their administrations, the pharaohs took ownership of enormous royal estates and used these agricultural resources to support a bevy of advisors, priests, scribes, artisans, and merchants.

- The early pharaohs associated themselves with Horus, the sky god, and often chose to be depicted with the image of a falcon or hawk, the symbol of Horus. Later pharaohs saw themselves as offspring of the more powerful sun god Amon, and the idea emerged that after his death the pharaoh would merge with Amon.

- The pharaohs were also depicted in monumental sculpture as enormous figures towering over their people, projecting the strength and awesome power needed to protect the Egyptians and their lands through their domestic and foreign policies.

- Toward the end of the 6th dynasty, Old Kingdom prosperity came to an end, partly because the enormous cost of building the pyramid tombs exhausted the state treasury and also because the power of the king was increasingly challenged by regional rulers, who eventually succeeded in fragmenting the state.

- The environment also played a role, because a 50-year-long severe drought after 2200 B.C.E. disrupted the Nile floods, leading to famine and social unrest.

- During the so-called First Intermediate period that followed the collapse of the Old Kingdom, civil war raged in Egypt, and power was divided among regional rulers. Stability was restored by the rulers of the 11th and 12th dynasties around 2030 B.C.E., which marks the beginning of the Middle Kingdom.

- During the reign of the 12th-dynasty warrior-king Senusret III, the Egyptian military was once again very active in Nubia, where a series of forts were built to try to retain control. But the 12th dynasty came to an end with the death of Queen Sobek-neferu; she left no heirs and her reign was succeeded by the much weaker 13th dynasty.

- Late in the 13th dynasty, much of northern Egypt was conquered by a group of mysterious invaders known as the Hyksos. This conquest marks the end of the Middle Kingdom and the beginning of the Second Intermediate period. The Hyksos had a number of military advantages over the Egyptians, including the chariot, bronze weapons, battle-axes, and composite bows.

- The Hyksos eventually formed their own 15th dynasty, but Upper Egyptian rulers of the 17th and 18th dynasties adopted Hyksos military technologies and waged a series of campaigns to drive the foreigners out.

- Working from Thebes and later Memphis, Egyptian leaders gradually pushed the Hyksos out of the Nile delta, and by the mid-16th century, Egyptians had regained their independence and founded a powerful new state, the New Kingdom, which would last from 1550 to 1150 B.C.E.

- During the New Kingdom, Egyptian experiments in managing a huge and wealthy state reached their zenith. For half a millennium, Egypt was an imperial power and tribute flowed in from all over western Eurasia and North Africa.

PHARAOH AMENHOTEP III

- The empire reached its peak of wealth and power during the four-decades-long reign of Pharaoh Amenhotep III, between 1386 and 1349 B.C.E.

- It was during the reign of Amenhotep IV, the son and successor of Amenhotep III and the father of Tutankhamen, that the Egyptian state was weakened by a power struggle between the king and the priests of the sun god Amon.

- Amenhotep IV caused chaos within the religious hierarchy of Egypt, particularly the powerful priesthood of Amon, by changing his name to Akhenaton to demonstrate his personal loyalty to an alternative sun god, named Aton. Akhenaton's "conversion" to the worship of Aton was followed by great religious conflict and civil unrest, and during that turbulent time, much of the Egyptian empire was lost.

- But Akhenaton's son Tutankhamen restored order to the state during his reign, and the priests of Amon destroyed the temples and public inscriptions dedicated to Aton.

- After King Tut's death, an ambitious army commander named Horemheb usurped the throne. Childless late in his reign, Horemheb appointed as crown prince an army friend, Ramses, and Ramses attempted to regain control of Syria and Palestine. His efforts led to conflict with the Hittites, who had invaded Mesopotamia and large regions of the eastern Mediterranean.

- The climax of these attempts to rebuild the Egyptian empire occurred during the reign of Ramses II, also known as Ramses the Great. He did succeed in regaining control of Palestine but was unable to drive the Hittites from Syria. In the end, the two sides signed a peace treaty.

- Rameses II's long reign was Egypt's last era of national grandeur. After his death, royal authority was lost to the priests of Amon in Thebes, who established their own dynasty to rule Upper Egypt in the Third Intermediate period, from 1070 to 332 B.C.E.

- The once-mighty Egyptian state fragmented, and merchant princes established their own dynasties in the delta. Libyans invaded from the west and also established their own dynasty. In 760, Egypt was

Rameses II at Luxor
Temple in Egypt

conquered by its old foes and trading partners, the Nubians—specifically, the rulers of the powerful Nubian Kush Kingdom.

■ King Kashta of Kush founded his own dynasty that ruled Egypt for a century, before the Assyrians, who had seized control of Mesopotamia, invaded Egypt and drove out the Kushites.

■ Egyptian prestige was briefly revived during the 26th dynasty between 663 and 525 B.C.E. But Egypt, like much of western and central Eurasia, was conquered by the Persians in 525, and then conquered again by Alexander of Macedon in 332.

■ For the next 2,000 years, Egypt was relegated to the status of a province in a series of powerful empires, beginning with the Romans. Egypt would not regain independence again until the advent of Gamal Abdel Nasser in the mid-20th century. The great age of Egyptian civilization, and of all-powerful semidivine pharaohs like the boy-king Tutankhamen, was over.

SUGGESTED READING

Kemp, *Ancient Egypt.*

Roehrig, Dreyfus, and Keller, eds., *Hatshepsut.*

Welsby, *The Kingdom of Kush.*

QUESTIONS TO CONSIDER

1. How does the brief life of a relatively inconsequential ruler like Tutankhamen help nonetheless quintessentially exemplify the era of agrarian civilizations?

2. What role did the environment of Egypt play in generating the incredible wealth of Egyptian civilization?

SOCIETY AND CULTURE OF EGYPT

This lecture will explore some of the fascinating social, economic, and cultural achievements of the Egyptians, with a focus on the main cities of the Egyptians and on the social hierarchies and relationships that emerged in those cities. You will consider the flourishing trade that developed between Egypt and its many regional commercial partners, as an early example of the exchange networks that were so important in ultimately tying agrarian civilizations to one another. You will also consider two aspects of Egyptian civilization that remain enormously interesting today: its rich hieroglyphic writing system and its complex polytheistic religion.

URBAN LIFE

- In several respects, urban life in ancient Egypt's agrarian society mirrors that of Mesopotamia. Just as in Mesopotamia, successful farming in Egypt led to the emergence of dense populations along the Nile valley, and these populations evolved into a complex, interconnected society with a wide range of social roles, professional positions, and economic opportunities. Social hierarchies emerged in both civilizations, as they did in all ancient societies.

- Also, as in Mesopotamia, a river valley was an essential element in the development of cities in Egypt. Not only did the Nile make agriculture possible, as did the Tigris and Euphrates in Mesopotamia, but the Nile valley also functioned as a natural highway that connected much of eastern and central Africa to the Mediterranean. This in turn facilitated high levels of trade and cultural exchange throughout the region.

- However, the nature of urban life in Egypt differed from life in Mesopotamia. Successful farming, and population and resource increases, led to the appearance of enormous cities in Mesopotamia. The cities of Egypt were nowhere near as large, nor as prominent, as those in Mesopotamia.

- The reason is tied closely to the environment of the Nile valley.

- Throughout the thousands of years that Egyptian civilization flourished, the great majority of Egyptians remained living in villages spread along the valley—villages that used the Nile River and simple irrigation systems to water their fields and also to trade surplus foods and goods up and down the valley.

- Egyptian farmers, with ready access to rich alluvial soil and irrigation water, did not need to cluster together in vast cities, where powerful administrations took on the responsibility of constructing and managing huge state-run irrigation systems.

- In addition, because the Egyptians—with their divine pharaoh and centralized, unified administration, along with their relative geographical isolation—were never as troubled by interstate warfare or regular invasion as were the Mesopotamians, they did not need to build the walls and defensive structures that were a necessary feature of Sumerian cities.

- While ancient Egyptian civilization did construct some impressive cities, and decorated them with huge monuments of deep symbolic power, it was nevertheless much less urbanized than virtually all other ancient civilizations.

GREAT EGYPTIAN CITIES

- The semilegendary founder of the Egyptian state, Menes, sometimes also called Namur, created a unified Egypt by bringing together separate kingdoms around 3000 B.C.E. Menes is also recognized by historians as the probable founder of the first city in Egypt, Memphis, which he had constructed as a convenient and strategic site for his capital, right at the midpoint between Upper and Lower Egypt, about 15 miles south of modern Cairo.

- Memphis was an important city during the 500-year-long Old Kingdom period. Memphis remained important throughout the centuries of Persian, Hellenistic, and Roman control of Egypt, but thereafter the city was ransacked by Christian and Islamic rulers and was largely abandoned by the 7th century C.E.

- Another Egyptian city of great symbolic power was Thebes, built on both banks of the Nile about 420 miles south of Cairo. Thebes contains some of the most iconic religious and burial sites in all of Egypt's long history. The city reached its peak of splendor and power in the 18th dynasty, when pharaohs constructed great palaces, while the bustling city streets were full of foreign traders and citizens from all walks of life.

- During the religiously troubled reign of Akhenaton, the city fell on hard times and was abandoned by the court. But Akhenaton's son Tutankhamen restored the city and its centrality. Thebes declined again late in the 2nd millennium but had revived sufficiently by the 7th century B.C.E. But after being sacked by the Assyrians around 663 B.C.E., the city dwindled and was a more-or-less abandoned tourist attraction for the Romans by the 1st century B.C.E.

- Another fascinating Egyptian city is Heliopolis, which was founded around 2900 B.C.E. but now lies about 50 to 60 feet below a suburb of Cairo. Heliopolis became the headquarters for the worship of the sun god Re and also a major cultural center that reached the height of its influence during the New Kingdom.

- Like the cities of Mesopotamia, all of these Egyptian cities were centers of considerable resource accumulation, and this led inevitably to the appearance within them of social hierarchies based on wealth.

- A series of well-defined classes emerged, with slaves and peasants on the bottom, religious and political elites on top, and an urban middle class of artisans and merchants in between. Within this middle class, pottery, textile weaving, woodworking, leather working, stonecutting, and masonry all became distinct trades.

- But here is another significant difference between Mesopotamia and Egypt: Although the city-states of the Tigris and Euphrates valleys were often ruled by individual kings and their elites, and sometimes by imperial conquerors like Sargon, in Egypt the entire state was almost always under the control of a single, all-powerful, centralized ruler.

- This meant that there was little room for a land-owning nobility with personal armies in Egypt, so it was the priesthoods and scribal administrators that formed the upper social strata, below the pharaoh.

- And because many of these bureaucratic positions were open to different classes, it was theoretically possible for members of the middle class to work their way into positions of high social status through their administrative talents, something that was less common in Mesopotamian society.

MEN AND WOMEN

- A clear similarity between Egyptian and Mesopotamian societies is that both built patriarchal societies that vested authority over public and private affairs in men. Yet this also provides another important difference: Women in Egypt appear to have had more rights than women in Mesopotamia, and considerably more than Greek and Roman women would enjoy millennia later.

- Some Egyptian women became scribes; others worked as priestesses, musicians, dancers, and artisans. Many royal wives had great influence.

- Egyptian women also enjoyed greater legal protections than in almost any other ancient society. They could manage, own, and sell private property; institute legal settlements before the courts; free their slaves; and adopt children.

■ Egypt was always a patriarchal society in which men held public and private power. But quite exceptionally in the era of ancient civilizations, not only did women enjoy unusual protection in law, but they were also able, at various times, to rule the state as pharaohs in their own right.

TRADE

■ The wealth that Egyptian society had available, thanks largely to its agricultural prowess, also enabled it to engage in trade, and not only in agricultural products. Artisans and craftsmen of the Nile valley employed an ever-expanding range of technologies, many of them borrowed from Mesopotamia.

■ Some of these technologies seem to have taken a surprisingly long time to diffuse from West Asia, a delay that we can only attribute to the relative geographic isolation of Egypt.

■ Bronze metallurgy, for example, eventually made its way from Mesopotamia into Egypt and Nubia, allowing the Egyptians to also cross that important threshold of complexity by moving from stone to metal tools and weapons.

■ But although bronze production was flourishing in Mesopotamia from as early as 3000 B.C.E., its use in Egypt only became widespread around 1700, after the Hyksos invaders used bronze weapons to take control of Lower Egypt.

■ After the Hyksos were expelled, the armies of Thutmose and other pharaohs used up-to-date bronze weapons to conquer neighboring lands, but the metal was expensive to manufacture, so its use was closely monitored by royal workshops.

■ It wasn't until centuries later, sometime after 1000 B.C.E., that serious iron production began in the Nile valley. The Hittites had developed smelting techniques in Anatolia around 1300 B.C.E., but it also appears to have emerged independently in some regions of Africa that had particularly plentiful supplies of iron ores.

■ Along with these developments in metallurgy, Nile merchants and craftsmen also worked to continuously devise more efficient means of transportation, another development that had a significant impact on trade.

■ Egyptians were traveling up and down the Nile in boats well before 3500 B.C.E. The Nile flows south to north, which meant that these boats could easily ride the currents in that direction, except where the river's cataracts created an obstruction. Because the winds generally blow from the north, boats could almost as easily sail back up the river.

■ These developments in river-transportation technologies led eventually to the establishment of long-distance trade networks that linked the Nile to the wider world. This Egyptian trade, with multiple commercial partners in the Mediterranean and sub-Saharan Africa, facilitated widespread cultural exchange and interaction throughout the region.

WRITING

■ Closely associated with trade, and with keeping state and commercial records, was the development of writing in Egypt, a common threshold invention of virtually every agrarian civilization.

■ Writing first appeared in Egypt around 3200 B.C.E., possibly borrowed from Mesopotamia. The earliest script was pictographic, but the Egyptians soon began to add symbols representing sounds and ideas, facilitating more sophisticated written communication and collective learning.

Egyptian papyrus

- This writing system came to be known as hieroglyphic, because it appeared especially prominently on temples. The hot, dry climate of Egypt also preserved for thousands of years many papyrus rolls, which contain written administrative and commercial records as well as literature.

- The importance of writing and record keeping meant that formal education and literacy became well rewarded in Egyptian society.

RELIGION
- As with all ancient civilizations, religion was central to the lives of the Egyptian people, who believed that their gods played an active role in human affairs. Over time, the Egyptians came to worship hundreds of gods and goddesses, so on any given day, people would be sacrificing to

their household gods for health and well-being, and also worshipping a range of local and regional gods.

- It was the early Old Kingdom pharaohs who elevated their own gods and religious centers to the level of state gods. All of the most important gods had their own temples and priesthoods, and the temples owned vast properties that supported their often huge priesthoods.

- The Egyptian belief in the possibility of resurrection marks a particularly significant difference between the two first great civilizations of Mesopotamia and Egypt.

- The Mesopotamians believed, as epitomized by King Gilgamesh, that death brought an end to human existence; they appear to have had no concept of an afterlife. The Egyptians, in contrast, believed that death was a transition to a new existence.

- It is this belief in immortality that underlies the practice of mummification. And it was an incredibly old belief, dating from the early stages of the Old Kingdom, when it was already believed that through mummification ruling elites could be resurrected.

SUGGESTED READING

Foster, *Ancient Egyptian Literature*.

Hawass, *Silent Images*.

James, *Pharaoh's People*.

QUESTIONS TO CONSIDER

1. Why would women in ancient Egypt have had more rights and power than women in Mesopotamia?

2. Is it valid to argue that ancient Egyptians were essentially more optimistic than ancient Mesopotamian peoples, and if so, to what extent did the environmental context of both civilizations contribute to this?

EARLY MEDITERRANEAN CIVILIZATIONS

I n this lecture, you will explore four smaller cultures of the ancient Mediterranean whose influence on subsequent history has been surprisingly profound, given their relative lack of political power. None of them was a military match for such great imperial civilizations as the Egyptians or Hittites, but each of them was destined to leave their mark on the Mediterranean and indeed the wider world for different reasons. And none of them would have existed or developed as they did had it not been for the chance creation of the Mediterranean itself.

THE CREATION OF THE MEDITERRANEAN

- The Mediterranean was central to life in some of the world's most ancient civilizations and to the trade in goods that linked those civilizations to one another. But 5.5 million years ago, the Mediterranean basin was an almost completely dry expanse of land, lying at elevations of between one to two miles below sea level.

- The basin had been formed by the collision between the African and Eurasian plates in the Early Jurassic period, and it was completely sealed off from the Atlantic Ocean by a ridge of high mountains that connected Spain and Morocco, ancient mountains that essentially joined Europe with Africa.

- Then, around 5.3 million years ago, a tectonic subsidence in the seafloor caused that mountain range to collapse, and water from the Atlantic began to pour through the breach. It quickly became a catastrophic flood, discharging 100 million cubic meters of Atlantic water per second down the slopes into the low-lying Mediterranean basin at speeds of about 100 kilometers per hour, leaving scars on the seabed that are still visible today.

- This Zanclean flood, as it is known to geologists, tore open a great gash in the earth that became the Straits of Gibraltar, and in less than two years, it created the Mediterranean Sea, which today contains about 4 million cubic kilometers of water.

- So, the Mediterranean was no longer landlocked; it was, and is, connected by the narrow Straits of Gibraltar to the Atlantic Ocean in the west and by the even narrower Hellespont and Dardanelles waterways to the Black Sea in the east.

- The coastline of this sea in the middle of the earth is almost 29,000 miles long, and it is on this extensive littoral that a range of human communities found themselves—at various times incorporated into expansive agrarian civilizations, but at other times enjoying their independence.

THE PHOENICIANS

- Around 1200 B.C.E., both the Hittite kingdom in Mesopotamia and the New Kingdom in Egypt had entered a period of decline, allowing for smaller groups to assert their independence. Significant among these were the Semitic-speaking Phoenicians, descendants of Canaanite peoples who had dwelt along the shore of the eastern Mediterranean for centuries.

- Their ancestors probably migrated out of the Arabian Peninsula to the coast around 3000 B.C.E.; once resettled, they organized themselves into a confederation of independent city-states along the coast of modern Lebanon, Syria, and Israel.

■ Many of their settlements have persisted to the present day, including Tyre, Sidon, and Beirut, and these larger cities had considerable influence over smaller settlements—particularly Tyre, which by the 10th century B.C.E. dominated much of southern Phoenicia.

■ The Phoenicians were always more interested in trade than empire building, however, so even the largest Phoenician city-states often found themselves political subjects of larger regional powers.

■ But despite not ever being particularly numerous or powerful, Phoenician influence on the Mediterranean basin was strong because of their well-developed trade networks and their supreme skill as shipbuilders and mariners.

■ As successful as they were as traders, the Phoenicians had an even greater influence on subsequent world history because of the alphabetic writing system they devised. Adapting Egyptian hieroglyphs through a series of experiments, Phoenician scribes eventually devised an alphabetic system consisting of 22 letters, each one a consonant. The spread of the alphabet increased literacy levels throughout the eastern Mediterranean.

■ The Phoenicians contributed to a broader historical development, one that continued into the early modern era—namely, the dynamism of small commercial states. The Phoenicians established a series of purely commercial city-states that were similar in nature to the subsequent ancient Greek *poleis* and also much later to the great trading cities of the Indian Ocean, even the Italian city-states of the early modern era.

■ Eventually, many of these geographically small states with limited resources became politically and militarily powerful enough to challenge and even defeat the vast tributary civilizations, with profound ramifications for the modern world.

THE HEBREWS

■ Another example of a small, militarily inconsequential society that was nonetheless destined to play a major role in world history is that of the Hebrews. Despite being minor players in the history of the ancient world, the Hebrews laid the foundations for three of the great world religions: Judaism, Christianity, and Islam.

■ The only source for much of the history of the Hebrews is what Jews call the Tanakh, essentially the Old Testament of the Judeo-Christian Bible, and this makes it difficult to provide a definitive chronology for their political history.

■ The term "Hebrew" refers to all who were speakers of ancient Hebrew, a Semitic language related to that spoken by the Canaanites, the ancestors of the Phoenicians. The ancestors of the Hebrews were probably pastoral nomads who inhabited lands between Mesopotamia and Egypt during the 3rd millennium B.C.E.

■ As Mesopotamian civilization prospered, some Hebrews settled in the great cities of the region. As they migrated, the Hebrews appear to have taken with them a number of elements of Sumerian culture, including Hammurabi's codes of law and many of the fascinating stories from the *Epic of Gilgamesh*. These elements can be found woven into the Old Testament.

■ While internal divisions and conflicts with other peoples always limited the Hebrews' political and military power, their increasingly distinctive religious beliefs came to have tremendous historical influence.

■ The early Hebrews, living in the cities of Sumeria, had venerated many of the Mesopotamian gods, and they also believed that nature spirits dwelt in trees, rocks, and mountains.

■ Yet the Hebrew patriarch Abraham, who would come to play a crucial role in both Christian and Islamic tradition, and later Moses, who is said to have led the exodus out of Egypt, explicitly embraced monotheism.

They believed that there was only one god, called Yahweh, who was a supremely powerful deity and the creator of the world.

- Even in the midst of the Persian, Hellenistic, and Roman empires, small Jewish states were able to maintain their distinctive religious and cultural identity, based on their perceived special relationship with Yaweh and the teachings of the Torah. And that was how their beliefs survived to have such a substantial influence on the world, both in themselves and through Christianity and Islam.

THE MINOANS

- To the west of Israel, on the islands and mainland of the Aegean Sea, another group of mariners were carving out their own cultural space in the region even before Abraham is thought to have led his family out of Mesopotamia.

- These were the Minoans, named after their legendary founder King Minos, and they established themselves on the island of Crete before gradually spreading to other islands in the Aegean, the coast of ancient Turkey, and mainland Greece.

- Minoan culture was influenced by trade with Egypt and West Asia, facilitated by the central location of Crete. For 750 years between 2200 and 1450, Crete was a major center of Mediterranean commerce. Minoan merchants used advanced sailing craft of Phoenician design to became actively engaged in long-range trade all across the Mediterranean.

- The Minoan state was governed by rulers who used both Egyptian hieroglyphics and also a script known as Linear A to keep records.

- Historians have long characterized the Minoan political structure as monarchial, but more recently scholars have started to question whether there was ever a single male king of the Minoans.

Ruins of the palace of Knossos in Crete

■ Elite Minoan women appear to have enjoyed relative freedom and equality. Minoan religion also appears to have been focused on female divinities, and women played the lead role as officials at religious ceremonies.

■ After 1700 B.C.E., Minoan society experienced a series of natural disasters, as plate tectonic movements under the Mediterranean Sea triggered earthquakes and volcanic eruptions. The Minoans rebuilt their palaces to include the latest technology, but after 1450, the wealth of their civilization attracted a series of invaders.

■ By 1100, Crete had fallen under foreign control, yet Minoan maritime skill, colonization, and building traditions went on to profoundly influence the inhabitants of nearby mainland Greece, including new groups of Indo-European–speaking nomads who had settled there during the previous millennium.

- These migrants mingled with earlier farming cultures and settled in fortified citadels at places like Athens and Mycenae, from which this new culture derives its name: the Mycenaeans.

THE MYCENAEANS

- Although they were influenced by Minoan culture, the Mycenaeans were essentially militarized sea raiders. They built massive stone fortresses throughout the southern parts of the Greek peninsula that offered protection and thus attracted settlers who built agricultural settlements around them.

- Most of the Mycenaean population were tenant farmers who lived in villages but recognized the masters of the fortresses as their leaders, a militarized nobility that was in turn under the control of a king, who lived in the nearby palace.

Mycenaean palace ruins

- The king, who possessed large estates and may have been seen as semidivine, appointed individuals to powerful administrative positions. Below the noble and administrative classes were laborers who worked in agriculture or in textile or metal production. There is no evidence of a merchant class, suggesting that the elites probably used their monopoly control of trade to further strengthen their power and wealth.

- After they became aware of Minoan culture, Mycenaean women adopted some elements of Minoan fashion. But Mycenaean society was decidedly more patriarchal than Minoan.

- The Mycenaeans adopted a form of Minoan Linear A writing, but they developed it further into a syllabic script known as Linear B, essentially an early form of Greek.

- The Mycenaeans also adopted the Minoan practice of colonization and established commercial settlements in Turkey, Sicily, and southern Italy.

- Perhaps to eliminate a commercial rival, in about 1250 B.C.E., the Mycenaeans launched a hostile expedition to the city of Troy on the coast of modern Turkey. The Trojan War was part of a much broader period of chaos in the region, and it coincided with invasions of the Mycenaean homeland by mysterious foreign mariners wielding iron weapons.

- Between 1150 and 800 B.C.E., a period sometimes termed the Greek Dark Ages, chaos reigned throughout the eastern Mediterranean. This turbulence may have been related to the climate change and migrations that roiled southwest Asia starting in 1200 B.C.E.

- Invasions and civil unrest made it impossible to maintain stable government or productive agriculture. Mycenaean palaces fell into ruin and population declined sharply as settlements were abandoned, and both Linear A and B writing disappeared.

- But in the wake of social conflict and military chaos, new civilization eventually emerged in the eastern Mediterranean: Hellenic Civilization.

Greece has been known as Hellas since ancient times, and its innovations in philosophy, the sciences, the arts, and government continue to exert a powerful influence on the world today.

■ Many of those innovations were grounded in the achievements of the Phoenicians, Hebrews, Minoans, and Mycenaeans—small but immensely influential players in history.

SUGGESTED READING

Casson, *The Ancient Mariners.*

Finkelstein and Silberman, *The Bible Unearthed.*

QUESTIONS TO CONSIDER
1. In what ways can smaller states with little political or military power nonetheless have a profound impact on world history?

2. How do historians explain the chaos that engulfed the eastern Mediterranean region between the 11th and 8th centuries B.C.E.?

MYSTERIES OF THE INDUS VALLEY

J ust as agrarian civilizations were flourishing in Mesopotamia and Egypt, and smaller states such as the Phoenicians, Minoans, and Mycenaeans were active in the Mediterranean basin, a new civilization was also emerging in South Asia. For you to better understand the early history of South Asian civilization, this lecture will return to one of the key themes of the course and consider the environmental and cultural context in which this civilization unfolded.

GREATER INDIA

- The geographical entity known as Greater India, which includes the modern nations of India, Pakistan, Bangladesh, and Sri Lanka, is shaped like a diamond jutting southward into the Indian Ocean.

- The northern regions are hemmed in by the highest mountain ranges on earth, including the mighty Himalayas and Karakoram Range that geographically separate the subcontinent from the rest of Asia and that have, to a certain extent, helped protect the Indus valley and India from invaders.

- These formidable ranges are intersected by only a small number of viable passes, across which a long series of migrating peoples, armies, traders, merchants, and travelers came to explore, influence, and shape South Asian history.

- Along with the northern mountain ranges and their passes, the history of Greater India has also been strongly influenced by two other distinct geographical features.

- To the south of the Himalayan foothills is the Indo-Gangetic Plain, sometimes also called Hindustan, which stretches from the Indus valley in the west to the Bay of Bengal in the east. This enormous plain contains two of the most important river systems in the world, those of the Indus and Ganges. The great fertility of the Indo-Gangetic Plain sustained all of the great civilizations of ancient South Asia.

- The Indus valley, which is created by rivers that begin high in the Hindu Kush and Himalayas, consists of a rich upper alluvial plain called the Punjab and a drier lower Indus region called Sind. As with the river valleys of Mesopotamia and the Nile, the Punjab floodplain of the Indus River consisted of rich agricultural land bounded by highlands, desert, and ocean.

- The Indus River also carries huge quantities of silt that are eventually deposited lower down the valley; today a series of dams has tamed the Indus, but for most of history, it was subject to regular, often devastating floods.

- The climate of Greater India is varied, but of particular importance to the way human history unfolded here are the monsoon winds. The southwest summer monsoon, which blows up from the Indian and Arabian Seas and deposits substantial amounts of water on the continent, is the most productive wet season on the planet and is responsible for 80 percent of all the rainfall in India. Most of this rain falls in the summer and autumn, often torrentially, brought in by winds from the Arabian Sea.

- The monsoon process is essentially reversed in winter, when much dryer northeast monsoon winds blow down from the arid heart of central Asia, creating an extensive dry season over much of the subcontinent.

- These wind systems have had huge ramifications for South Asian history, affecting not only patterns of agriculture and settlement, but also the region's long and vital role in trans–Indian Ocean maritime trade.

- The broad cultural context of South Asia is also fascinating; the region is essentially home to two quite distinct language and ethnic groups. Indo-European–speaking peoples generally dwell in the north, the descendants of Indo-Aryan migrants who arrived in India during the 2nd millennium B.C.E. These northern Indo-Aryan peoples include the Kashmiri, Gujarati, Punjabi, and Hindi cultures and languages.

- Much of the south of Greater India is occupied by Dravidian peoples, descendants of the original occupants of India who were pushed south by the Indo-Aryan migrants. They include the Tamil, Kannada, Teluga, and Malayalam cultures and languages, which are still spoken widely in the south today.

- Despite this pronounced linguistic and ethnic division, the eventual adoption of the Hindu religion culturally unified most of India, in the same way that Christianity tended to unify culturally and ethnically distinct peoples in Europe in the centuries following the disintegration of the Roman Empire.

THE INDUS VALLEY CIVILIZATION

- Humans were living in South Asia during the Paleolithic era, and like all human communities during that long period, they survived by pursuing foraging lifeways.

- By 7000 B.C.E., the transition to agriculture had begun. As was the case in the river valleys of Mesopotamia and Egypt, successful agriculture resulted in increased populations and the emergence of towns, cities, and eventually complex states.

- The earliest complex urban society we are aware of in South Asia, and one of the most intriguing agrarian civilizations of the ancient world, is known to historians today as the Harappan or Indus valley civilization. Its establishment might have been caused by the response of local farmers to climate change.

- Evidence indicates that a period of increasing aridity during the 4th millennium perhaps forced people to move from the highlands down to the river valleys for survival, just as people in Mesopotamia and Egypt also did. The population of the valley is estimated to have tripled between 3000 and 2600 B.C.E., leading to very rapid urbanization by 2500 B.C.E.

- The Indus Civilization is generally dated to between 2500 and 1500 B.C.E., but much less is known about the early history of Indus cities and culture than any other early civilization that we will consider. This is because the oldest physical remains of Indus civilization are now covered by water. Silt deposits along the Indus River have raised the level of the land, and the water table has risen along with it, meaning that much early history is now inaccessible to archaeologists.

- Another very considerable problem with our understanding of the Indus civilization is that the Indus valley writing system has not yet been deciphered, and perhaps never will be.

- But the other evidence we do have of the Indus valley civilization is spectacular, including the remains of two very large cities: Harappa in the

north and Mohenjo-Daro about 250 miles farther south. Both cities had up to 40,000 inhabitants by 2300 B.C.E. They were superbly planned, produced exceptional pottery, and used a system of uniform weights and measures.

- The Indus River helped maintain communications and a certain cultural, political, and economic uniformity between the cities, and indeed throughout the entire civilization, which covered much of modern-day Pakistan and a large part of northern India, a combined area of half a million square miles.

- The Indus civilization was undoubtedly the most extensive of the world's three earliest civilizations and was also much larger than early Chinese dynastic states.

- Despite the similarities in agricultural and urban evolution between the Indus and other ancient civilizations, there was one crucial difference: A political hierarchy, or even any form of central administration, seems not to have existed in the Indus civilization. Archaeologists also find virtually no evidence of large-scale conflict anywhere in the Indus valley during the thousand years of its existence.

- Despite this apparent lack of central political and military administration, clear signs of order and cooperation abound. The cities themselves were superbly planned, with straight streets intersecting at right angles, sophisticated drainage systems featuring underground channels, and multistory houses constructed of strong baked bricks.

- Based on irrigation agriculture as the Indus economy was, whatever state administrators were in place collected agricultural surpluses through tribute taking, storing them in huge state-owned granaries.

- Trade within the Indus valley was lively; pottery, tools, and decorative items produced in Harappa and Mohenjo-daro were exported all over the region. Indus merchants also carried on an energetic trade with their

Ruins of Mohenjo-Daro

regional neighbors, including Persia, central Asia, and Mesopotamia. Much of this trade was maritime.

■ As was also the case with all ancient civilizations, the wealth of the Indus civilization led to the emergence of social classes; the dwellings in both Harappa and Mohenjo-daro show us that the rich and the poor lived very different lives.

■ Indus civilization attitudes toward gender relations are difficult to determine, but what we can tease out about them is critically important, because they offer further evidence of the powerful Indus influence on subsequent South Asian society.

■ As far as we can tell, the Indus Civilization was strictly patriarchal; Indus women were completely at the mercy of adult males and enjoyed few of the legal protections and rights that were specified in Babylonian society, let alone Egyptian society.

■ Yet Indus religion in general does seem to reflect a strong concern for fertility; like other agricultural societies, Indus peoples venerated gods and goddesses associated with procreation, associating human fertility with the fertility of the land.

■ Whatever held Indus valley civilization together, sometime after 1900 B.C.E., it entered a period of decline. By 1700 B.C.E., people in Harappa and Mohenjo-Daro had abandoned those cities for smaller ones, and by 1500, cities everywhere in the Indus valley had almost entirely disappeared. Society lost its urban traits and reverted to local traditions.

■ Climate change is one possible explanation. Evidence suggests that a series of prolonged droughts affected the region around 2200 B.C.E., although they seem to have ended by 1900 to 1700 B.C.E., so their role in the civilization's collapse, if any, is unclear.

■ Other theories for Indus decline are epidemiological: Some historians argue that malaria and cholera may have hit the urban areas. Still other theories are agricultural: Farmers from the Indus valley may have moved elsewhere as domesticated rice and millet arrived in the region. The truth is that we don't know why this extraordinary civilization disappeared.

■ But we do know that soon after the great cities had been abandoned, around 1500 B.C.E., newcomers began to filter into the Indus valley from the north. Who the attackers were is matter for conjecture, but one thing is clear: The city was already in an advanced stage of economic and social decline.

■ Today, only ruins of the Indus valley civilization remain, but it's possible that a significant aspect of its culture endures. If the lack of evidence of military conflict or autocratic leadership in Harappa and Mohenjo-Daro suggests a culture of nonviolence and respect for life, perhaps that is the original source of those ideas in the religions and philosophies of India.

■ Some scholars agree with this conclusion; others argue that the Indus people experienced as much violence as the Sumerians, but they do not appear to have celebrated or ritualized it in the same way.

■ Whatever the case, and in spite of everything we do not know about the Indus valley civilization, it remains one of the most advanced and intriguing early civilizations of the ancient world.

SUGGESTED READING

Anthony, *The Horse, the Wheel, and Language.*

Kelekna, *The Horse in Human History.*

Mallory, *In Search of the Indo-Europeans.*

QUESTIONS TO CONSIDER

1. Why were Indus cities so much more sophisticated in their planning and infrastructure than most other ancient cities?

2. Although Indus writing has never been deciphered, what does the visual evidence they left behind tell us about the influence of Indus beliefs on later classical Indian religions?

SOUTH ASIAN CIVILIZATIONS AND BELIEFS

I n this lecture, you will learn about the religious developments during
the Vedic era in South Asia. You will also learn about the political and
social history of South Asia during the 1st millennium B.C.E., when
migrants known today as the Indo-Aryans slowly expanded throughout
the subcontinent. Evidence for this history comes from epic poems,
such as the Mahabharata and the Ramayana, and also from the work of
archaeologists.

RELIGIOUS HISTORY

- Soon after the great cities of the Indus had been abandoned, sometime
  around 1500 B.C.E., bands of Indo-European–speaking migrants
  from the north began to filter into the Indus valley and assimilate with
  local populations. These migrants are known to historians today as
  the Indo-Aryans; they spoke the Indo-European language of Sanskrit,
  and they identified themselves as Aryan (or "noble people") and thus
  different from, and even superior to, the indigenous peoples.

- Although they pursued pastoral nomadic lifeways and herded cattle,
  they also were highly militarized and skilled charioteers. Quite rapidly,
  the Indo-Aryans became the dominant elite across extensive northern
  regions of South Asia, although the newcomers also borrowed many
  ideas and technologies from the Indus civilization.

- During the half millennium between 1500 and 1000 B.C.E., the Aryans settled across the fertile plain of the Punjab, adopted many of the farming practices of the natives, and became the masters of modern Pakistan and northern India.

- They assimilated the indigenous peoples or drove them south across the Vindhya Mountains to join the darker-skinned Dravidians of the Deccan Plateau, helping to create the cultural and linguistic divide between northern and southern India that endures to this day.

- The Indo-Aryans brought with them new ideas about religion, notably the singing and chanting of hymns known as *ric* to accompany their sacrificial rituals. These hymns were created by an elite class of priests and seers called Brahmans, who claimed the ability to communicate directly with the gods.

- During this 500-year period between 1500 and 1000 B.C.E., the Brahmans composed more than a thousand of these hymns and brought them together into the *Rig-Veda*, a spiritual collection that is the oldest of the sacred books of what would became the Hindu religion. It has been used in worship in South Asia for more than 3,000 years.

- In addition to being a religious document, the *Rig-Veda* has also proven invaluable to historians as a source of information about early Indo-Aryan culture. In terms of political organization, the hymns of the *Rig-Veda* describe a multi-tribal structure in which each tribe was led by some sort of a warlord, called a raja.

- The *Rig-Veda* also shows that the conflict between the Indo-Aryans and the Dravidians for control of the Indus valley was ongoing between 1500 and 1000 B.C.E., leading to much destruction and devastation in towns and farmlands.

- Gradually, the Indo-Aryans were able to take control of most of India, settling down to become farmers and transforming their original pastoral nomadic tribal structures into political institutions more suited to sedentism. Rather than constructing imperial states, however, the Indo-Aryans built smaller regional kingdoms that reflected the long history of competitive disunity between the original tribes.

■ During the next phase of South Asian history, after 1000 B.C.E., the continuing influence of the Indus civilization contributed to the emergence of a new, more rigid social structure that explicitly divided the people into four distinct classes, or varnas.

■ These classes were the Brahmans, the priestly class; the Kshatriyas, which was made up of nobles and warriors; the Vaishyas, who were the common people, such as artisans and merchants; and the Shudras, who were the equivalent of serfs in a feudal system. Sometime later, a fifth category of "untouchables" was added, so called because members of other castes would be defiled if they were touched by one.

■ The varna, or caste, system has deeply influenced the lives of Indians ever since it emerged. The system also had powerful implications for religion. The important Hindu text the Bhagavad Gita, which consists of a dialogue between the Kshatriya warrior Arjuna and the Hindu god Vishnu disguised as a charioteer, explicitly states that membership in each caste demands the carrying out of certain mandated duties and that failure to do so will bring disgrace.

Sanskrit verse from the Bhagavad Gita

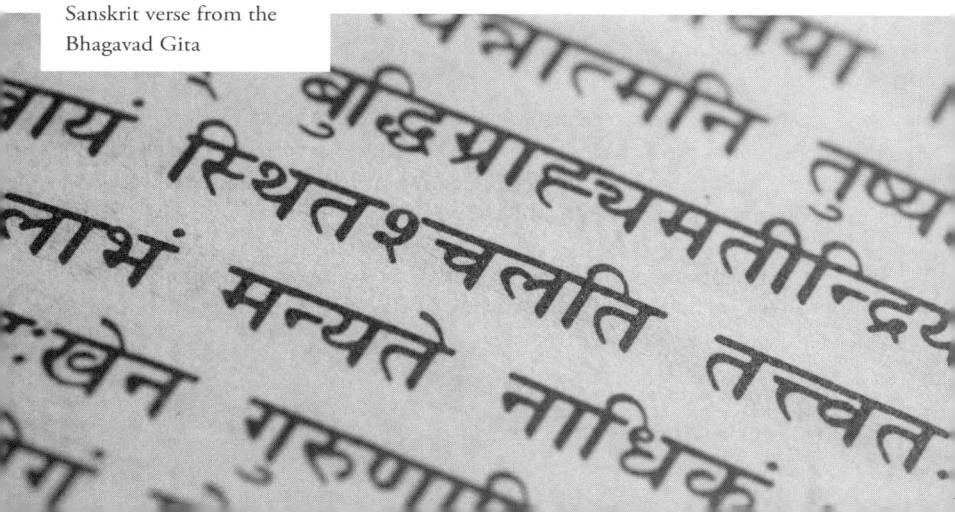

- Despite the deeply entrenched and religiously sanctioned nature of the varna system, members of lower castes resented their inferior status. Around 600 B.C.E., a radical Brahman sect emerged that openly embraced mysticism, spiritual discipline, and yogic meditation and rejected the standard rituals of Vedic religion.

- These new approaches to traditional Vedic religion were written down in a collection called the Upanishads, which was soon recognized as the supreme realization of Vedic religion. These texts advanced an idea that consciousness within individuals comes from an eternal, sacred energy at the heart of the universe.

- The Upanishads also articulated the notion of the transmigration of the soul. The premise for this is that people's deeds in life stayed with them in the form of an unseen power called karma. After death, a person's karma might be insufficient to keep the soul in heaven, at which time the soul would descend to earth and be reincarnated in another body.

- Bad deeds, therefore bad karma, lead a soul to hell, and rebirth in subhuman form is a consequence of violating the basic doctrine of the religion.

- This rebirth of the soul in a new body was an endless and tedious process, and the only way to avoid this fate was to adopt the ascetic life of pure dharma, or deep meditation. This led to the appearance of gurus, who wandered the country as meditating ascetics, all of which had a powerful effect on society.

- However, even this reformed version of the Vedic religion was still dependent on ritual sacrifices offered by Brahman priests, who remained at the highest strata of society, were exempt from taxation, and received generous fees and gifts for their services.

- Resentment increased among the lower castes against Brahman pretensions and superiority, leading to the emergence of new sects that openly attacked the Brahmans, claiming that they were charlatans who hoodwinked the people.

- But the most important development in this period of intense thinking about religion was the emergence of new ideologies—particularly Jainism, Buddhism, and later Hinduism—which incorporated many Vedic practices and works.

JAINISM

- Jainist ideas date to the 7th century B.C.E., but the ideology was fully developed in the late 6th century by semilegendary teacher Vardhamana Mahavira, a member of the elite Kshatriya caste.

- Jains believe that almost everything that exists in the universe has a soul, including humans, plants, animals, and insects. But trapped in their physical bodies, these souls are in a constant state of suffering that can only be eased through purification, which will release the souls from their prisons.

- Purification is obtainable through adopting the principle of ahimsa, which means practicing no violence toward any other living thing that possesses a soul.

BUDDHISM

- A more accessible alternative to the classical Vedic religion came in the form of Buddhism, which shares some beliefs with Jainism. Both stress the humanity of their founder rather than his divinity, teach nonviolence, and developed monastic traditions of celibacy and asceticism.

- Like Mahavira, Siddhartha Gautama, who became the Buddha, was a member of the elite Kshatriya caste, and he also gave up his privileged social position in a quest for personal enlightenment.

- Buddhism is called the Middle Way because it lies somewhere between normal human life and extreme asceticism and demands only a moderate form of renunciation. Like Jainism, Buddhism rejected the caste system and offered all humans an escape from the tedious cycle of reincarnation without the help of Brahman priests, so it appealed strongly to the lower classes. And because Buddhism did not demand the extreme behaviors of the Jains, it became much more popular.

- Eventually, a new version of Buddhism emerged called Mahayana, which spread rapidly throughout India, and then along the Silk Road into central Asia, China, Japan, Korea, and Southeast Asia.

- However, practitioners of traditional Vedic religion did not take the rise in popularity of Buddhism lightly; instead, they worked to reform the religion of the Brahmans and create a much more popular and accessible version of the religion. That version is known today as Hinduism.

POLITICAL AND SOCIAL HISTORY

- In South Asia during the 1st millennium B.C.E., the Indo-Aryans continued to slowly expand throughout the subcontinent, fighting many epic battles among themselves as they did so. The warriors were now armed with iron weapons, which made warfare increasingly bloody, but iron was also used to make tools that increased agricultural production.

- Eventually, all of the Ganges basin was divided into a series of independent city-states, each with its own state army and a powerful king known as a maharaja, or "great king."

- The maharajas collected tribute from the farmers, artisans, and merchants of their states and used this to build palaces and other examples of monumental architecture in their cities and to maintain their courts and armies.

- These developments had further political and social ramifications, leading to the entrenchment of three key pillars of Indian society that continue even today: the caste system, the semiautonomous individual village, and the extended family.

- The autonomy of Indian villages and their governing structure of headman and council of elders was critically important in maintaining cohesion within the kingdoms. Known as the panchayat raj system, these self-governing and often self-sufficient villages offered political stability across eons of Indian history, even as great empires rose and fell. This crucial role for autonomous villages has persisted even into the political structures of modern India.

- The consolidation of the three-generation family also assumed tremendous significance in the 1st millennium B.C.E. Within the extended family, women were put into a position of subordination to men. Women were also expected to have a male protector at all times. Women were not able to inherit property and could not participate in Vedic religious rituals.

- As Indian society took shape under the rule of the maharajas, outside peoples began once again to play a role in South Asian affairs. Late in the 6th century B.C.E., Persian king Darius expanded the Persian empire into the Indus valley.

- This remained the political reality for the next two centuries, until in the 320s Alexander of Macedon destroyed the Persians at Gaugamela, crossed the Hindu Kush mountains, and campaigned vigorously along the Indus valley. He defeated a series of local maharajahs, including the most powerful, King Porus, and this created a power vacuum.

- After Alexander withdrew, an ambitious local prince known as Chandragupta Maurya used his small but well-trained army to conquer a series of regional states until much of northern India was under his control, thus uniting a significant part of South Asia into a single imperial state for the first time.

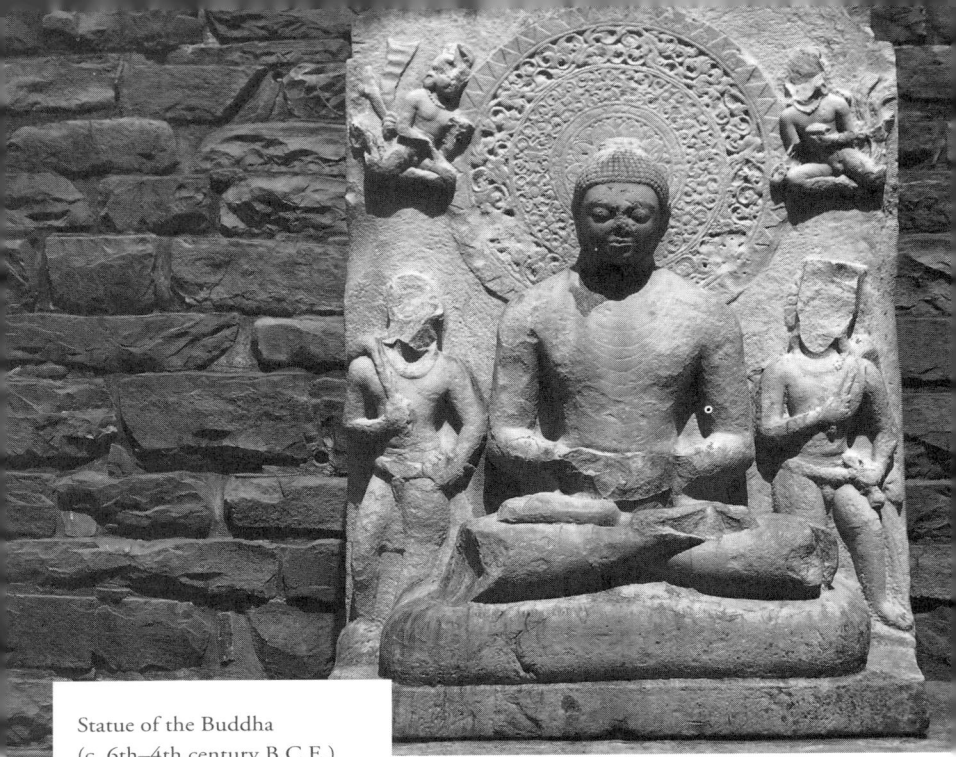

Statue of the Buddha
(c. 6th–4th century B.C.E.)

■ Chandragupta was succeeded briefly by his son, and then by his grandson Ashoka, one of the most successful and revered rulers in the history of India. Ashoka communicated his policies and Buddhist beliefs in a series of edicts that were inscribed in stone and erected all over the Mauryan realm. He also had an extensive road network constructed, which encouraged trade within the empire and also with surrounding states.

■ Modern Indians revere the legacy of Ashoka. But the empire constructed by his grandfather Chandragupta could not survive the death of his able and charismatic grandson for long, and the 150 or so years that followed witnessed a steady economic decline because the expense of administering this large South Asian empire could not be met by revenues.

■ By 185 B.C.E., the Mauryan empire was no more and India was fragmented once again. South Asia—the home of powerful maharajas and emperors, several of the world's most fascinating religions, and a rich and complex society—was destined not to be reunited again for another 500 years.

SUGGESTED READING

McIntosh, *A Peaceful Realm.*

Possehl, *The Indus Civilization.*

Ratnagar, *Trading Encounters.*

QUESTIONS TO CONSIDER

1. How do historians use ancient religious texts like the *Rig-Veda* as evidence for social, political, and military life during the Vedic age?

2. How do we explain the universal appeal of some religions, such as Buddhism, whereas others seem destined to remain much narrower in their appeal? Are there any features common to all global religions that offer some insights?

CHINA: BORN IN ISOLATION

As civilizations were emerging in Mesopotamia, Egypt, and South Asia, fascinating and even unique civilizations were also being established in East Asia. Despite the fact that in many ways the evolution of agrarian civilization in that part of Eurasia mirrored what happened in other regions, the relative geographic isolation of East Asian civilization enabled it to develop some original and fascinating ideas about government, society, and the role of the individual. This lecture's exploration of East Asian civilization begins with a consideration of the geographical and environmental characteristics that enabled these original ideas to emerge.

EAST ASIAN CIVILIZATION

- The term "East Asia" refers to a huge mainland area dominated by China, as well as the Korean Peninsula, the long archipelago of Japan, and the thousands of other islands that populate the Yellow and South China Seas, including Taiwan.

- China is an enormous country with a total land area of more than 3 million square miles, land borders 13,500 miles long, and a coastline almost as long at 11,000 miles. Given its great size, it is hardly surprising that China has tremendous variety of topography, climate, and vegetation.

- The country can be divided into four key regions: the eastern plains, the northern grasslands, the southern hill regions, and the mountainous and arid west. This combination of geographical barriers has meant that for much of its ancient history, China was protected from competing civilizations in the west, so China was never actually incorporated into anyone else's empire until Europeans and their gunboats turned up in the 19th century.

■ This also meant that China experienced little cultural influence from the early civilizations of the Indus, Mesopotamia, or Egypt—which, in contrast, had engaged in high levels of trade and cultural exchange almost from the beginning of their history.

■ For centuries, China's occasional contact with the militarized nomads on its northern and western borders were its primary cultural conduit to the outside world. This relative isolation forced China's early dynasties to focus on internal cultural and ethnic integration rather than on external expansion.

■ Probably the most significant geographical feature in understanding the emergence of civilization in China are its two major river systems, which have tended to divide China into two distinct cultural halves.

■ The southern regions are dominated by the mighty Yangtze River, which flows nearly 4,000 miles from the Tibetan Plateau to the sea. In the north, the nearly 3,000-mile-long Huang He is called the Yellow River because of huge amounts of yellow, mineral-rich soil that it carries out from the plains into the sea. It was in the valley of the Huang He that the earliest settled communities and cultures of East Asia appeared.

■ Archaeological evidence shows that by 7000 B.C.E., farmers had learned to domesticate a drought-resistant and very nutritious wild grass called millet. Sedentary populations increased until, by 5000 B.C.E., hundreds of villages were flourishing in the middle Huang He valley.

■ The complex farming culture that operated in these villages is known to archaeologists as the Yangshao culture, identified through its very fine painted pottery and distinctive bone tools. About 200 Yangshao villages have been excavated by archaeologists.

- As populations continued to increase and society became more complex, a new and more sophisticated agrarian culture emerged in the Huang He valley after roughly 3000 B.C.E., which archaeologists call the Longshan culture. The Longshan were responsible for the domestication of a new species that was destined to have a significant impact on world history: the silkworm.

- The absence of any early irrigation structures suggests that rainfall was sufficient for growing crops. But between 2500 and 1500 B.C.E., the climate of the Huang He valley gradually changed from warm and humid to cooler and more arid.

- This led to significant population increase in the heart of the Huang He valley, as early farmers were forced to migrate into the still-sustainable areas from increasingly arid regions farther afield, similar to the process that occurred in the Indus valley.

- Early in the 2nd millennium, a new culture appeared in the Huang He valley, a culture that has been tentatively identified with a dynasty named the Xia in certain ancient Chinese texts. For centuries, Chinese scholars assumed the Xia dynasty to have been only a legendary creation of early authors, but archaeological discoveries made in 1959 at the site of Erlitou, near Luoyang, gave material support to the stories.

- We know little about the Xia but a lot more about the succeeding Shang dynasty, whose more than 500-year rule between about 1600 and 1045 B.C.E. is supported by an enormous amount of evidence.

- The Shang controlled a large territory, much larger than that of the Xia, and were responsible for so many significant advances in governance, technology, writing, and urbanization that they are deservedly credited with establishing many of the core foundations of East Asian civilization.

- The Shang established a rigid pyramidal society, with the king on top followed in descending order by the members of his family, a noble class, court officials, local aristocrats, peasants, and slaves.

- Another important element that emerged in Shang society has parallels with ancient India: the role of the extended family. This became particularly influential in Chinese society because families venerated both their living and their dead ancestors.

- The Shang demonstrated a high level of sophistication in bronze metallurgy, which was exclusively reserved for, and monopolized by, the royal family and other elites.

- The Shang kings moved their capital city several times; at least five different capital cities have been discovered, and these constitute the first cities in East Asia. Although they were nowhere near as large and densely populated as the early cities of Mesopotamia, they were nonetheless impressive, particularly Yin, near Anyang, which was probably the last Shang capital.

WRITING SYSTEM

- Despite these many achievements, perhaps the most important contribution of the Shang to subsequent Chinese civilization was the invention of the first writing system in East Asia, one of the key thresholds of complexity that had to be crossed by all ancient agrarian civilizations.

- The roots of Chinese writing probably extend much earlier than the Shang, but the oldest actual evidence we have of writing in China comes from the Shang period, and—unlike in Mesopotamia, Egypt, or the Mediterranean region—it is not a system of accounting.

- Interestingly, the earliest Chinese writing was used as a means whereby the kings and their elites could communicate with the gods by writing questions on animal bones, so-called oracle bones.

- Of the more than 2,000 characters inscribed on the oracle bones, most of them have a modern recognizable counterpart, which means that, unlike cuneiform or hieroglyphics, the Chinese writing system that

The most important contribution of the Shang dynasty to subsequent Chinese civilization was the invention of the first writing system in East Asia.

emerged under the Shang has been in continual use for more than 3,000 years.

MILITARY

■ The Shang kings used their strong military to suppress other regional powers and to demand tribute and slaves from rival states, but ultimately they were unable to deal with the increasingly powerful Zhou state, which controlled the Wei River valley in the west.

■ In time, the Zhou military came sweeping out of the Wei Valley and destroyed the Shang. The beheading of the Shang king in 1045 B.C.E. marks the end of the Shang and the beginning of the Zhou dynasty, which would go on to rule China for the next 800 years.

- The arrival of the Zhou marks a new phase in the way elites validated their violent seizure of power. The Zhou promoted the idea that there was a parallel between affairs on earth and affairs in heaven and that divinities in heaven had the ability to bestow power on terrestrial political regimes.

- Indeed, the Zhou claimed to have received the mandate of heaven, arguing that heavenly support was bestowed or withdrawn as a direct result of the quality of leadership. This mandate of heaven political theory would go on to dominate Chinese imperial politics for the next 3,000 years, until the abdication of the last emperor in 1912.

- Because the territory of the Zhou state was much larger in area than that of the Shang had been, the Zhou put in place a decentralized administrative structure in which local leaders were allowed to rule their own kingdoms as long as they supported the Zhou with tribute and troops.

- For several centuries, this structure worked surprisingly well, but eventually regional leaders amassed enough power to set up their own bureaucracies and military forces. By the 8th century B.C.E., all sense of unity had disappeared, and widespread conflict broke out between the regional kingdoms—conflict that was destined to last for the next 500 years.

- This half millennium of civil warfare in China is divided into the Spring and Autumn period, during which the state was especially fragmented, and the aptly named Warring States period, in which seven states contended for dominance. These were tumultuous historical eras in which, nevertheless, important social, technological, and philosophical advances were made.

PHILOSOPHY

- This was also an extraordinarily creative age for Chinese philosophy, as intellectuals pondered the sorry state of Chinese affairs and considered the best way to end the almost continuous warfare and restore effective and ethical governance to the state.

- So many philosophers were active that the period has come to be known as the Hundred Schools of thought, and a handful of these schools have gone on to dominate Chinese thinking ever since— notably Confucianism, Daoism, and Legalism.

- In an attempt to create a more ethical leadership class, a lower-level aristocrat from the State of Lu, Kong Fuzi, better known as Confucius in the West, attempted to redefine the criteria for status in society. He argued that a superior individual was not necessarily someone born into a superior class, but someone who had attained the rank of *junzi*, or "princeling," through pursuing high levels of intellectual and ethical cultivation.

- An alternative to the educational activism of the Confucians was the ideology proposed by the Daoists, who were more pessimistic about the ability of humans to construct harmonious, ordered societies. Not really trusting governments, the Daoists proposed instead that humans need to modify and tailor their behavior to live in harmony with the Way— the great, nameless, intensely creative force at the heart of the universe.

- As attractive as both Confucianism and Daoism have been to East Asian people ever since they first emerged about 2,500 years ago, it was a very different philosophy that ultimately succeeded in reuniting China.

- One of the warring states, the powerful Qin from northwestern China, adopted the ideology of Legalism, which insisted on achieving social cohesion through the application of strict laws and harsh, collective punishments.

- Using often brutal legalist tactics, it was the Qin who finally succeeded in 221 B.C.E. in reuniting China and establishing their own short-lived but astonishingly successful Qin dynasty. Their extraordinary first ruler was

Shi Huangdi, whose success as the first emperor of China paved the way for centuries of stable rule that followed under the mighty Han dynasty.

SUGGESTED READING

Embree, ed., *Sources of Indian Tradition*.

Thapar, *Early India*.

Wolpert, *A New History of India*.

QUESTIONS TO CONSIDER

1. How did the environmental context of China influence the way its unique history and culture evolved?

2. Why did the political situation in Late Zhou China lead to the emergence of several of the most influential philosophies in all of world history?

CHINA'S DYNASTIES AND INFLUENCE

D uring the final decades of the Warring States era, a young king named Ying Zheng came to the throne of the western state of Qin. Working closely with his Legalist advisers and military officials, King Ying was amazingly successful—so successful that desperate rulers of the rival warring states sent assassins to try to kill him. After King Ying Zheng conquered his rivals, he ended the Warring States era and unified much of China under the Qin dynasty, with himself as absolute ruler. Although the Qin's reign was brief, only 15 years, their achievements made it possible for their successors, the Han, to establish a truly enormous Chinese empire that would last for 400 years, utterly transforming East Asian civilization.

THE QIN DYNASTY

- In 221, the victorious Qin king proclaimed himself Shihuangdi, a title he coined meaning "First Emperor." In a reign of just 11 years, he undertook a stunning series of reforms that few rulers in history have matched in reigns four times as long.

- To unite the divided kingdoms and peoples of China, he needed to first weaken the power of the nobility, which he did by moving its leading members to the Qin capital and keeping them as virtual hostages. In place of Zhou dynasty feudalism, China was now divided into 36 provinces, each under the control of administrative bureaucracies rather than noble lords.

- To guard against future rebellions, the First Emperor ordered the civilian population to surrender all the weapons they had amassed after centuries of warfare, and private possession of arms now joined the prohibited list in the new Qin law codes.

■ This rigidly Legalist code was promulgated throughout the empire and regulated all aspects of society. Lawbreakers were subject to harsh punishments. What was not in keeping with the objective spirit of Legalism, however, was the fact that the emperor and his advisors would not tolerate criticism of the government.

■ Realizing that scholars were using historical and philosophical texts to criticize government policies, the emperor passed a law banning "dangerous" books, excepting only treatises on divination, medicine, forestry, and farming. He ordered all banned books to be burnt.

■ The First Emperor next passed a series of linguistic and economic reforms aimed at further unifying the state. The writing system was reformed by the introduction of a new style called Small Seal script, which now was to be used throughout the Qin empire and which persisted as the official script well into the Han dynasty. All weights, currency, and measurements were also standardized.

■ The First Emperor also introduced reforms that allowed for private ownership of land by the peasants, although the lives of the peasants remained little better than those of serfs. Their lot was made worse by the massive building projects started by the First Emperor, the most impressive of which resulted in the construction of two of the great wonders of the world: the First Emperor's tomb and the Great Wall of China.

THE HAN DYNASTY

■ As has often been the case throughout history, the charismatic First Emperor was succeeded by a relatively inept son who could neither control the nobility nor feed the peasants, so rebel armies arose across China, leading quickly to the collapse of Qin authority.

- The most formidable of these rebel armies was led by a peasant named Liubang. By 206 B.C.E., Liubang had defeated his rivals and established the Han dynasty, destined to rule China for more than four centuries between 206 B.C.E. and 220 C.E. These centuries were mostly characterized by a strong central government, a well-organized bureaucracy, and extensive imperial expansion.

- Under the Han, China grew into a huge empire that stretched from Vietnam to Korea and from the China Sea deep into the heart of central Asia. This dramatic expansion of Chinese civilization had world historical implications, because it was under the Han that East Asia began to engage with the rest of Eurasia for the first time. Eventually, much of Afro-Eurasia was connected through a network of trade routes, which facilitated extraordinary levels of material and cultural exchange.

- The Han era is divided into two periods, the Early and Late Han, separated by a period of non-Han rule under an emperor named Wang Mang. The Early Han ruled from the city of Changan, which is modern Xian; the Later Han ruled from Luoyang.

- The Early Han was the more successful period of the two, reducing taxes on the peasants and enlisting the support of Confucian scholars to create a large bureaucracy staffed by skilled salaried administrators to rule their empire.

- The country was divided into new administrative structures: 10 kingdoms and 83 commanderies. The commanderies were further divided into prefectures, which were divided into districts, and the districts were divided into smaller units known as wards. This was the most complex and carefully organized imperial administrative structure of the ancient world, and it was only possible because of the quality of the bureaucracy.

- During the reign of Emperor Wudi, the "Martial Emperor," who ruled from 140 to 86 B.C.E., the Han government adopted Confucianism as the official philosophy of the state. This adoption is one of the reasons why Confucianism remained at the core of Chinese government for the next 2,000 years and is still employed to a degree by China's communist regime today.

- Wudi established a state educational system based on knowledge of the Confucian classics, topped by an imperial Confucian academy to train future officials. He also strengthened the examination by basing it squarely on the knowledge candidates possessed of the Confucian classics.

- This meant that candidates for high office needed to have had considerable training as scholars before they could take up an administrative position, and these Confucian scholar-bureaucrats now gained prominent status as the new elite.

- Emperor Wudi, like his predecessors, still combined brutal Legalist methods with Confucian ideals. Recent discoveries by archaeologists of Han official documents have revealed that the Han had very harsh

Confucianism was adopted in China as the official philosophy of the state by Han-dynasty emperor Wudi and is still employed to a degree by China's communist regime today.

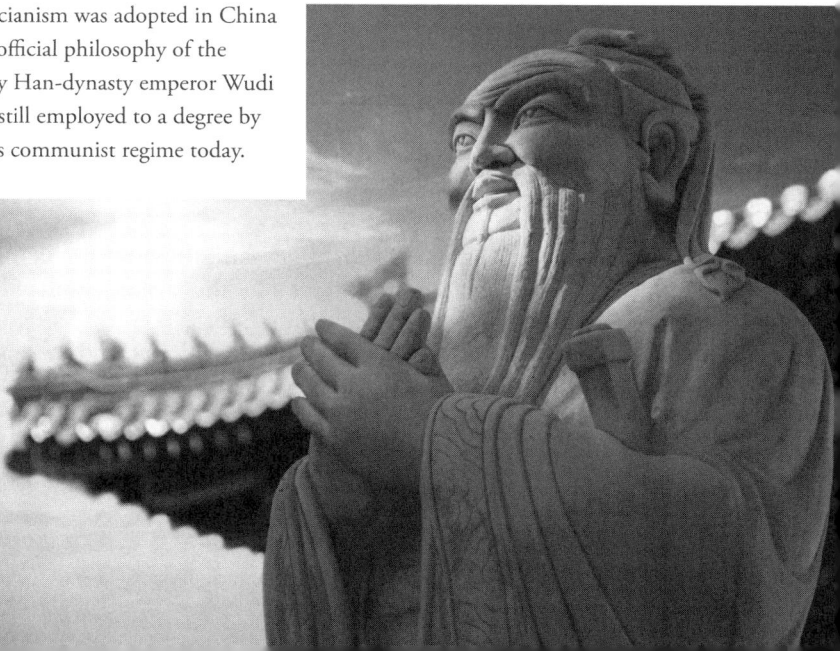

laws and punishments in place, and like the Qin, the Han government demanded conscripted labor service from its population.

- The duties of the conscripted labor force included lengthy military service, particularly after Wudi instigated a period of aggressive imperial expansion late in the 2nd century B.C.E. Before long, Han armies were marching all over East and central Asia, and under Wudi, the Han empire reached the heights of its power and size.

- But the Martial Emperor was followed by a succession of weaker emperors that hastened the demise of the Early Han dynasty. In 8 C.E., a well-meaning Confucian chief minister named Wang Mang overthrew the Han and enacted reforms to try to bring relief to the peasants, including the abolition of debt slavery and the introduction of a system to try to more equitably apportion land to peasant families.

- Wang Mang also tried to stabilize the prices of basic commodities by establishing government agencies to buy and stockpile surpluses when prices were low and sell them at a subsidized rate when scarcity forced prices to rise, something similar to what reformist Roman politicians were trying at the opposite end of Eurasia.

- Ultimately, Wang Mang's attempts to radically redistribute wealth and taxes failed, and he was killed in battle in October of 23 C.E. Two years later, Liu Xiu, a distant relative of the Liu family that had founded the Han dynasty, declared the start of the Later Han dynasty, which went on to rule for almost another two centuries.

- The reigns of Liu Xiu and his son and grandson were the high points of the Later Han dynasty, but thereafter the dynasty suffered from corruption and political infighting among three powerful elite groups: the clans of the empresses, the Confucian bureaucrats, and the eunuchs. But none of these were able to improve the harsh lives of peasants.

- In 153, China was beset with a series of natural calamities, including massive locust swarms and devastating floods along the Huang He.

These forced hundreds of thousands of people off the land and on the roads in a desperate search for food.

- The government could do little to help, and Confucian scholars were so disgusted by the conniving and corruption in court that they organized mass protests against the eunuchs, who in turn orchestrated purges of Confucian officials, who were exiled, jailed, or killed. Meanwhile, the reigning Emperor Huan chose to ignore the growing economic and political storm and instead entertain thousands of concubines in his harem.

- By the late 2nd century, Daoist demands for equal land distribution had spread throughout the peasantry, and peasant insurgents of an uprising known as the Yellow Turban Rebellion swarmed across the North China Plain, destroying the principal agricultural sector of the country.

- Then, in 184, a massive rebellion led by radical Daoists, who were generally distrustful of government, resulted in widespread attacks on government officials all over the country. The result was that power once held by the Liu royalty now fell into the hands of regional warlords, such as Dong Zhou, who attacked and burned the Han capital in 190 C.E., and the brilliant but ruthless general Cao Cao.

- The last figurehead Han Emperor Xian was allowed to continue his nominal reign until 220, when Cao Cao's son Cao Pi forced his abdication and brought to an end the Han dynasty era of Chinese history.

- Despite the extraordinary political and military history of the Han dynasty, perhaps even more memorable is its technological and cultural achievements. The Han were responsible for the development of the world's first wheelbarrow, the first water mill, a type of seismometer to measure the strength of earthquakes, extraordinarily accurate astronomical observations, piston bellows to assist in the manufacture of high-quality iron, and paper.

■ In the realm of social relations, the Han dynasty is also noteworthy for its attitudes toward women and gender relations. During the Later Han, Ban Zhao, the only woman ever appointed to the position of official court historian, made an explicit demand for equal education for girls and boys, which led to more opportunities for elite women to receive higher levels of education in imperial China.

SUGGESTED READING

di Cosmo, *Ancient China and Its Enemies.*

Loewe and Shaughnessy, eds., *The Cambridge History of Ancient China.*

Thorp, *China in the Early Bronze Age.*

QUESTIONS TO CONSIDER

1. How was Qin Shihuangdi able to accomplish so much in his short reign as First Emperor of China?

2. What is the meaning of the essay "Lessons for Women"? Is Ban Zhao making an argument for or against the maintenance of a patriarchal gender structure in ancient China?

THE IMPORTANCE OF THE NOMADS

I n this lecture, you will consider the role of militarized pastoral nomads in the history of civilizations, to try to understand why they had such a devastating impact on all the states and civilizations they interacted with over thousands of years. You will also consider the enormously positive effect they had in providing vital links between one civilization and another and examine the forces that governed their lives and compelled them to thrust themselves into the lives of neighboring peoples.

PASTORALISM

- Pastoralism emerged as a viable lifeway several thousands of years ago, when some human communities realized that it was possible to live well by exploiting the products of domesticated animals, such as cattle, sheep, camels, goats, or horses.

- This lifeway was seminomadic, and as a result, pastoralists never established civilizations like those of Mesopotamia or Egypt, with their great cities and stable, stratified societies. But their interactions with virtually every complex state across Afro-Eurasia over thousands of years were crucial to the way history unfolded in that vast world zone.

- Following the agricultural revolution, some communities embraced farming and became solely dependent on agriculture for their survival, a lifeway that required full-time sedentism. Other communities preferred to continue as nomadic foragers, often by migrating into areas outside of the sedentary zones.

- Yet others, the pastoralists, embraced a third lifeway, a specialized hybrid that incorporated elements of both farming and foraging. Pastoralists opted for a semisedentary, seminomadic existence that was dependent on the domestication of certain species, so this was a specific survival choice that some communities embraced within the broad framework of the agricultural revolution.

- But pastoralism did not appear 10,000 years ago with the transition to agriculture. Archaeologist Andrew Sherratt points out that pastoralism was only able to emerge early in the 5th millennium B.C.E., after humans worked out new ways of using animal products.

- Although sheep, goats, and cattle had all been domesticated from at least 6000 B.C.E., it was only when humans had learned to exploit the traction power of these animals—as well as their secondary products, such as blood, milk, and hair—that some communities were able to use

Pastoralism emerged as a viable lifeway several thousands of years ago, when some human communities realized that it was possible to live well by exploiting the products of domesticated animals, such as cattle, sheep, camels, goats, or horses.

them to greatly extend their range and eventually colonize large areas of grassland otherwise unsuitable for farming.

- The specific environment in which pastoralists lived—the Eurasian steppe—was critical for the operation of pastoralism, because, although the steppe cannot support sustained cultivation, it can sustain seasonal pastures of grasslands. Humans cannot eat the grass that grows in this steppe environment, but they can eat and use the animals that graze on it, thus tapping into an otherwise unusable energy source.

- The Eurasian steppe is a vast belt of grassland that extends 5,000 miles from the Alfold plain in Hungary and Rumania in the west, through the Ukraine and central Asia, all the way to Manchuria in the east.

- Far from being a uniformly flat expanse of grassy plains, however, the steppe varies considerably in its geography. At various places, the steppe is interrupted by rivers, hills, high mountains, and arid deserts, effectively dividing the vast ocean of grass into different regions.

- These often-forbidding dividing features were never a real barrier to the pastoral nomads, so various groups could and often did interact with each other, and with sedentary societies, across the entire length and breadth of the Eurasian steppe. But often, these dividing features did serve as places of refuge for nomads fleeing pursuing armies sent by the sedentary societies that the nomads had probably just finished raiding.

- Two examples of the extraordinary reach of militarized pastoral nomads are the Huns, who proved problematic for the German tribes and Romans late in the Roman imperial period; and the Mongols, who in the 13th century carved out the largest contiguous empire the world had ever seen.

- But the Huns and Mongols are simply the best known of a large number of powerful militarized nomadic confederations that proved difficult for even the most powerful agrarian civilizations to deal with, even as they also proved beneficial to these same civilizations by linking them together into networks of trade and exchange.

ORIGINS AND SPREAD OF PASTORALISM

- Although Andrew Sherratt has estimated the arrival of pastoral nomadism at some time after 5000 B.C.E., the chronology of its historical origins and spread remains obscure. Archaeologists have found evidence of farming communities that seemed particularly dependent on domesticated animals, including the horse, within certain early cultures that appeared in the Ukraine and parts of southern Russia.

- By the time the first cities and states appeared in Afro-Eurasia late in the 4th millennium B.C.E., pastoralist lifeways had become so productive that entire communities were now able to depend almost exclusively on their animals.

- The more they did this, however, and with the proviso of still having to trade or raid periodically with sedentary societies, the more nomadic they had to be, so that they could graze their animals over large areas.

- The appearance of burial mounds called *kurgany* scattered across the steppe is evidence of increasing nomadism in some of these communities, and the distribution of kurgans shows a gradual eastward spread.

- There were various degrees of pastoral nomadism, ranging from groups that had no permanent settlements to communities of largely sedentary pastoralists who lived in permanent settlements.

- The impact of migrating pastoralists across Eurasia, an impact that resulted from their mobility and ability to survive in marginal environments, was immediate and profound. Archaeologists trace cycles of expansion across the steppe, with periods of semisedentism in between—cycles probably explained by climate and demographic pressures.

- In periods of warmer and wetter weather, agriculture may have become a more viable alternative in regions once suited only to nomadism, and in time, large sedentary communities developed around the winter camps of regional leaders. But once conditions changed and became less favorable to farming, the pastoralists returned to nomadism, often migrating vast distances across Eurasia.

- Russian archaeologists have distinguished three cycles of large-scale migration in the millennia before the Common Era: between roughly 3400 and 3200, 2600 and 2400, and 2000 and 1800 B.C.E. These migrations represent the invasion of large regions of Eurasia by various groups of Indo-European–speaking pastoral nomads, who traveled eastward from their probable homeland somewhere in southern Russia.

- With each wave of migration, the pattern of kurgans shows that pastoralists were spreading farther and farther to the east, through southern Siberia and central Asia, extending eventually into Mongolia and western China.

- Much of the archaeological evidence for the Early Bronze Age cycle of expansion comes from the western steppes, particularly the pit-grave *yamnaya* pastoralist culture that flourished from the region between the Bug and Dniester Rivers in the west and the Ural River in the east. These so-called pit-grave cultures provide evidence of horse riding and also of the use of wheeled vehicles on the steppe that might have been vital in the logistics of mass migration.

- Many of the metal goods discovered in *yamnaya* sites, including weapons, had been imported from agricultural metal-working zones— evidence that pastoralists, farmers, and artisans of the western steppes were already linked into a regional system of commercial exchanges by the late 4th millennium.

- By the Middle Bronze Age, Indo-European–speaking pastoral nomads had migrated farther to the east, occupying parts of southern Siberia and the central Asian steppe, driven most probably by overpopulation and climate change in the western steppe.

■ The most important pastoralist culture of the central and southern steppe is that of the Afanasevo, named after the site of Afanaseva Gora in southern Siberia, first excavated by the Soviets in 1920. Afanasevo artifacts show distinct similarities to those of the pit-grave cultures, suggesting that the Afanasevo was an extension of pastoral nomadic migrants from the west, combined with the assimilation of local indigenous populations.

■ By the Late Bronze Age, there is evidence of a new wave of large-scale migration, which seems to have caused widespread disruption across many regions of the steppe. The steppe-bronze culture that emerged in the wake of this invasion is known as Andronovo, whose lifeway varied between mobile pastoralism and occasional periods of semisedentary agriculture.

■ During the 1st millennium B.C.E. a number of pastoral nomadic communities emerged with the military skills and technologies, and the endurance and mobility, to raid at will and even dominate their sedentary agrarian neighbors.

■ Some of these militarized groups, such as the Xiongnu, Yuezhi, Huns, and Scythians, formed powerful state-like confederations in the steppe lands between the agrarian civilizations.

■ As with other pastoral nomads, these were not civilizations, because they lacked many crucial features. They had no cities; no large, dense populations; no monumental architecture; and, in most cases, no writing.

■ However, their political structure and military prowess allowed these often very substantial confederations to not only live well on the steppes, but also to develop military horse-riding contingents that became formidable opponents of the armies of all sedentary civilizations.

THE SCYTHIANS

- The Scythians were a nomadic confederation whose appearance on the edges of civilizations terrified the Greeks and many other ancient states. At its height, the Scythian realm stretched from the Black Sea to the Altai Mountains in Siberia.

- Like most pastoral-nomadic confederations, the Scythians did not leave any written sources, so for much of their history, we have to depend on accounts from sedentary cultures such as the Greeks and also archaeological evidence from thousands of excavated tombs.

- Even with this evidence, we don't really know if there was a single Scythian group or several different groups who shared a common culture that archaeologists describe as Scythian because of certain similarities. Their ethnic identity is also uncertain, although they were most probably Indo-European–speaking migrants who intermingled with other sedentary and nomadic groups.

Scythian stone sculptures

- The Scythian confederation contained its fair share of fast-moving horse archers, but it also included various sedentary cultures who dwelt along the northern coast of the Black Sea.

- In the 700s B.C.E., the Scythians forced a rival militarized nomadic confederation, the Cimmerians, to move away from the Black Sea steppes and south into the Middle East. The Scythians pursued their enemies, which brought them into conflict with powerful sedentary states, including the Assyrians and the Medes, who seemed to have no idea of how to deal with this first wave of militarized nomads to contest with sedentary civilizations.

- The tables were turned on the Scythians when they were attacked by the armies of the Persian empire. For more than a century, powerful Persian kings such as Cyrus the Great and Darius I attempted to subdue the Scythians. But these campaigns generally failed because the Scythians, like all militarized nomadic armies, used their mobility to simply retreat back into the steppe and, from their strongholds there, send troops out to harass their less-mobile opponents.

- During the 4th century B.C.E., the political structure of the Scythian confederation was centralized until all the tribes were united under King Atheas. Trade and agriculture now became important parts of the Scythian economy, and this, along with increased contact with Greek colonies, increased the sedentization of the nomads.

- By the 2nd century B.C.E., Scythian dominance in the Black Sea region was waning after invasions by Celts and Sarmatians, although they still possessed sufficient military power to conquer Greek Black Sea colonies to maintain their dominance in regional trade.

- However, even as Scythian power waned in the west, by this stage they had spread extensively eastward across much of Inner Eurasia. In the Black Sea region, however, the Scythians were reduced by Roman military actions to the status of a minor threat. And when the Goths moved into the Black Sea Scythian heartland in the 3rd century C.E., the Scythians essentially ceased to exist as they mixed into the Gothic population.

SUGGESTED READING

Ebrey, *The Cambridge Illustrated History of China.*

Lewis, *The Early Chinese Empires.*

Schirokauer, et al, *A Brief History of Chinese and Japanese Civilizations.*

QUESTIONS TO CONSIDER

1. In what ways did the environment of the steppes influence the abilities, attitudes, and beliefs of the people who dwelt in these regions?

2. Has any animal played a more crucial role in world history than the horse?

OXUS CIVILIZATION AND POWERFUL PERSIA

T he story of civilization in central Asia provides an ideal example of how the key themes in big history offer new insights on the past. In this region of shifting rivers, ephemeral oases, high mountains, and steppe grasslands, early attempts to construct permanent farming settlements were faced with many environmental challenges. Because of this, we see a close correspondence between the rise and fall of towns, cities, and even entire civilizations and natural changes in climate and geography. Despite these environmental challenges, great civilizations did indeed appear in the region. In this lecture, you will learn about the Persians and the cultures that preceded them.

CENTRAL ASIAN CIVILIZATIONS

- All the ancient civilizations we have so far considered were established along major river valleys, including those of the Tigris, Euphrates, Nile, Indus, Huang He, and Yangtze.

- Central Asia had no suitable dominant river to integrate peoples and resources along a trunk corridor, but at various locations, alluvial deposits and oases produced by rivers that essentially drained into the desert were sufficient to be exploited by early farmers.

- With good soil, abundant sunshine, and a ready supply of water, these farming communities prospered; populations and resources increased, and so did the size of settlements until the first towns appeared.

- This meant that when Indo-European–speaking pastoral nomads started migrating into central Asia in the 3rd millennium B.C.E., they did not move into virgin territory; the region was already occupied by farming communities speaking a range of indigenous languages.

- The numbers of these farmers were sparse in most places, because the oases could not support large populations. But in a handful of environmentally conducive locations, really big settlements had already appeared before the nomads arrived, including the ancient city of Anau, located in modern Turkmenistan.

- Anau was inhabited from the 4th millennium B.C.E., making it one of the oldest urban areas on the planet. Excavation of this site began in 1904 by the American archaeologist Raphael Pumpelli. The excavations at Anau have not only yielded abundant material on the origins and growth of agricultural settlements in central Asia, but they have also proved the existence of early trade and exchange links between central Asia and the city-states of the Indus valley and Mesopotamia.

- But the findings at Anau also illustrate the eternal story of civilizational expansion and contraction: By 2400 B.C.E., all urban centers in central Asia, including Anau, were in a state of collapse. The reasons remain a mystery, although environmental factors, such as climate change and the drying up of oases, must have played a major role.

- However, if this was the case, the environment must have stabilized quite quickly, because within a few centuries, new urban settlements appeared in the region, in particular those associated with the Oxus civilization.

THE OXUS CIVILIZATION

- The appearance of the Oxus civilization was probably influenced by new waves of migration into central Asia by Indo-European–speaking pastoral nomads, whose tribal confederations, with well-developed political structures and powerful chiefs, occupied the more sparsely populated lands.

- The impact of Indo-European migrations across much of ancient Eurasia varied considerably according to the level of sociopolitical and technological development already achieved in the regions they moved into.

- The distinctive culture that emerged in the region toward the end of the 3rd millennium was thus a result of the mixing of preexisting agrarian peoples and pastoral nomads, a mixing that led eventually to the development of distinctive new central Asian cultures, such as the Sogdians and Bactrians.

- This also helped firmly establish central Asia as one of the major centers of a trans-Eurasian network of cultural exchanges, a situation that was fully realized during the period of the Oxus civilization.

- Until the late 20th century, there was virtually no evidence of the existence of the Oxus civilization. But thanks to work of the late Greco-Russian archaeologist Vicktor Sarianidi, we now have striking evidence of this complex urban culture.

- Like the settlements at Anau, Oxus sites were clustered around a series of oases in the harsh deserts of central Asia. Viktor Sarianidi declared the Oxus civilization to be the fifth oldest civilization on earth—not just an urban culture but an entire lost civilization. And he noted that it was one of just a handful of ancient civilizations that did not emerge in a river valley.

- These Oxus urban sites, which appeared between about 2200 and 2000, helped facilitate trade between sedentary agriculturists and neighboring nomadic pastoralists and brought central Asia into the preexisting exchange network that already linked Egypt, Mesopotamia, and the Indus civilization.

- Oxus centers also represent new developments in settlement patterns in the region, with communities centred around large fortified complexes that Soviet archaeologist Sergei Tolstov named *qala*.

- The most important of these fortified *qala* are Gonur in Turkmenistan, Sapalli in Uzbekistan, and Dashli in northern Afghanistan, archaeological sites that have yielded evidence of high levels of craftsmanship and also of the early use of spoked wheels and horse riding.

- There is also considerable evidence of mercantile activity, with the influence of steppe nomadic culture obvious in many of the trade goods discovered, particularly the iconography on the seals, cylinders, and metal ornaments discovered at Oxus sites.

- But the environment in this part of the world is always changing, so it is not surprising that urban activity was renewed several centuries later, during the 1ˢᵗ millennium B.C.E. This is evidenced by the construction of new irrigation systems and fortifications, probably in response to increased levels of nomadic militarization during the Scythian era.

THE PERSIAN EMPIRE

- In spite of these efforts at self-defense, the relative isolation of these new fortified centers left them vulnerable to attacks from the Scythians and other militarized nomads, and also from the armies of powerful sedentary states, as the Achaemenid Persians were about to demonstrate.

- It wasn't just central Asia that was about to be incorporated into an expansive Persian state, but huge swathes of Eurasia. During the 1ˢᵗ millennium B.C.E., they all found themselves absorbed by the Persians into the greatest empire the world had ever seen. The Persians essentially brought Europe and Asia into direct contact with an intensity never seen before, and this had tremendous ramifications for trans-Eurasian cultural exchange.

- The Persian heartland is the Iranian plateau, a high and semiarid region located to the east of Mesopotamia and separated from the valleys of the Tigris and Euphrates by the Zagros Mountains. The plateau has long functioned as a natural crossroads between west and central Eurasia, an area through which numerous migrating peoples have passed, virtually since the time humans started moving out of Africa 100,000 years ago.

- Late in the 2nd millennium B.C.E., two groups of Indo-European–speaking pastoral nomads, the Medes and the Persians, settled on the plateau and organized themselves into tribal confederations. The Medes and Persians were highly militarized, and as the Babylonian and Assyrian empires waned in Mesopotamia, both groups began to use their military prowess to construct their own imperial states.

- The Medes were the first to strike. King Cyaxares established Median hegemony over large areas of Mesopotamia and western-central Asia after forming an alliance with the Scythians and destroying the Assyrians at Nineveh in 612 B.C.E.

- The founding ruler of what would become the Persian empire was Cyrus, a leader of the Achaemenid family. The Greek historian Herodotus is our most important source for the life of Cyrus.

- Herodotus tells us that Cyrus came to the throne in 559 or 558 B.C.E. and that between 553 and 550, he overthrew the Median king and adopted the Median royal title of "Great King, King of Kings, King of Lands." He then led his forces out of Iran on a series of successful expansionary campaigns, and during the next two decades, he established an empire that stretched from Afghanistan to Turkey.

The Greek historian Herodotus is our most important source for the life of Cyrus.

- Cyrus owed his success—and his title, Cyrus the Great—to his ability to achieve clear-sighted military objectives, despite the formation of alliances against him by the rulers of Lydia, Babylon, and Egypt.

- Cyrus eventually died around 530 while fighting the powerful nomadic Massagetae, under their ruler Queen Tomyris, during a failed campaign to conquer the steppes of modern Uzbekistan. With the death of the king, many parts of the empire quickly rebelled, and the whole structure could have fallen apart had it not been for the exceptional ability of Cyrus's successors, beginning with Cambyses, who ruled between 530 and 522.

- Cambyses was a skilled military leader and administrator. Cambyses added Egypt and parts of North Africa to the Persian realm. Cambyses assumed authority as a pharaoh, thus bringing to an end millennia of Egyptian autonomy and starting a long period of Egyptian colonization by powerful empires like the Persians. But the successful Egyptian campaign was also Cambyses's last; he died from an accident during his return from Egypt in 522.

- While Cambyses had been campaigning in Egypt, a revolt led by a usurper named Gaumata had broken out in Persia. Cambyses's son and successor Darius, an officer in the army for the Egyptian campaign, immediately marched back to the Persian homeland and defeated Gaumata. Darius, the third in a line of superb Achaemenid leaders, went on to rule for 35 years, from 521 to 486.

- After being crowned king of Persia, he quickly restored order all over the empire by suppressing a series of revolts during the first year of his reign and then increased the size of the already-massive empire through expansionary campaigns until it stretched from India to the Balkans.

- During a seven-year campaign between 520 and 513, Darius captured Sind and the Punjab in India, bringing the entire Indus valley under Persian control. In the west, Darius crossed the narrow Bosporus into Europe in 513 and campaigned against the Scythians north of the Black Sea, bringing much of Thrace and Macedonia under his control.

- Darius and his successors were then faced with the task of administering this huge multicultural empire in which a range of languages, religions, and cultures coexisted. In tackling this daunting challenge, they succeeded in creating an administrative system that offered valuable lessons to many civilizations that followed.

- Realizing that it would be futile and even unwise to attempt to standardize these cultural differences, the Persians focused on constructing an empire that achieved a fine balance between centralized and local administration.

- Through their far-sighted administrative policies, the Persians learned to administer the largest empire the world had ever seen, and in so doing, they established a model for subsequent imperial governments, such as the Mauryans, Kushans, and Romans, as well as their regional Iranian successors, the Parthians and Sasanians.

- But in the end, the Persians overreached themselves; it was Achaemenid expansion into the eastern Mediterranean that led to the demise of this first Persian empire.

SUGGESTED READING

Brosius, *The Persians.*

Foltz, *Spirituality in the Land of the Noble.*

Frye, *The Heritage of Central Asia.*

QUESTIONS TO CONSIDER

1. How did early farmers, nomads, and merchants create the prosperous Oxus civilization deep in the harsh desert environment of central Asia?

2. What administrative techniques did Cyrus and his Achaemenid successors use to construct and govern the greatest empire ever seen in world history? How did these differ from the techniques tried by previous imperial rulers in the region, beginning with Sargon?

GREECE IN ITS GOLDEN AGE

This lecture is about the civilization of classical Greece and the various experiments the Greeks carried out in how to effectively govern a complex state for the benefit of all its citizens. Geography and the environment often dictate the cultural and historical evolution of civilizations both ancient and modern, and this is certainly the case with the Greeks. But as you will learn in this lecture, the genius of the system of government that the Greeks developed made it both adaptable and inspirational to cultures around the world.

ANCIENT GREEK CIVILIZATION

- Greece is essentially made up of a mainland region that juts into the Mediterranean and also of thousands of islands. The mainland is a mountainous peninsula, and its rugged mountain interior made internal communications difficult.

- So, the cities that eventually emerged on the mainland were isolated from each other to the extent that, throughout the long history of ancient Greece, they generally preferred to remain independent. There was never any such thing as a Greek empire then, although different states would form alliances in times of conflict.

- Along the west coast of the peninsula, the mountains fall so steeply into the sea that there are no safe harbors. But much of the rest of the mainland is indented with natural harbors, particularly the east coast and the land south of the Gulf of Corinth, the Peloponnesus.

- The challenges of travel in the Greek interior and the nature of the region's coastline acted as a natural encouragement to the development of robust maritime trade and communication by sea.

- Another geographical feature of critical importance to Greek history is the serious lack of arable land in the country, which forced the mainland city-states to establish colonies abroad—both to serve as supplementary sources of food and to provide more space for rapidly increasing populations.

- Because of its geography, and the widespread unrest across the eastern Mediterranean during the so-called Greek Dark Ages from roughly 1100 to 800 B.C.E., no central power emerged in the region during this period. Instead, it was left up to local institutions to try to restore civil society.

- In the context of this ongoing conflict, it is hardly surprising that the most common local institution to emerge toward the end of this period was the polis, a Greek word for a fortified citadel that offered refuge for surrounding communities when needed. What is remarkable, however, is the new species of political system that evolved in the poleis over time.

- Because they were defensible and strategically located, these poleis began to attract larger and denser populations, becoming increasingly urbanized commercial and political centers that took control of surrounding regions.

- To support the functions of government, elites within the poleis extracted tribute from the hinterlands in the form of a proportion of agricultural surplus, and much like the early Mesopotamian city-states, this tribute was used to support urban populations.

- By 800 B.C.E., many mainland poleis had evolved into bustling city-states, which functioned as the principal centers of Greek civilization throughout its history.

- The next century was characterized by political tension in the poleis after elite noble classes gained power. They established an aristocracy (a Greek word that means "government by the best") or an oligarchy ("government by the few").

- But over the century that followed, increasing maritime trade in pottery, textiles, and wine, as well as the minting of the first coinage in the world to facilitate these commercial transactions, led to the emergence of a new middle class that began to challenge the elite monopoly on power.

- At the same time, with arable land in short supply, rising populations put increasing pressure on resources, which is why many poleis established overseas colonies, encouraging commoners to resettle as a safety valve against potential political unrest.

- Greek colonization did help temporarily ease political tensions within the poleis, and it had the larger effect of intensifying commercial and cultural exchange between the various peoples that lived in these regions and spreading Greek language and culture.

- However, despite the establishment of these colonies, political unrest continued to ferment as both commoners and middle class chafed at the power and political presumptions of the nobility.

- Soon after 650, political revolutions broke out in several of the poleis, leading to the appearance of a new type of ruler known as a tyrant, another Greek word that means one who "usurps power." Many tyrants seized power with the explicit support of the poor and middle class, and then passed laws to redistribute land to the poor and promote commerce and economic development.

- They also encouraged middle-class citizens to take a larger role in civic and military life, leading to the creation of a new heavily armed, citizen-based military force. In this environment of political and military reform, new ideas about the best way to organize and govern a society were constantly swirling about.

THE PERSIAN WARS

- As Athens, Sparta, and other mainland Greek poleis prospered in their own ways, Greek colonies and merchants continued to gain prominence in the Mediterranean and Black Sea basins, from Spain in the west to Crimea in the east. It was this expansion of Greek interests that eventually brought the Greeks into conflict with the rapidly expanding Persian empire.

- The protracted conflict between the Greeks and Persians, which lasted for nearly three decades, is known to history as the Persian Wars, thanks mostly to the superb account of the conflict written by the great 5th century B.C.E. Athenian historian Herodotus.

- The spark that ignited the conflict was an aggressive move by the Persian king Darius to incorporate the prosperous Greek colonies into the Persian empire by force. The colonies revolted in 499 and appealed to their fellow Greeks for help; in response, Athens sent ships and burned the Persian city of Sardis, invoking a furious Persian response.

- Persian king Darius sent 20,000 troops across the Aegean in 490 B.C.E. in an attempt to force the Athenians to accept a pro-Persian tyrant. The Persian fleet landed at Marathon, but the Greeks outflanked the Persians, forcing them to retreat to their ships with the loss of about 6,400 men.

- Ten years later, the new Persian king Xerxes launched a second campaign, dispatching possibly the largest force ever assembled to that point in history across the swift-flowing water at the Hellespont, the narrow strait between Asia Minor and Europe.

- To make the crossing, the Persian army constructed two pontoon bridges, marched over them, and then headed down the coast toward Athens, accompanied by a formidable fleet of 350 ships. Athens hastily assembled its own fleet of 200 war ships, while Sparta formalized a defensive alliance of 31 states.

- A force of 300 Spartans, supported by several hundred allied troops, prepared to confront the massive Persian army at a narrow pass at Thermopylae. Although the Persian military strategy had allowed them to create the largest empire in world history, the particular geographical circumstances of Thermopylae were much better suited to the Greek formation.

- The Spartans and their allies all died but have been immortalized ever since in Western culture for the courage of their stand against overwhelming odds.

- The Persian forces continued down the coast and sacked the polis of Athens.

- But at the ensuing Battle of Salamis, the ships of the outnumbered Athenian navy, with the assistance of some very fortuitous winds, managed to destroy the Persian fleet, and the Persians were effectively driven out of Greece forever.

- Despite the courage of the Spartans at Thermopylae, it was Athens that emerged as the de facto leader of the Greek world after the defeat of the Persians, and during the ensuing Golden Age, Greek civilization went on to achieve the fullest development of its genius.

- Ultimately, the triumphs and failures of classical Greek society ended in bitter self-destruction through civil war. Although the Persians had been driven out of mainland Greece, they still ruled many Greek colonies along the Ionian Coast.

- The Athenians addressed the situation by establishing a defensive alliance of several of the Aegean city-states, the Delian League, in 478 B.C.E. Sparta, for its part, returned to its preferred policy of isolationism.

- From the beginning, Athens dominated the Delian League, insisting that the allied states pay large amounts of cash to Athens to maintain its navy and thus protect members of the league in case of renewed conflict with the Persians.

- But what many allies resented as the years went by, with no further outbreak of hostilities with the Persians, was that the coins they were paying to Athens were really being used to finance Athenian building projects, such as the Acropolis and the Parthenon.

THE PELOPONNESIAN WAR

- Resentment grew stronger during the 32-year reign of the great Athenian statesman and orator Pericles. Other Greek city-states that were not in the Delian League began to ally themselves with Sparta in a new power block that came to be known as the Spartan League.

- In 431 B.C.E., tensions between Sparta and Athens reached a boiling point, and Sparta declared war on Athens. The war would drag on for 27 years and was superbly catalogued by the ancient Greek historian Thucydides in his account of the conflict, *History of the Peloponnesian War.*

- The indecisive conflict dragged on until a treaty was signed in 421, which included a 50-year pact of nonaggression and concluded the first phase of the war. In the end, the treaty held for six years, but war parties in both Athens

and Sparta kept resentment on the boil, particularly a hot-headed kinsman of Pericles named Alcibiades.

■ War resumed in 415, when the Athenians received word that one of their allied colonies in Sicily was under attack from the city-state of Syracuse, a Spartan ally. The Athenians felt obliged to assist their ally and sent Alcibiades and their forces on what turned out to be an utterly disastrous expedition against Syracuse.

■ Alcibiades soon defected to the Spartan side, leaving a general named Nicias to lead the Athenian force. Procrastination by Nicias meant that virtually nothing was accomplished during the expedition's first season. And when reinforcements arrived the following spring, poor decisions made by the Athenian leaders resulted in the utter defeat of the Athenians in a great sea battle in Syracuse harbor.

■ The Athenians managed to recover from this disaster, and political revolution in the city saw a group of 400 oligarchs placed in power, under whose leadership Athens won several victories and recovered much of its territory.

■ But the Spartans ended up winning the final, decisive conflict of the war when, in 405, their brilliant commander Lysander annihilated the Athenian fleet in a great sea battle, sinking 168 Athenian ships and capturing thousands of sailors. Athens was utterly defeated and surrendered the next year.

■ The Golden Age of Greece was over. In Sparta, a reactionary oligarchy was put in place, and in Athens, democracy was suspended and replaced by the rule of Thirty Tyrants. Intellectuals had lost faith in democracy, and some of them hoped for the intervention of new leaders who would reunify Greek civilization. They found them—not in Athens, but to the north, in Macedonia.

SUGGESTED READING

Demand, *A History of Ancient Greece in its Mediterranean Context.*

Harris, ed., *Rethinking the Mediterranean.*

Kagan, *The Peloponnesian War.*

QUESTIONS TO CONSIDER

1. Why did the physical environment of Greece make it difficult to form a unified Greek civilization?

2. After their success in defeating the mighty Persians, what caused Greek civilization to implode in a bitter civil war?

GREEK GODS, PHILOSOPHY, AND SCIENCE

The ancient Greeks were a naturally curious people. The belief systems they constructed were motivated by a need to discover some sense of meaning and order in the natural world and in the world of human society. As in Western society in our day, some pursued these ends through faith or creative expression while others pursued them through rational inquiry. It was the achievements of the Greeks that laid the foundations on which much of the West's later intellectual accomplishments are built.

GREEK RELIGION

- The Greeks constructed one of the richest and most influential cultures in history. This is nowhere more obvious than in the realm of philosophy, a field in which the towering figures of Socrates, Plato, and Aristotle used reason and logic to construct sophisticated explanations of the natural and moral world and the place of humans in it.

- But despite the monumental achievements of Greek thinkers, most Greeks did not have an advanced education, nor a sophisticated ability to rigorously apply logic to questions of meaning and purpose.

- Rather, most Greeks relied on religion to help them understand the world and their place in it, and given the often-spiteful and willful behavior of the many gods and goddesses who dwelt on the lofty slopes of Mount Olympus, what a confusing and arbitrary world this must have seemed to them.

- Greek religion was the epitome of polytheism—a pantheon of deities that represented all the phenomena of the world and whose relationships explain why and how the world became what it is.

- The Greeks constructed epic myths to explain this world, beginning with the creation of Mother Earth out of a formless void of chaos, as revealed to the poet Hesiod. According to Hesiod, Earth generated a partner in the Sky, and together they gave birth to day and night, to sun and moon, and to all the other natural phenomena.

- From the beginning, the Greek pantheon was a place of struggle between these various spirits, and out of early conflicts, the god Zeus, grandson of Earth and Sky, emerged as the most powerful ruler of the divine realm. The court of Zeus and his wife Hera was populated by all manner of gods and goddesses, each with their own special powers and responsibilities.

- The fascinating stories about the various gods and goddesses can be understood as metaphors to explain the world and the powerful forces within it. But they also served a civic function in that they allowed for the formation of religious cults that provided an outlet for various groups within Greek society.

- The cults established rituals that were known only to initiates. The rites of even the most famous cult, the cult of the Eleusian Mysteries, are still largely unknown, although they apparently included a purification process, a ritual bath in the sea, and three days of fasting.

- Of particular importance to gender relations in Greece were the cults that were open to women, which allowed them to find a place in wider society beyond the confines of the home.

Zeus and cupid

- Eventually, the rituals associated with the cults moved from the mountains to the city center. The drama that emerged was innovative, provocative, and profoundly influential.

- The plays were presented in magnificent, semicircular open-air theaters that seated up to 20,000 spectators. The dramas performed in these theaters, which were usually presented as part of a competition, played out in full view of the audience on a small performance space called the orchestra.

- The playwright Aeschylus, a veteran of the Persian Wars, is credited as the first great innovator of Greek drama, adding more actors, more elaborate costumes, and genuine dramatic monologues to his plays. Yet many of these dramas were deeply conservative and promoted the values of Greek religion.

- Another brilliant Athenian dramatic innovator was the highly educated actor and musician Sophocles, who wrote more complex, psychological roles for his protagonists.

- A lifelong friend of Sophocles, Euripides, was another brilliant dramatist who wrote experimental, even scandalous plays that led to him being accused of using immorality to subvert the state.

- The different opinions expressed by these dramatists on the role of the gods in the life of humans reflected a broader dichotomy between those Greeks who sought an understanding of the world through religion and those who sought it through reason.

- The rich schools of Greek philosophy that emerged set out to explain not only the purpose for human existence, but indeed the very nature of the physical world and the structure of the universe itself, using rational, logical arguments that had no need to resort to polytheistic beliefs.

- It was the pursuit of knowledge of the natural world by early Greek thinkers, an approach we would describe as scientific today, that paved the way for the later moral and ethical philosophy of Socrates, Plato, and Aristotle.

GREEK PHILOSOPHY

- The birthplace of Greek philosophy—a word that means "lovers of wisdom"—was not Greece itself, but the colonies established by the mainland city-states along the Ionian coast of modern Turkey and in Sicily and southern Italy.

- One of the first Ionian thinkers was Thales of Miletus, who flourished around 600 B.C.E. Thales was an extraordinary mixture of philosopher and pragmatic scientist, and as far as we are aware, he was the first Western intellectual to argue that the universe could be completely understood by natural laws and reason—not by mythology and religion.

- Anaximander, a student of Thales, attempted to accurately describe the true shape of the earth in relation to the other celestial objects.

- The Pythagoreans, a semireligious society founded by Pythagoras in a Greek colony in Sicily, adopted an approach to knowledge that combined mathematics and metaphysics into the first known system that used numbers to understand the nature of the universe. Another influential discovery of the Pythagoreans was that musical harmony was based on mathematical proportions.

- The philosopher Democritus, who was born in northern mainland Greece around 460 B.C.E., was part of a group of materialist philosophers who approached the world from a pragmatic perspective. They were not so much interested in the purpose of events but in explaining the events themselves. Democritus and his colleagues accurately suggested that everything in the universe consisted of atoms.

- Attempts to understand the world from a scientific point of view are also evident in the work of Greek physicians such as Hippocrates. The great text that Hippocrates produced, the *Hippocratic Corpus*, is another milestone in the history of rational science in that it attempts to expand the knowledge of diseases and treatments by observing the course of illnesses and describing rational medical interventions.

- The final group of pre-Socratic philosophers are the Sophists, intellectuals who were more interested in human behavior than the natural world. Their skepticism of the accepted ideas and standard mores of human behavior often made them figures of suspicion, potential corruptors of the young, and dangerous intellectuals who were attempting to undermine the state. Sophists were master lecturers, renowned for their skills at rhetoric.

SOCRATES, PLATO, AND ARISTOTLE

- The predecessor of both Plato and Aristotle is one of the most famous philosophers who ever lived: Socrates. Like his pupil Plato, and Plato's pupil Aristotle, Socrates disagreed with the Sophists. He suggested that only by asking meaningful questions and subjecting the answers

Socrates (c. 470 B.C.E.–399 B.C.E.)

to logical analysis—that is, not by using mere rhetoric and sophistic tricks—could agreement be reached about ethical and moral behavior.

■ The only evil for Socrates was ignorance; human virtue and excellence were the products of constant intellectual activity in the pursuit of genuine knowledge. Socrates took this idea into the realm of ethics, arguing that the wise man who knows what is right will also do what is right—that intellectual cultivation will inevitably lead to ethical cultivation, surely the aim of all educators ever since.

■ But like the Sophists, Socrates's constant questioning of everything, including the political leaders of Athens, raised the suspicions of the state. Socrates was arrested as a subversive radical, tried by his peers, and condemned to death.

■ The death sentence against Socrates revealed that even the Athenians had a limited tolerance toward efforts at understanding nature and explaining it rationally, without recourse to the gods. But thinking of this kind could not be suppressed, as Plato and Aristotle demonstrated.

■ Plato, who lived a long life between 427 and 347, was Socrates's most famous disciple. He established a school of higher education in the Athenian suburb of Akademia, the name that has been applied to the world of professors and intellectuals ever since.

■ In addition to being known for his theory of the nature of the universe and the creation of the world, Plato also produced some of the most famous works in the history of philosophy, using Socrates as his main character and pursuing philosophical questions through his depictions of dialogues between Socrates and others.

■ Plato's greatest pupil, Aristotle, also went on to found his own institute of higher learning in Athens, the Lyceum. And Aristotle also profoundly impacted history as a teacher—in particular, through his role as tutor to Alexander of Macedon.

- Aristotle's intellectual interests were incredibly varied; he essentially invented the modern academic disciplines of biology, mathematics, astronomy, physics, literature, rhetoric, logic, politics, ethics, and metaphysics.

- One of the most remarkable things about the achievements of these Greek thinkers is that they made their arguments about the power of human reason to decipher the truth and the purpose of existence in the midst of a profoundly religious age.

- This profound dichotomy between understanding the universe as an entity created by a god or gods—and therefore knowable only through submission to gods—or of the ability of humans to understand everything through reason and rational logic has remained the defining eternal question faced by human beings ever since.

SUGGESTED READING

Burkert, *Greek Religion.*

Colaiaco, *Socrates against Athens.*

Sourvinou-Inwood, *Athenian Myths and Festivals.*

QUESTIONS TO CONSIDER

1. What was the real function of the enormous range of deities in the ancient Greek pantheon? Were they taken literally or metaphorically by the Greeks?

2. How persistent has the Greek dichotomy between trying to understand the universe through rational enquiry or through submission to divine spirits been throughout subsequent human history?

ALEXANDER'S CONQUESTS AND HELLENISM

Philip II, king of Macedonia, with the assistance of his son Alexander, defeated Greek armies at the Battle of Chaeronea in 338 B.C.E., which gave the Macedonians control over much of Greece. But this victory was intended to be just the prelude to Philip's real aim of leading a combined Macedonian and Greek army against the Persians. Philip's assassination meant that the task would be taken up by Alexander, who set out in 336 B.C.E, on one of the most audacious campaigns in history. Alexander's campaign marked the beginning of a fresh chapter in the history of civilization; it ushered in a new era during which Greek civilization expanded across vast regions of Afro-Eurasia.

PHILIP II

- Since the end of the Peloponnesian War, the Persians had continued to meddle in Greek affairs, pursuing policies that aimed to keep Greece fragmented. Many Greeks lost faith in democracy, and some openly called for the appearance of a benevolent tyrant who could reunite the poleis, although few would have expected this champion to come from Macedonia.

- Until the mid-4th century, Macedonia had been seen as little more than a rugged frontier state to the north of Greece, home to peasant farmers and seasonal pastoralists. But Macedonian elites had quietly prospered through trade with the wealthy cities of Greece, and this commercial relationship had allowed the elites to become increasingly well acquainted with Greek culture.

- One such member of the Macedonian nobility was Philip II, and during his lengthy reign as king between 359 and 336 B.C.E., Macedonia emerged as a powerful and sophisticated state in its own right.

- In his youth, Philip had gained considerable expertise in Greek military history and strategy, and once he became king, he used this knowledge to build a formidable military by uniting the experienced and well-trained Macedonian cavalry with the Greek infantry.

- With these forces, Philip methodically annexed the northern Greek cities, and although all Greeks recognized the threat posed by Philip, the Peloponnesian War had so poisoned the atmosphere that the formation of any sort of alliance to stop the Macedonians was impossible. Even when Athens and Thebes did act belatedly to join forces against the Macedonians, their armies were destroyed at the Battle of Chaeronea.

- Philip allowed the Greek poleis to retain their own governments, vowed that he would crush any who rose up against him, and then began to make preparations to invade the Persian empire. It was on the eve of departure that Philip was assassinated, perhaps with Persian complicity.

- Alexander quickly assumed control, gained the support of the Macedonian nobility, and crushed the only attempted Greek uprising against him in Thebes. At the age of 21, he prepared to carry out his father's aim of destroying the Persian empire.

ALEXANDER THE GREAT

- Alexander was a superb athlete and horseman, charismatic leader, and gifted military strategist. The new king of Macedonia and Greece was also highly educated; his tutor had been the great philosopher Aristotle. By the age of 20, Alexander was ready to wage war against the Persians.

- Crossing the Bosporus and marching into Asia Minor, Alexander's force of 43,000 infantry and 6,000 cavalry gained an early victory over the Persians in 334 B.C.E. at the River Granicus, a victory that liberated the Greek colonies along the Ionian coast.

- Alexander again defeated King Darius and the Persians in a second battle south of the ancient city of Issus in Turkey.

- After being held up for six months by a siege of the Phoenician city of Tyre, Alexander marched into Egypt, where at a small coastal village he decided to found a new city. He named the city Alexandria, which would turn out to be not only the first but also the greatest of the 70 or so cities he founded in his campaign.

- In Egypt, Alexander was greeted as a liberator, and after visiting the oracle of the Egyptian god Amon, whom the Greeks identified with Zeus, he began to see himself as semidivine.

Alexander the Great
(356 B.C.E.–323 B.C.E.)

- Alexander now took an unexpected northern route to march rapidly into Mesopotamia for a fateful third confrontation with Darius and the Persians. After crossing the Tigris River with great difficulty due to its strong current, Alexander prepared to confront Darius on an open, flat plain just east of the city of Mosul in modern Iraq. Darius chose this field at Gaugamela.

- Despite being grossly outnumbered, Alexander struck the decisive blow of the Battle of Gaugamela by forming his units into an unstoppable wedge that he personally led deep into the Persian center, completely unnerving Darius and changing the course of history as a result.

- In the aftermath, Alexander captured or killed large numbers of Persian soldiers and also captured a huge treasure before marching triumphantly into Babylon. After resting for a month, Alexander continued on to the Persian capital of Persepolis, capturing an even greater quantity of treasure and allowing his drunken soldiers to burn and loot the city.

- Marching next toward modern Tehran to try to capture Darius, Alexander was dismayed to find that the Persian king had already been murdered by a kinsman named Bessus. This gave Alexander the excuse he needed to push on deep into central Asia, ostensibly to punish Bessus for his act of regicide.

- After capturing several of the great trading cities of central Asia, Alexander took his men across the snow-covered Hindu Kush and into Bactria, where he married Roxana, the beautiful daughter of a Sogdian nobleman.

- With central Asia now more or less secured, Alexander marched south across the Khyber Pass into the Indus River valley, where he was confronted by a powerful local ruler named Porus at the Battle of the Hydaspes.

- Once again, Alexander's audacious strategy paid off. Crossing the Jhelum River in secrecy with a small force, he attacked Porus's flank, and even though the battle was costly for the Macedonians, Porus surrendered. Creating a power vacuum in the region allowed the young Indian prince Chandragupta to build the Mauryan empire. The battle also opened up much of India to Greek political, economic, and cultural influences in the centuries that followed.

- With all of India now open to him, Alexander was keen to press on, but after this bloody battle, his troops refused to go any farther; reluctantly, Alexander was obliged to abandon his campaign and turn for home. He took up residence in the palace of Nebuchadnezzar II in Babylon.

- The king of Europe and Asia began to make preparations for new campaigns, but following a prolonged bout of drinking and feasting, Alexander fell ill and died on June 11, 323 B.C.E., at the age of 33.

- Alexander had ruled for only 13 years, but by facilitating a changing of the guard from Persian to Greco-Macedonian rule, he had irrevocably altered the geopolitical context of a huge region of western Afro-Eurasia and also made possible the colonization of much of the region by the conquerors. Alexander's campaign also led to an astonishing flow of wealth from the Persian realm to the Mediterranean.

THE HELLENISTIC ERA

- When Alexander died, the seemingly unified Greco-Macedonian empire he had created was quickly plunged into crisis as his generals fought to carve up the empire. What emerged after 50 years of conflict was a three-part polycentric Hellenistic empire that survived until the Romans eventually incorporated much of the region into their own expansive state.

- Several of the new cities that Alexander had established were at the center of this Hellenization of much of Afro-Eurasia, from the Mediterranean to central Asia. Some never evolved to be more than fortified settlements or administrative centers, but others developed into thriving metropolises that attracted large numbers of Greek and Macedonian colonists.

- All the Hellenistic cities show evidence of a surging economy based on commerce, with new centers of wealth emerging particularly in Syria and Egypt and new middle-class commercial elites becoming powerful enough to challenge the traditional nobility.

- As the political, intellectual, and economic center of the Greek world shifted from the classical Greek poleis to these new cities, Greek civilization lost its inward-looking, civic-focused character and became increasingly cosmopolitan.

- The mainland Greek cities also turned away from their earlier experiments in democratic government, which no longer worked in poleis that were now small parts of much larger imperial structures. This meant that one of the most cherished contributions of ancient Greece to modern civilization essentially disappeared for millennia.

- No city typifies the cosmopolitanism of the Hellenistic era more than the city that Alexander had personally founded on the shores of the Mediterranean in Egypt: Alexandria. Enormous wealth flowed through Alexandria, the greatest bureaucratic, economic, and intellectual center of the Hellenistic world.

- Alexandria's enormous harbor could accommodate 1,200 ships at any one time, making it the most important port—not just in the Mediterranean but indeed the entire world—in the 3rd century B.C.E.

- People from all over Afro-Eurasia resided in this huge megalopolis. These residents were of very different religious and cultural traditions, all learning to conduct their affairs in a spirit of multiculturalism and tolerance.

- Alexandria also became the intellectual center of western Afro-Eurasia after the government established the Alexandrian Museum, an institute of higher learning where philosophers, writers, and scientists were able to carry out advanced research. Attached to the center was the famous Alexandrian Library, which by the 1st century B.C.E. had a collection of hundreds of thousands of scrolled manuscripts.

■ The growth of new cities like Alexandria across the Hellenistic world tended to eclipse the reputation and wealth of the ancient poleis on mainland Greece. This had ramifications for Greek philosophy, which now had to function in a much larger, more cosmopolitan context.

■ Because the ancient poleis were no longer self-governing states but small parts of much larger imperial structures, their residents were forced to become more "international" in outlook. At the same time, Greeks were now living all over the Hellenistic world, from India to Egypt, so the new philosophical schools that emerged were designed to help people, wherever they dwelt, make sense of this vast and confusing new geopolitical environment.

■ Three of those schools proved very attractive to the Romans, and as a result, they have remained deeply embedded in the Western psyche ever since. Epicureanism, skepticism, and stoicism each in its own way addressed the problem of how to find purpose and calm in the midst of a chaotic world.

■ Science and technology also made some fascinating advances in Alexandria during the Hellenistic era, including in agriculture. Two other quite extraordinary fields in which Alexandrian scientists made technological advances were automata and pneumatics.

■ Hellenistic sculptors also produced some of the abiding masterpieces of all Greek art. A large number of magnificent sculptures have survived the centuries, each of them expressing an extraordinary sense of realism and movement that has inspired artists ever since, from the Romans to Michelangelo.

- In so many ways, Hellenistic civilization was the context for extraordinary innovations, functioning as a commercial and cultural bridge between Europe and Asia and between the Persian and Roman empires. But like every civilization we will consider in this course, with the exception thus far of modern civilization, because of internal revolts and civil war, the Hellenistic kingdoms eventually began to crumble.

- The immediate fate of the Hellenistic world was now to be incorporated into the Roman Empire, and this would be the context through which Greek civilization would become deeply embedded into Western civilization.

SUGGESTED READING

Hammond, *The Genius of Alexander the Great.*

Sherwin-White and Kuhrt, *From Samarkhand to Sardis.*

Shipley, *The Greek World after Alexander.*

QUESTIONS TO CONSIDER

1. What was it about Alexander's personality and education that produced one of the most extraordinary generals in history?

2. What changes in the geopolitical context of Greek civilization led to the emergence of new philosophies like epicureanism, skepticism, and stoicism, and why do they still seem so relevant today?

BUILDING THE ROMAN REPUBLIC

The civilization that came to supersede the Greeks as masters of the Mediterranean world was Rome. While the Greeks were establishing their poleis in the Aegean and their colonies around the Mediterranean and Black Seas, a group of elites in a small city in central Italy revolted against their king and established a new form of government based on the rule of an aristocratic assembly they called the Senate.

THE ETRUSCANS

- Late in the 6th century B.C.E., Rome was considerably less distinguished than a score of other cities scattered about the Italian peninsula. The ancestors of the Romans had established their settlement around a group of seven hills on the banks of the Tiber River, in the central Italian plains of Latium.

- The settlers had chosen their site well; the seven hills were easy to defend, the village was built beside a ford across the Tiber River, and the central location of Latium made it easy for the Romans to eventually divide and conquer the entire peninsula.

- The long-booted peninsula played an additional critical geographic role in the story of Rome. Because it juts far out into the heart of the Mediterranean Sea, it effectively divides the Basin in half, which would help the Romans eventually take control of the whole of it.

- To the south of Rome were well-established Greek colonies that flourished along the coast of the mainland and the island of Sicily. To the north were the Etruscans, migrants from Asia Minor who were flourishing in the region called Tuscany today.

■ According to some of the early foundation myths of the Romans, Etruscan kings gained control and ruled Rome for a while, but they were overthrown in a series of events that revolved around female virtue and male honor. The expulsion of the last Etruscan king is dated to 509 B.C.E., which marked the end of Rome's monarchical period and the dawn of the Republic.

■ Whether or not Rome was ever ruled by Etruscan kings, it went through significant changes during its monarchical period. It became a real city with walls and temples, paved roads, and a drainage system. The Romans adopted the Etruscan alphabet, which the Etruscans had adopted from the Greeks.

ROME

■ To replace the monarchy, the Romans established a new form of government that placed executive power in the hands of two officials, the consuls, who were elected annually by the nobility. But the decisions of the consuls had to be ratified by the Senate, which thus constituted the real source of power in Rome.

■ The Romans called this new form of government the res publica, which essentially means the commonwealth. This Republican government would last, despite increasing strains, for almost half a millennium.

■ Senators and consuls were members of the aristocratic patrician class. Privileged status was determined by birth into elite families, much like the elite lineages that gave certain members of earlier human communities automatic status. Patrician men dominated the affairs of state, provided military leadership, and monopolized knowledge of law and legal procedure.

- The common people of Rome, the plebeians, were free citizens with some voice in politics but few of the patricians' political and social advantages. Some plebeian merchants did eventually come to rival the patricians in wealth, but most plebeians were craft workers, peasant farmers, or landless urban poor.

- As was the case in Greece, this social inequality led to conflict; the plebeians sought to increase their political power by taking advantage of the fact that Rome's very survival depended on its army, whose ranks were filled by the plebeians.

- According to tradition, in 494 B.C.E., the plebeians staged a general strike and refused to serve in the army, forcing the patricians to make important concessions. The plebeians were now given the right to elect their own officials, known as tribunes, who were able to veto unfair consul decisions. Plebeians were also made eligible for other important offices. In 450 B.C.E., many of these provisions were enshrined in Roman law.

- By these various compromises, the power base was expanded, although the patricians still managed to maintain their privileged position through their ownership of agricultural land and their ability to "buy" the votes of elected plebian officials. These privileges culminated in a renewed class struggle in the 2nd century B.C.E., which set in play a chain of events that led ultimately to the collapse of the Republic.

- Even as these political changes were occurring, the core social structure of the Roman state remained unchanged. We have quite a detailed understanding of gender roles in Roman society. The male head of the household was called the paterfamilias, and he had tremendous power over his wife and children.

- Beyond the domestic sphere, the Roman Republic regularly found itself in conflict with its neighbors. It conducted its foreign affairs so effectively, however, that it eventually came to dominate the entire Italian peninsula.

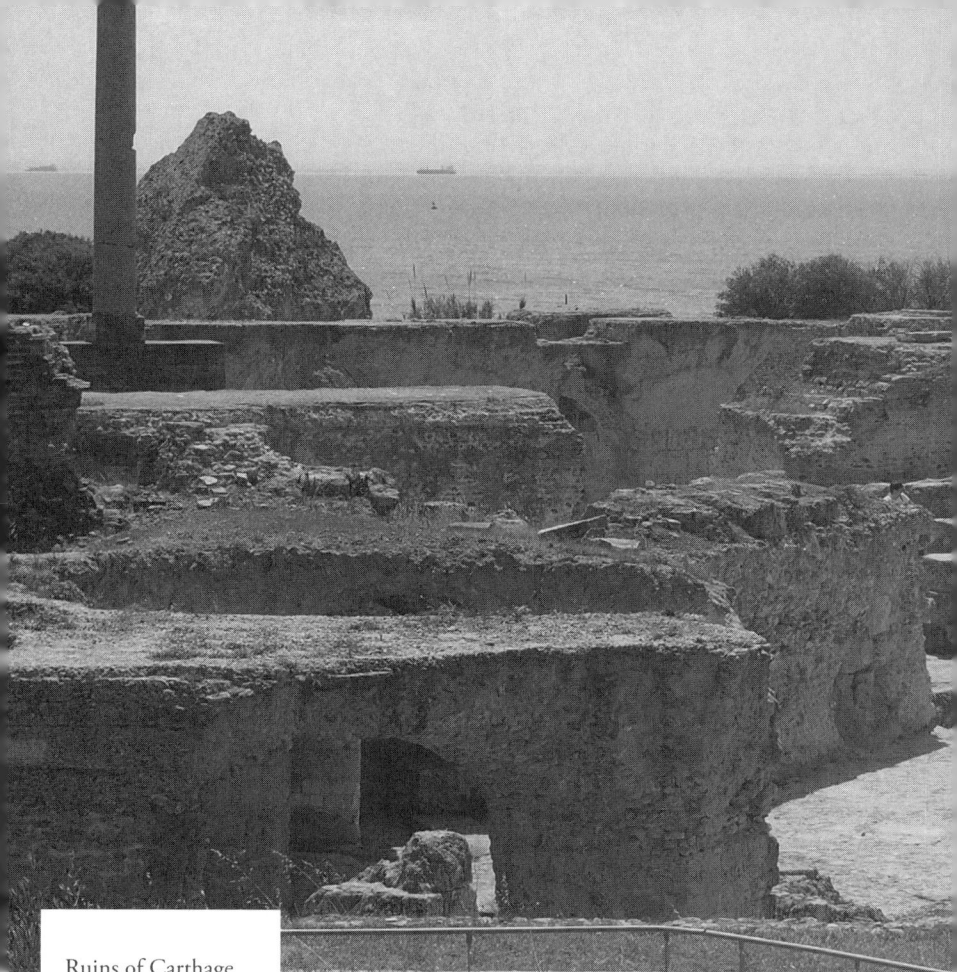

Ruins of Carthage

- The Romans did not impose harsh sanctions on defeated peoples, however, allowing conquered states to remain self-governing so long as they provided levies of troops and supported Roman foreign policy. This enlightened form of hegemony paid enormous dividends when the Republic faced its sternest challenge in a life-and-death struggle with Carthage.

FOREIGN POLICY MATTERS

- By 270 B.C.E., Rome's one remaining rival in the Mediterranean was Carthage, a city established centuries earlier as a Phoenician trading colony on the coast of North Africa. Carthage was now a wealthy state and possessed a superior navy to the Romans, but the Mediterranean was too small to accommodate two such expansive powers.

- In a series of three conflicts known as the Punic Wars, Rome and Carthage battled for survival and control of the Mediterranean basin. By the end of the protracted conflict, Carthage was in ruins, and its culture was extinguished.

- Rome not only survived but evolved from a regional Italian power to a position of unrivalled dominance in the Mediterranean world. By 146 C.E., the year in which Carthage was finally destroyed, Rome was well on its way to creating a vast empire that would gain control over much of western Eurasia and North Africa.

- The struggle with Carthage thus enabled the Romans to conceive of themselves for the first time as a world power and accustomed them to sending armies over large distances to fight in several international theaters simultaneously. This was something that the Romans would continue to do successfully for the next 500 years.

- With the defeat of Carthage, the Romans turned to other foreign policy matters. Eventually declaring the Mediterranean to be *mare nostrum*, or "our sea," the Romans began to create administrative machinery to hold their growing state together through a provincial system ruled by governors.

- With the conquest of the Mediterranean world, Rome became a great city, spending the massive amount of war booty it had accumulated to build theaters, stadiums, and other magnificent structures.

- Even though the Romans began to spend more of their time in leisure pursuits influenced by Hellenistic culture, the Roman state was careening into a series of economic, social, and political crises.

- Many small farms had been destroyed by military operations, and many farmers had been recruited as soldiers by the Romans. After the wars, these veterans joined the ranks of the unemployed in Rome, where they became known as the proletariat.

- Wealthy senators bought up the abandoned farm land and used it to grow cash crops like olive oil and wine instead of grain, working their estates with prisoner of war slave labor, further exacerbating the unemployment problem for free farm laborers.

- These senators were also appointed as governors of the new Roman provinces, where they took advantage of easy corrupt profits and made sure their elite colleagues received lucrative government contracts to supply armies and materials.

- Despite the class wars of centuries earlier, Roman government remained a senatorial oligarchy focused solely on protecting the rights of the rich and powerful. With no solutions to the problems of an impoverished lower class and an inefficient system for governing a world-state based on the corrupt rule of senatorial governors, Rome seethed with discontent. It was the failure of the Senate to address these problems that led ultimately to the collapse of the Republic and the emergence of the Roman Empire.

FROM REPUBLIC TO EMPIRE
- Some patricians did attempt to relieve the situation, such as the tribune Tiberius Gracchus, who, in an attempt to limit the size of senatorial farms, tried to introduce a law that would limit the amount of public land individuals could hold.

- The Senate persuaded the tribunes to veto this measure, so Tiberius had the popular assembly depose the tribunes and still pass the law. The Senate accused him of acting like a king and had Tiberius and 300 of his followers murdered.

- Tiberius's younger brother Gaius was elected tribune in 123 and proposed establishing colonies for military veterans in Italy and Africa. To protect the urban poor against price gouging in the grain market, he also legislated for the government to subsidize grain distribution at half the market price. This became known as the dole and was later used by unscrupulous politicians to buy votes.

- Gaius ran for reelection in 121, but he and 3,000 of his followers died during violent rioting, with nothing having been achieved to redress the social problems.

- Then, between 111 and 105 B.C.E., Roman legions were defeated in Africa and Germany, and in the crisis that followed, the people's assembly elected a tough soldier named Gaius Marius as consul in 107.

- Marius put down the foreign uprisings and professionalized the Roman army, recruiting it from landless peasants who now owed their loyalty to their commander rather than to the Senate. This marked the beginning of the "personal armies" that powerful men could use to threaten the government.

- In 88 B.C.E., the Senate sent their general Sulla to put down an uprising in Asia Minor, but the people chose Marius to go and fight the same war, leading to the first civil war. The war was won by Sulla, who proved to be even tougher than Marius. The Senate appointed him sole dictator, which gave the senatorial elites complete control of legislation until Sulla retired in 79.

- More ambitious men now appeared on the political scene, determined to gain personal power. Pompey Magnus was elected consul in 70

B.C.E. Julius Caesar was elected consul in 59 and then immediately left Rome and spent the next nine years campaigning in Gaul, building a personal fortune and a well-trained personal army.

■ Upon Caesar's return from Gaul, Pompey and the Senate demanded that he disband his army before crossing the Rubicon River, which marked the boundary between Gaul and the territory controlled by Rome and its allies.

■ But Caesar refused and marched on Rome, causing Pompey and most of the Senate to flee to Greece. Caesar pursued and defeated them, and this second civil war was over by 45 B.C.E.

■ Victorious, Caesar assumed the title of "dictator for the administration of public affairs" and moved vigorously to reduce the social tensions in Rome. He passed laws to reduce debt, established colonies outside of Italy, and declared that one-third of all laborers on estates had to be free.

■ Caesar now argued that the Republic was dead, which led some patricians to view him as a tyrant. He was assassinated on March 15, 44 B.C.E., by Brutus and others claiming they were attempting to restore Roman liberty.

■ In the aftermath, Caesar's 18-year-old adopted son Octavian stepped forward, formed an alliance with Mark Antony and the Senate, and pursued and defeated the conspirators.

■ But the allies fell out when Antony was put in charge of the eastern reaches of the state and promptly fell in love with Cleopatra, who was destined to be the last of the line of rulers established by Alexander's former general and boyhood friend, Ptolemy.

■ Octavian, declaring that Rome had been polluted by this alliance, defeated Antony's armies. Antony and Cleopatra committed suicide, and the Roman state was unified under Octavian, who was hailed as "father of the country" by the Senate. This is the moment that the Republic gave way to the permanent dictatorship of the Roman Empire—not yet in name, but certainly in fact.

■ Octavian shrewdly governed as a dictator while appearing to rule in conjunction with the Senate, which renamed him Augustus, or the "revered one." After a century of civil war, Augustus now concentrated on restoring the integrity of the state and traditional Roman values. By reducing corruption, professionalizing the army, and founding more than 40 colonies for its veterans, his reforms led to a new age of peace and optimism.

SUGGESTED READING

Bradley, *Slavery and Society at Rome.*

Cunliffe, *Greeks, Romans, and Barbarians.*

Toner, *Popular Culture in Ancient Rome.*

QUESTIONS TO CONSIDER

1. Was the expansion of the Romans driven by imperial ideology or defensive necessity?

2. Why did the constitution of the Republic fail, leading to the emergency of the permanent dictatorship of the Roman Empire?

TRIUMPHS AND FLAWS OF IMPERIAL ROME

The advent of Julius Caesar's adopted son Augustus as "imperator" of Rome ushered in a golden age for Roman literature, art, science, and commerce. After more than a century of brutal civil wars, the success of Augustus in appearing to rule through the old Republican constitution while in reality wielding absolute power restored political stability to the state. This new political situation gave rise to a new era of optimism—the so-called *Pax Romanum*—in which the creative genius of the Romans was able to flourish.

GRECO-ROMAN CULTURE

- The question of how to define the essence of Roman cultural and technological creativity has divided historians for millennia. Some Western scholars have suggested that the cultural legacy that the Romans ultimately passed on to Western civilization was unoriginal, because this legacy was essentially Greek in nature.

- Some take this further by arguing that it was the preservation by the Romans of so many original Greek political, intellectual, and scientific ideas about the world that was the Romans' single greatest contribution to world history.

- There is no doubt that the Romans were fascinated by Greek achievements in many fields. But like the evolution of culture

177

throughout world history, what emerged from this fascination was not just a slavish copying of Greek ideas, but rather the creation of a new syncretic Greco-Roman culture that combined Greek traditions with Latin innovations.

- This trend toward cultural syncretism continued when, late in the Roman empire, Greco-Roman culture was further infused with Christian and Germanic ideas, and it is this polyglot that essentially became the cornerstone of Western civilization.

- The emergence of a Greco-Roman syncretic culture became obvious during the Augustan golden age. A fascination by early Republican Roman authors with Greek literature was followed by an Augustan period in which Roman poets and historians began creating their own unique masterpieces that proved every bit as influential on Western civilization as the earlier works of the Greeks.

- The Roman senator and orator Cicero, who lived from 106 to 43 B.C.E., rose from the ranks of the middle class to the position of undisputed master of the Greek Sophist craft of rhetoric. Instead of

Cicero
(106 B.C.E.–43 B.C.E.)

Greek, however, Cicero used Latin in his powerful speeches and essays, helping turn that language into something every bit as expressive, and literary, as Greek.

- During the golden age, many Roman writers followed Augustus's lead in celebrating the traditional values of Roman civilization: family, dignity, civic duty, and even a renewed appreciation of the simple life of the countryside.

- Literature, art, and architecture were also given a tremendous boost in Augustan Rome through the benevolence of wealthy patrons such as Augustus's friend Maecenas, who had the resources to commission talented Romans to create everything from poetry to magnificent new buildings.

JULIO-CLAUDIAN AND ANTONINE RULE

- Augustus died peacefully in 14 C.E., and the period following his reign posed serious challenges for Roman intellectuals. Augustus's Julio-Claudian family provided a series of successors for the next half century.

- Two of Augustus's successors, the sadistic Tiberius and the hunchback Claudius, were actually quite able administrators, but Caligula was a madman who thought he was a god, and Nero murdered his own wife and mother and persecuted Jews and Christians. The authors and poets who lived through this later Julio-Claudian era were only too aware of the foibles of their rulers and also the dangers of openly mentioning these in their works.

- In 69 C.E., a year of chaos in Rome, four emperors contested the throne, but order was restored by the hard-nosed soldier Vespasian and his sons, who ruled as the Flavian dynasty for the next 30 years. They were effective but autocratic rulers who stabilized Roman government after the extremes of the Julio-Claudians.

- This brings us to a period of 84 years between 96 and 180 C.E., when a group of five Antonine emperors built on the work of the Flavians to provide generally excellent leadership. Under the Antonines, Rome reached the height of its prosperity and power, with Trajan, Hadrian, and Marcus Aurelius Antoninus serving as virtuous and able rulers.

- Trajan was born in 53 in the city of Italica in Spain. He was a superb soldier and rose quickly through the ranks of the Roman army, serving on some of the most contentious of the empire's frontiers, notably against the Germanic tribes.

- By the time the emperor Domitian was killed in 96 C.E., Trajan was recognized as one of the foremost military commanders of the empire, and this reputation served him well under Domitian's successor Nerva, who was unpopular with the army and needed to do something to gain their support.

- He accomplished this by naming Trajan as his adoptive son, a practice of Roman emperors that served as a way of appointing their successors. It was the future emperor Hadrian, Trajan's eventual successor, who brought word to Trajan of his adoption, which meant that he had Trajan's favor for the rest of his life.

- When Nerva died in January 98, Trajan succeeded him without incident, becoming the first non-Italian Roman emperor. Trajan's reign was distinguished by the expansion of the empire to its greatest extent, but his successor Hadrian realized that some of these new provinces were indefensible.

- When he came to power, he stabilized the empire by restoring some of these regions to autonomous rule and also erected key defensive walls in Germany and Britain. Hadrian also founded new cities to try to keep out the Germanic tribes, who, during his reign, seemed to be clamoring more and more at the very gates of the empire.

- Marcus Aurelius reigned for twenty years until 180. He was forced to spend much of his reign as a soldier fighting on the front lines, also trying to push back the Germanic tribes, but in his spare time, he wrote superb stoic philosophy collected and published as *The Meditations*.

- As we visualize the empire at the end of Marcus Aurelius's reign, we see a huge imperial state that stretched from Scotland to Iraq, home to 100 million people, connected to the rest of Eurasia by transregional trade and with the extraordinary megalopolis of Rome at its heart, a sprawling combination of magnificence and squalor.

- The stability and prosperity of the Antonine age produced many superb writers, such as the witty biographer of the great and powerful, Suetonius. As imperial librarian during the reign of Hadrian, Suetonius had unparalleled access to official records and used these to provide an intimate portrait of his age in *Lives of the Caesars*. Other writers grew cynical about the role of spectacular public entertainment in the Roman empire.

INNOVATIONS IN ARCHITECTURE AND SCIENCE

- The Roman calendar contained about 100 holidays a year on which some sort of public entertainment was provided by the wealthy elite and by ambitious politicians. On any given day, this entertainment might be in the form of chariot races in the Circus Maximus, a vast stadium holding up to 150,000 spectators, or gladiatorial games in the gigantic venue of the Colosseum, where armed men fought ferocious animals, or each other, in vicious combat.

- Appalling as the violent spectacles of Rome are to modern sensibilities, the venues in which they took place remain marvels of engineering construction. The gigantic stadiums of the Circus Maximus and Colosseum are some of Rome's most famous buildings, but Rome's superb engineers built impressive monumental structures all over the empire—aqueducts, temples, bridges, and a magnificent road network.

The Colosseum is one of Rome's most famous buildings.

- Engineering of this quality was based on a superb grasp of mathematics, and as we consider these sophisticated advances, we must inevitably return to the original question of Greek influence on Roman culture.

- We have seen previously the scientific advances that occurred in the Egyptian city of Alexandria during the Hellenistic age. Those advances barely slowed when Alexandria became part of the Roman world. And they weren't applied only to architecture; they also were essential in what were some of the earliest attempts to measure the planet and the solar system.

- Claudius Ptolemy, who worked in Roman-controlled Alexandria during the 2nd century C.E., had the longest influence on astronomy. His ingenious epicycle theory proved remarkably good at allowing astronomers to predict planetary movements—so good, in fact, that the Ptolemaic model held up for the next 1,300 years.

- But Ptolemy aside, few other scientific breakthroughs on this scale occurred during the Roman period. Rather, what we see are attempts by Roman authors to summarize Greek scientific discoveries, such as Pliny the Elder's *Historia Naturalis*, a comprehensive, multivolume encyclopedia of natural science.

THE RISE OF CHRISTIANITY

- One of the most enduring historical developments that occurred during the time of the Roman empire grew not out of the prosperity and relative peace that Romans enjoyed, but out of Rome's turbulent relations with its religious minorities.

- During the reign of the Julio-Claudian emperors, some sects of Judaism began to develop new beliefs as part of the endless search for spiritual meaning that all human societies have pursued since the Paleolithic. Groups such as the Essenes worked in secret on a radical new form of Judaism that scholars now recognize as the precursor to Christianity.

- Like all the great world religions, Christianity was a faith that offered something permanent and optimistic to believe in, and it was egalitarian in that it maintained that every soul was equally important.

- But Christianity also offered a sense of community based on concern for the welfare of its members, something that the Roman state was increasingly unable to offer in its later stages.

- Most of all, Christianity held out the hope of something that none of the other religions of the Roman world offered—the possibility of eternal existence in an afterlife.

- For the Roman state, the exclusive nature of Christianity made it a subversive sect, and many Christians were persecuted during the first two centuries of the Common Era, often scapegoated during times of political turmoil.

- By the early 3rd century, turmoil prevailed throughout the empire. The economy was in crisis, and about 26 despotic rulers reigned in just 50 years, most of them dying violent deaths.

- The able emperor Diocletian restored some semblance of order late in the 3rd century, dividing what had become an ungovernable empire into eastern and western halves, each with its own leadership.

- Then, civil war erupted, and Constantine fought his way to power. In the year 313 C.E., he decreed that Christianity would henceforth be "tolerated" throughout the empire. In 325, he invited all of the leading Christian thinkers to assemble at the Council of Nicaea, which resolved critical disputes over Christian beliefs. In 330, Constantine made the old Greek city of Byzantium the capital of the Eastern empire, and it was later renamed Constantinople.

- But the endgame of Roman civilization, at least in its classic form, was fast approaching. Various German tribes had been increasingly drawn into the power vacuum created by the Crisis of the Third Century.

- The Roman army recruited many Germans into its ranks and allowed others to cross the borders and settle on Roman land, although many of these communities were mistreated by corrupt Roman officials. German restlessness was exacerbated by the arrival of the militarized Huns from central Asia.

- As a result of Hunnish incursions, one Germanic tribal confederation, the Visigoths, attacked and defeated the Romans at the Battle of Adrianople in 378. The Romans managed to hold the German tide back for a few more years, but finally, under Alaric, they invaded Italy, and Rome was sacked in 410.

- Germans now settled all over Western Europe. Meanwhile, the Huns, led by the charismatic Attila, were finally defeated by a combined Roman and Visigoth army near Troyes, and their confederation completely disintegrated after Attila died in 453. It was German officers of the Roman army who now held real power in the Western Roman empire, and by 475, the Roman emperor was a German.

■ It's generally accepted that the new form of constitutional monarchy instituted by Caesar Augustus—that is, Octavian—was maintained, to varying degrees of effectiveness, by a series of emperors through the death of Marcus Aurelius in 180.

■ Thereafter, however, the imperial structure gradually disintegrated under the combined pressure of internal corruption and external threat.

■ Yet, the truly chaotic disintegration of the empire occurred in the west; the eastern half, based in Constantinople, would survive for another 1,200 years as the "shining light of the world" and the "second Rome."

SUGGESTED READING

Brown, *The Rise of Western Christendom*.

Kelly, *The Roman Empire*.

Romolo, *The Roads of the Romans*.

QUESTIONS TO CONSIDER

1. Horace once wrote, "Captive Greece captured her rude conqueror." Discuss in the context of the originality of Roman culture.

2. How accurately has the satirist Juvenal's phrase "bread and circuses" (*panem et circenses*), which captures the trade-off humans often make between political rights and distracting entertainment, continued to capture the intention of elites and governments in providing "diverting" education for the people?

NEW IDEAS ALONG THE SILK ROAD

Throughout the 4,000-year-long era of agrarian civilizations, few human communities existed in isolation. As various groups of pastoralists, complex states, and large-scale agrarian civilizations expanded their boundaries, they joined together to become smaller parts of much larger systems. These processes are complex, and the borders between civilizations were always fluid. From the big history perspective, the gradual linking up of different civilizations was immensely important because it led to a huge increase in the size, diversity, and intensity of opportunities for collective learning.

THE SILK ROADS

- Ever since the Paleolithic era of human history, the exchange of ideas between diverse peoples and cultures has been a prime mover in promoting historical change through enhanced collective learning.

- But during the Paleolithic and subsequent early agrarian eras, exchanges were limited by the small size of the groups involved. Only when exchanges began to dramatically expand in scope during the era of agrarian civilizations do we start to see a significant impact on collective learning.

- In Afro-Eurasia, as more and more agrarian civilizations became involved in transregional exchanges and enhanced collective learning, huge changes in the material, artistic, social, and spiritual domains of human history began to occur.

- Eventually, within the vast Afro-Eurasian world zone in particular, almost every human community was connected into a vast exchange web. Material and nonmaterial exchanges developed within Afro-Eurasia, the Americas, Australasia, and the Pacific, but these zones were so isolated from each other until roughly 1500 C.E. that human populations in each remained utterly ignorant of events in the others.

- The most influential of all the premodern exchange networks emerged along the Silk Roads. The trans-civilizational contacts that occurred through Silk Roads exchanges resulted in the most significant collective learning so far experienced by the human species.

- The term "Silk Roads" is a relatively new one. The geographer who coined the term initially used it in the singular form, imagining a single trade route linking China and the Mediterranean world through central Asia. Now we know that it was never a single road, but rather a network of shifting paths often dictated by environmental or political factors, so the plural form is much more accurate.

- The first important period of the Silk Roads was between roughly 50 B.C.E. and 250 C.E., when exchanges took place between the Chinese, Indian, Kushan, Iranian, steppe-nomadic, and Mediterranean worlds.

- The demise of the Western Roman, Parthian, Kushan, and Han Chinese empires resulted in several centuries of less regular contact, but a second Silk Roads era subsequently operated for several centuries between roughly 600 and 1000 C.E., connecting China, India, Southeast Asia, the realm of Islam, and the Byzantine empire into another vast web based on overland and maritime trade.

- The primary function of the Silk Roads during both periods was to facilitate trade in material commodities, but intellectual, social, and artistic ideas also traveled with the merchants, and these had an even greater impact on collective learning.

- The spread of ideas via the Silk Roads began primarily as a result of long-distance trade. Commercial and cultural exchange on the scale of Silk Roads trade became possible only after the small river valley states of the early agrarian era had been consolidated into substantial agrarian civilizations—a process that was largely the result of warfare.

- Continuing expansion by the major civilizations meant that, by the first Silk Roads era, just four imperial dynasties—those of the Roman, Parthian, Kushan, and Han empires—controlled much of the Eurasian landmass, from the Pacific to the Atlantic.

- The consolidation of these huge states established order and stability over a vast and previously fragmented geopolitical environment. By the middle of the 1st century B.C.E., conditions in Afro-Eurasia were ripe for levels of material and cultural exchange—and collective learning—hitherto unknown.

- Also critical in facilitating these exchanges were the pastoral nomads, who formed communities that lived primarily from the exploitation of domestic animals. By the middle of the 1st millennium B.C.E., several large pastoral nomadic communities had emerged with the ability to prosper in the harsh interior of Afro-Eurasia, and they served as the first tenuous links among the different communities along the Silk Roads and other networks.

- Once these preconditions were in place, it was the decision by the Han Chinese to begin to interact with their western neighbors and engage in long-distance commerce that turned regional trading activity into a great trans-Afro-Eurasian network.

- Half a century after the Han began to engage with their western neighbors, Augustus came to power in Rome following a century of civil war. This restored peace and stability to much of Western Afro-Eurasia, leading to a sharp increase in the demand for luxury goods in Rome, particularly for spices and exotic textiles like silk.

Silk trading route
between China and India

- As the name of this trading network suggests, the major Chinese export commodity in demand in Rome was indeed silk, an elegant material that came to be regarded as the last word in fashion by patrician women. The Chinese, realizing the commercial value of their monopoly on silk, carefully guarded the secret of silk production, and border guards searched merchants to make sure they weren't carrying any silkworms out of the country.

- Other imports into the Roman Empire—from China, central Asia, Arabia, and India—included superb Han iron as well as nutmeg, cloves, cardamom, and pepper. Importing these high-value goods cost the Romans a fortune. There was also a substantial volume of Roman exports to China, indicating the incredible scale of Silk Roads commercial exchanges.

- In return for their high-value exports, the Chinese imported a range of agricultural products, including grapes, Roman glassware, art objects from India and Egypt, and horses from the steppes.

TRAVELING THE SILK ROADS

- Traveling the Silk Roads could be challenging, but given the amount of money involved, and therefore the profits to be made by merchants, it is not surprising that so many traders were willing to risk the physical rigors of the journey.

- The animal that made Silk Roads trade possible in the eastern and central regions was the Bactrian camel, native to the steppes of central Asia. The bulk of overland Silk Roads trade was carried on the backs of these extraordinary animals.

- Whether by land or by sea, no traders we are aware of ever made their way along the entire length of the Silk Roads. Instead, merchants from the major eastern and western civilizations took their goods so far and then passed them on to a series of middlemen, including traders who were operating deep within the Kushan empire, which extended across most of modern-day Pakistan and Afghanistan.

- The Kushan empire, which can be dated from roughly 45 to 225 C.E., is one of the most important, yet least known, agrarian civilizations in world history. Located at the heart of the Silk Roads network, it straddled and influenced both the land and maritime routes.

- Descended from pastoral nomads, the Kushans maintained relatively cordial relations with the Romans, Parthians, Chinese, Indians, and steppe nomads and were thus able to play a crucial role in facilitating the extraordinary levels of cross-cultural exchange that characterize the first Silk Roads era.

- The Kushan monarchs were not only effective political and military rulers; they also demonstrated a remarkable appreciation of art and were patrons of innovative sculpture workshops within their empire. The output from these workshops reflects the sort of synthesis typical of the intensity of collective learning during the era.

- The sculptures produced in the Kushan cities of Gandhara and Mathura were created by the combined talents of central Asian, Indian, and Hellenistic Greek artists. It was apparently they who were commissioned to create the first images of the Buddha for worship. Influenced by depictions of Greco-Roman deities, the first representation of the Buddha spread along the Silk Roads, to Sri Lanka, China, Japan, Korea, and Southeast Asia.

- The spread of Buddhist ideology along the trade routes is an equally striking example of this cross-fertilization of traditions. Buddhism emerged in northern India in the 6th century B.C.E. Offering the hope of salvation to all, regardless of caste or status, Buddhist ideas spread along the well-traveled trade routes from India through the Kushan realm and into China.

- The Silk Roads also facilitated the spread of Christianity, Manichaeism, and, later, Islam. Christian missionaries made good use of the superb Roman road and sea transportation networks. Christianity eventually spread further to the east along the Silk Roads, through Mesopotamia and Iran, into India, and eventually into China. The Nestorian branch of Christianity became most deeply entrenched in central and eastern Asia.

- The central Asian religion of Manichaeism, which viewed the world in dualistic terms such as good and evil, also benefitted from the Silk Roads after it emerged in Mesopotamia in the 3rd century C.E. Eventually, most of the major Silk Roads trading cities contained Manichaean communities.

THE SECOND SILK ROADS ERA

- By the 3rd century C.E., the Silk Roads fell gradually into decline as both China and the Roman Empire withdrew from the network. Silk Roads trade itself was at least partly responsible for this disengagement, because it contributed to the spread of disastrous epidemic diseases, including smallpox, measles, and bubonic plagues.

- The Han dynasty disintegrated in 220 C.E., and the Kushan and Parthian empires collapsed under pressure from Sasanian invaders a few decades later. The Roman Empire experienced a series of crises throughout the first half of the 3rd century. For the next several centuries, the prevailing political situation in many parts of Afro-Eurasia was not conducive to large-scale commercial exchange.

- However, with the creation of the vast realm of Islam in the 8th and 9th centuries, and the establishment of the Tang dynasty in China at the same time, significant Silk Roads exchanges along both land and maritime routes revived. This period is known as the second Silk Roads era.

- Both the Tang dynasty and its successor, the Song dynasty, which ruled well into the 13th century, presided over a vibrant market economy in China, in which agricultural and manufacturing specialization, population growth, urbanization, and infrastructure development led to high levels of internal and external trade. New financial instruments, including printed paper money, appeared to facilitate large-scale mercantile activity.

- At the same time, Arab merchants, benefiting from the stable and prosperous Abbasid administration in Baghdad, began to engage with Chinese merchants in lucrative commercial enterprises. Large numbers of Muslim merchants moved to China, where they joined communities of Byzantine, Indian, and Southeast Asian traders in the great Chinese port cities.

- As maritime trade gradually eclipsed overland trade in volume, merchants and sailors from all over Afro-Eurasia flocked to southern port cities, such as Guangzhou.

- As with the first Silk Roads era, although the material exchanges were important and impressive, the cultural exchanges in this later period seem in retrospect of even greater significance.

- Long before the Tang came to power, many foreign religions had made their way into East Asia. With the advent of Islam and the establishment of substantial Muslim merchant communities in the centuries that followed, mosques also began to appear in many Chinese cities.

- Yet of all the foreign beliefs that were accepted in China, only Buddhism made substantial inroads against Confucianism. Between 600 and 1000 C.E., thousands of Buddhist stupas and temples were constructed in China.

- With its promise of salvation, Buddhism seriously challenged Daoism and Confucianism for the hearts and minds of many Chinese, and in the end, the syncretic version of Chan Buddhism (Zen Buddhism in Japan) emerged as a popular compromise.

- Buddhism remains one of the great cultural bonds shared by millions of Asian people, one of the many legacies that the modern world owes to the Silk Roads.

SUGGESTED READING

Franck, and Brownstone, *The Silk Roads*.

Liu, *The Silk Roads*.

Wood, *The Silk Road*.

QUESTIONS TO CONSIDER

1. What political, economic, and environmental conditions had to be in place before the Silk Roads could flourish?

2. What were the most important material and nonmaterial exchanges that occurred, and how did these influence subsequent human history?

CHAOS AND CONSOLIDATION IN EURASIA

By the mid-3rd century C.E., civilizations across Afro-Eurasia were in trouble; all of the imperial states that had been linked together by the Silk Roads faced serious internal and external problems. What was going on that explains this near-universal contraction? Although the reasons for this contraction were rather similar, the outcomes varied enormously. The dual task of this lecture is to trace the contraction of Afro-Eurasian civilizations and consider the different outcomes of this process—differences that have had a tremendous influence on subsequent world history.

EAST ASIA

■ In China during the Later Han dynasty, internal problems stemming from infighting between various elite groups resulted in a series of peasant revolts that, coinciding with an increase in the power of militarized nomads and regional warlords, led to the complete collapse of the Han in 220 C.E.

■ A comparison between the situation in China after the fall of the Han and that in Europe after the so-called decline and fall of the Roman Empire reveals that both regions were forced to deal with incursions by powerful militarized nomadic confederations at more or less the same time.

■ With the collapse of central government, both the western and eastern regions of Afro-Eurasia experienced centuries of fragmentation captured by the term "Dark Ages," although this is a label that historians seldom use today.

■ But there is a huge difference in outcomes: While western Europe was never effectively reunified after the fragmentation of the western Roman Empire—in spite of several relatively short-lived attempts in early and modern times—China was successfully reunified under strong central government, a situation that continued with only one serious interruption through the 20th century.

■ The three and a half centuries of disorder that followed the collapse of the Han are characterized by the rise and fall of regional states. Periods of political fragmentation are generally fertile breeding grounds for technological and cultural evolution, and this was particularly true in southern China.

■ For example, paper replaced older writing materials, so books were more numerous than ever before. In addition, agriculture and international maritime trade out of port cities surged. It was also during this Age of Disunity that Buddhism found its readiest acceptance in East Asia.

■ Buddhism traveled from China to Korea during the 4th century, arriving just when three separate kingdoms—Koguryo, Paekche, and Silla—were embarking on a long contest for control of the peninsula. Eventually, the kingdom of Silla formed an alliance with the Tang dynasty in China to defeat the other kingdoms, giving Silla control of much of the peninsula. Each of these three kingdoms contributed to what eventually became Korean culture.

■ Chinese influence was also strong in the nearby archipelago of Japan. During the 7th century, Japanese rulers adopted Chinese-style imperial titles and began to build a powerful state using Chinese administrative techniques.

■ In China, it was the short-lived but effective Sui dynasty that ended the Age of Disunity late in the 6th century, paving the way for the success of the Tang dynasty that followed. The Sui were responsible for reengaging China with the wider Eurasian world through commercial and military expeditions and also for extensive infrastructure improvements—particularly the construction of the Grand Canal, which helped unify the divided Chinese realm.

- This was the largest hydrological project attempted to this point in history. But construction on this scale made harsh demands on the peasants through high taxes and forced labor, and a military revolt capped by the assassination of the emperor brought the Sui to a rapid demise.

- Their successors, the Tang dynasty, which ruled for almost three centuries, until 907 C.E., returned China to strength and prosperity, creating what was undoubtedly the wealthiest and most powerful civilization on the planet. Under the Tang, China became a great imperial power; Chinese forces conquered Manchuria, Vietnam, much of Tibet, and large regions of central Asia.

- In stark contrast to most traditional agrarian civilizations, the Tang government supported agricultural innovation. Farming productivity soared, and China's population approached 100 million, leading to rapid growth in the number and size of cities. By the 10th century, Tang China was the most urbanized society ever seen.

- The vast, cosmopolitan, flourishing civilization of the Tang utterly dominated the eastern half of the Afro-Eurasian world zone, and their eventual collapse, a product of complacent rule by the later emperors, brought to an end an extraordinary chapter in the history of civilization.

- The end of the 1st millennium also represents a watershed in East Asian history more generally. In Southeast Asia, countries such as Vietnam shrugged off centuries of Chinese control and began to forge their own distinctive cultures. The Koryo dynasty in Korea replaced the Silla and went on to rule for the next 500 years.

- In Japan, Chinese-style imperial institutions became increasingly irrelevant as centralized imperial power disappeared and a new and uniquely Japanese class of regional warriors, the samurai, began to assert themselves.

- In South Asia, meanwhile, a century after the demise of the Kushan empire, imperial rule and unification returned to India with the establishment of the Gupta empire. Using marriage and diplomacy to forge links between regional states, Chandra Gupta created a dynamic kingdom in the Ganges Valley that was expanded by his able successors until it approached the territorial size of the Mauryan empire. Rather than establish centralized imperial administration over their realm, Gupta kings preferred to rule through a network of regional rulers.

- This Indian golden age declined during the 5th century in the face of a new wave of militarized nomads from central Asia, particularly the aggressive White Huns, who established their own kingdom in northern India.

- A brief attempt at South Asian reunification was made early in the 7th century by Prince Harsha, who brought a large area of the Ganges Valley under his control. But local rulers had amassed too much regional power to accede to a single, central authority, and following Harsha's death at the hands of an assassin, India reverted to a fragmented realm divided among regional polities, a situation that persisted until the arrival of Islam in the 9th century, which ushered in a new stage of commercial vitality but also of political and religious tension.

- North of the Himalayas in central Asia, the Parthian and Kushan empires were replaced in the early 3rd century by the Sasanians, who went on to create their own significant empire that would last for more than 400 years to 651 C.E.

- The Silk Roads remained a major land trade route during the Sasanian era, although maritime routes became even more important.

- Incessant wars between the Sasanians and the Romans disrupted land-based trade and brought the Arabs in southern Arabia into prominence as traders operating alternative routes from the Arabian Sea to the Mediterranean. Eventually, Arabia also came under Sasanian hegemony, which allowed the Sasanians to control the trade across the Arabian Sea.

- In the 6th century, meanwhile, a new group of migrating nomads appeared on the scene—namely, the Turks, who caused serious problems for the Sasanians and indeed for most of the agrarian civilizations of Eurasia.

- The Turks expanded out of their Mongolian homelands, disrupting the Tang Chinese and forcing the Hephthalites to move westward, the migration that led eventually to the destruction of the Gupta empire in India.

- The Turks eventually became a major trading partner of the Sasanians and Byzantines, but this was not the end of Turkic political ambitions, and as they continued to slowly move westward, they impacted every state they came in contact with through the early modern era.

- The Sasanians maintained commercial relationships with the Tang Chinese and the Byzantines. These three powerful new agrarian civilizations came to control much of Eurasia from the Yellow River to the Mediterranean Sea.

- In the mid-7th century, however, this Eurasian system was upturned by the appearance of yet another new major power, the Muslims, who destroyed the Sasanians and ushered in a new era in the history of Afro-Eurasia.

WESTERN EUROPE
- During the 5th century, the western Roman Empire fragmented into a series of fortified estates and competitive regional kingdoms, but the eastern half remained unified and strong as the Byzantine Empire, which was destined to last for another thousand years.

- The early Byzantine emperor Justinian, who reigned from 527 to 565 C.E., was responsible for much of Byzantium's success. He and his wife Theodora crushed an internal revolt, strengthened the defenses of Constantinople, published a complete codex of Roman law, and even attempted to reconquer parts of the western empire, although ultimately without success.

- In the 7th and 8th centuries, Constantinople was able to withstand concerted sieges by the expanding forces of Islam, although large regions of the empire were lost to the Muslims. The core empire survived, however, and used its strategic position to remain unconquered and wealthy through trade and innovative manufacturing until the middle of the 2nd millennium.

- The city lost some of its splendor in the 7th and 8th centuries following a series of natural disasters and desperate sieges. But in the 9th century, a military and economic recovery took place, leading to the great cultural achievements of the middle Byzantine period and the city's reputation as a place protected by military and commercial strength, and by God.

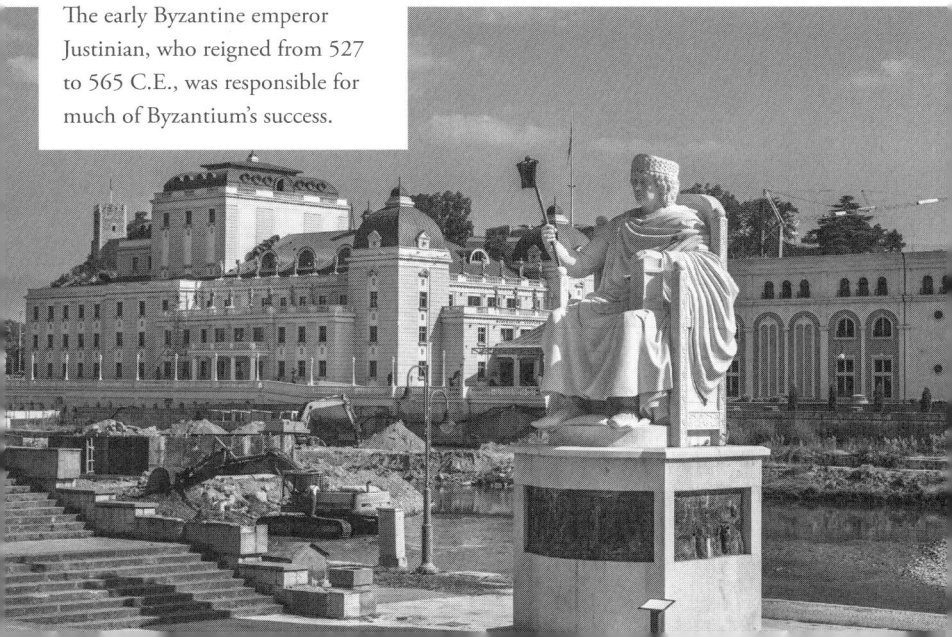

The early Byzantine emperor Justinian, who reigned from 527 to 565 C.E., was responsible for much of Byzantium's success.

- Further west, the western states of the former Roman Empire gradually lost the ability to tax their subjects or maintain a professional army in the centuries following the sack of Rome by the Visigoths. This led to political fragmentation and a new balance of power between monarchs, wealthy landholders, and the Christian church, which now began to play a significant role in the politics and culture of western Europe.

- However, the collapse of the Roman taxation and administration system made it difficult to maintain many of the Roman cities of the west. Some disappeared completely, while others broke up into areas of smaller settlements.

- Rome remained the largest city in the west, with a population of perhaps 25,000 in the 8th century. In Spain, the destruction of the Visigothic kingdom by the Muslims in 711 precipitated a wholesale economic collapse, although by the end of the 8th century, the unification of the territory that became known as al-Andalus under the Arab Umayyad emirate led to a gradual recovery.

- In Britain, many centuries of Roman occupation had increased the prosperity of a small class of villa owners. But by the mid-5th century, the breakdown of Roman control exposed these Romano-British to regular raids by Picts and Scots, and by Anglo-Saxons from the mainland.

- A counteroffensive led by a mysterious ruler stabilized the situation, preserving the status of the post-Roman elite. By the early 7th century, 10 or more small Anglo-Saxon kingdoms had been established in England.

- Further north, trading and raiding in the later 8th and early 9th centuries brought Scandinavian peoples into close contact with communities in both western Europe and Russia.

- The establishment of wealthy trading centers along the English Channel and North Sea coasts encouraged Scandinavians to link the northern European exchange network into the Baltic region.

- But political instability in Denmark led to expeditions by armed bands of Vikings out of Scandinavia in the mid-9th century and to their raiding and eventual settlement in Britain, France, and Russia.

- Scandinavian peoples also played a critical role in the emergence of the first Russian state. Vikings established commercial bases in Ukraine and Russia and took control of regional exchange networks, establishing themselves as a new elite that would evolve into rulers of the first real Russian state, Kievan Rus.

- The development of Russia was tied to the emergence of another group destined to play an important role in the future history of both Europe and Russia, the Slavs, who eventually occupied a wide region stretching from the Balkans to Russia, setting up a contest for their conversion between the Pope in Rome and the Patriarch in Constantinople.

- The year 1000 C.E. marks something of a watershed in the big history of civilization. Before 1000 C.E., many of the world's societies were relatively isolated and diverse in their lifeways, ideologies, and languages. But after 1000 C.E., the balance tipped, and processes of convergence became more and more important.

- Contacts between once-isolated regions multiplied, and migration, travel, and trade increased, creating new links between different communities and regions and much larger networks of exchange.

- It was the multiplication of these the links during the 2nd millennium that established the framework for today's globalized world—although these frameworks were still only functioning within the world zones, not between them.

SUGGESTED READING

Brown, *The Making of Late Antiquity.*

Herrin, *Byzantium.*

Lewis, *China's Cosmopolitan Empire.*

QUESTIONS TO CONSIDER

1. How do we explain widespread political collapse across Afro-Eurasia in the 3rd century C.E.?

2. Why were some regions able to reconstitute themselves into large unified civilizations while other regions remained politically divided, and what would be the long-term historical consequences of this?

ISLAMIC EXPANSION AND RULE

B etween the 8th and 10th centuries of the Common Era, the histories of many of the states and cultures of Afro-Eurasia became even more interconnected because of the expansion of Islamic civilization. Created by Muslim warriors, merchants, and administrators, the vast Dar al-Islam—the "abode or realm of Islam"—became one of the most important economic, intellectual, and cultural structures anywhere in the world. It dominated the western half of Afro-Eurasia in the same way that the Tang dynasty in China dominated the eastern.

ISLAM AND MUHAMMAD

- The word "Islam" means "submission," essentially submission to the will of Allah, the only god in this monotheistic religion. One who accepts the Islamic faith is a Muslim, or "one who has submitted."

- The Islamic faith and the early cultural practices associated with it were influenced by the desert environment and Bedouin traditions of the Arabian Peninsula. In this harsh and arid region, agriculture is only possible at a few oasis and coastal settlements, yet nomadic Bedouin peoples had learned to prosper through trade, organizing themselves into fiercely loyal clan groups.

- Arabia is surrounded on three sides by ocean, so it has always been strategically well placed to link into long-distance trade routes via maritime trade ports in the Red Sea and Persian Gulf, but also by overland routes via Palmyra and Damascus to the Mediterranean.

- Muhammad ibn Abdullah was born about 570 C.E. in Mecca, a city about 40 miles inland from the Red Sea coast. Around the year 610, Muhammad had a profound spiritual experience and became convinced that, rather than the host of deities worshipped by some of his fellow Meccans, there was only one all-powerful God named *Allah* (the Arabic word for God) and that recognition of other gods was wrong.

- Muhammad interpreted the visions he was experiencing as revelations from Allah, delivered through his messenger the archangel Gabriel. Without necessarily meaning to found a new religion, he told his family and friends about these revelations, and by 620, a loyal group of followers had joined Muhammad's circle.

- As Muhammad recounted the messages he had received, some of his followers began to write them down. By the early 650s, these written texts had been compiled as the Quran, a word that means "recitation." The Quran quickly became the holy book of Islam.

- But the growing popularity of Muhammad's preaching brought him into conflict with the rulers of Mecca, both for political reasons and because Muslim monotheism offended the polytheistic Arabs.

- As tensions with Arab elites increased, some of his followers were forced to flee to Ethiopia, the first of several waves of Muslim migrants and conquerors that would move into the African continent.

- Eventually, the pressure became so intense that Muhammad and about 70 of his followers left Mecca and moved to the rival trading city of Yathrib, about 200 miles north of Mecca. Various Arab and Jewish clans living in the city soon converted to Islam, and Muslims later started referring to Yathrib as Medina, a word that means "the city" but in this context means "the city of the prophet."

- This migration in 622, the *hijra*, marks the first year of the Islamic calendar and also the moment at which the spiritual visions experienced by Muhammad were transformed into a serious religious, but also social and political, movement.

- At the head of a growing society in exile, Muhammad organized his followers into a cohesive community called the *umma*, the community of the faithful. This was a society within a society, with its own law code, social welfare system, educational institutions, and income.

- Muhammad personally led the *umma* in daily prayers, and also in three major military confrontations with his enemies, who sent forces from Mecca to try to destroy the Muslim community. As an experienced merchant, Muhammad was able to organize successful commercial ventures and use the profits to support the *umma*.

- As the *umma* grew in size and confidence, Muslims aggressively sought converts and engaged in a *jihad*, or "struggle," to enlarge the size of their congregation and territories. By 629, Muhammad and the *umma* were powerful enough to return to Mecca, which they entered without battle, quickly replacing the Arab government with their own theocratic administration.

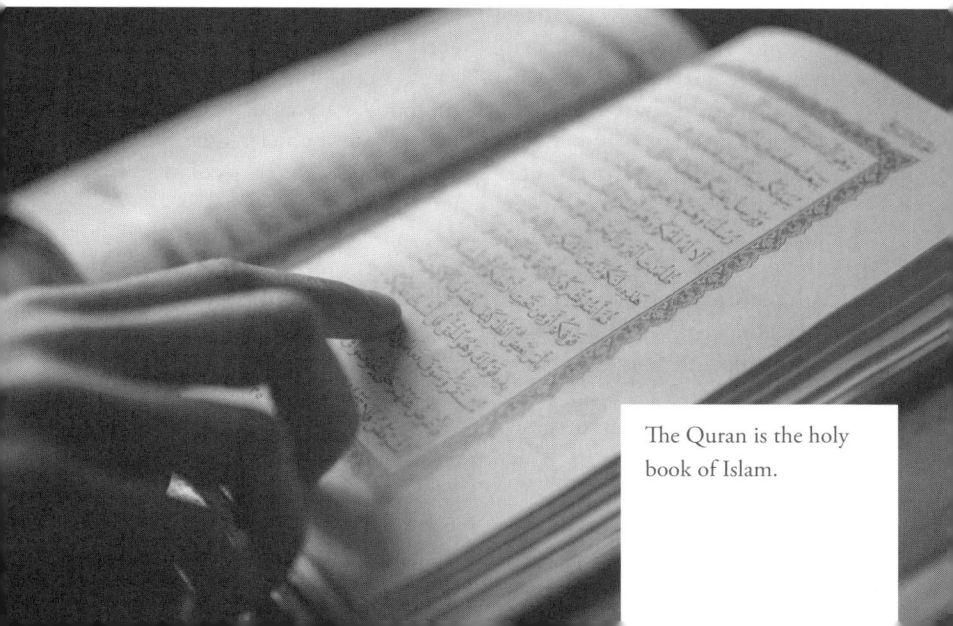

The Quran is the holy book of Islam.

- The Arab elites now accepted Allah, and the Muslims destroyed the old pagan shrines and built mosques instead. They did retain one old pagan shrine, the Ka'bah, which was transformed into a shrine to Allah that only the faithful could approach. Muhammad led the first pilgrimage, or hajj, to the Ka'bah, establishing the hajj as an example for all devout Muslims.

- As with most world religions, an associated law code—the sharia law—later emerged to offer the faithful guidance on all aspects of daily life. The sharia was inspired by the Quran and compiled by religious experts. It offers precise guidance on a range of social, political, and economic behaviors. It was partly because of the comprehensiveness of the sharia that Islam became more than a religious doctrine; it became a way of life with a complete set of social and ethical values.

The Expansion of Islam

- By the time of Muhammad's death in 632, a substantial part of Arabia was under Muslim control. The prophet was buried in Medina, and his advisors selected one of his closest disciples to serve as caliph, or civil and religious head, of the Muslim state.

- The question of Muhammad's succession remains, however, one of the most controversial in all of Islam. According to Sunni tradition, this first caliph was Abu Bakr al-Ṣiddiq, who was recognized as head of state, military commander, chief judge, and chief religious leader, a prime example of the evolution and consolidation of secular, spiritual, and legal power during the era of agrarian civilizations.

- Under Abu Bakr and his successors, the *jihad* continued. After conquering the remaining non-Muslim tribes of Arabia, Muslim armies turned northward to confront the huge but now somewhat complacent Byzantine and Sasanian empires.

- The lightning-fast expansion of the Dar al-Islam was unprecedented, even during an era in which many great empires grew rapidly to enormous size in their search for tribute and land. By 637, just five years after Muhammad's death, Syria, Palestine, and all of Mesopotamia had fallen.

■ During the 640s, much of North Africa was incorporated into the Islamic realm, and by the time the Sasanian imperial heartland of Persia fell to the Muslims in 651, the Dar al-Islam stretched from the Mediterranean to Afghanistan.

■ After a period of political consolidation, Islamic armies resumed the *jihad* early in the 8th century. Several kingdoms of northern India were conquered in 711, and Muslim hegemony in North Africa was extended to Morocco and then across the Straits of Gibraltar and into Spain by 718.

■ In an era characterized by substantial civilizations, the Islamic realm had expanded in less than a century to be the largest civilization the world had ever seen.

■ Despite the successful expansion of Islam, disagreements over Muhammad's succession led to a fatal split between the Shia and Sunni versions of the faith. Their political and spiritual differences have continued for almost 1,400 years and remain a source of great tension within the Islamic world in the 21st century.

■ While this split was occurring, Islamic authorities were faced with the same challenges that the Akkadians, Persians, Romans, Mauryans, and Han before them had been forced to confront: how to effectively administer a vast, multicultural empire.

■ The solution they came up with was to establish an administrative structure known as the caliphate, which was consolidated under a relatively stable dynasty, that of the Umayyads, who ruled from 661 to 750. Their successors were the Abbasids, who provided another period of stable rule that lasted almost 500 years.

THE GOLDEN AGE OF ISLAM

- In the vast region controlled by the Abbasids, millions of people converted to Islam and enriched the Islamic realm by bringing into it their own cultural traditions. Muslim administrators and intellectuals adapted many of these traditions for their own purposes, particularly cultural and scientific ideas.

- This cultural and linguistic synthesis resulted in an explosion of intellectual activity throughout the Muslim world, in a period historian Frederick Starr has called the Lost Enlightenment. The establishment of formal educational institutions facilitated this great age of learning.

- In this intellectual environment, many of the great literary and scientific works that had been produced by more ancient societies were translated and incorporated into the Islamic cultural realm.

- With all of central Asia and the Middle East now under control of the Muslims, regions that for centuries had been divided among different political powers, an economic golden age also ensued.

- Under the Abbasids, agriculture thrived in Egypt, Syria, and Mesopotamia during an era of increased productivity and population growth that stimulated the economy of the region like never before.

- Commercial activity also flourished across the Islamic world. Under the Abbasids, elaborate trade networks linked all of the regions of the Dar al-Islam together, connecting them to an even larger Afro-Eurasian-wide network. Muslim sailors and their ships linked East and Southeast Asia to the Indian Ocean, the Persian Gulf, and the coast of East Africa in a thriving commercial network.

- Whether by land or sea, trade also benefited from sophisticated Muslim business organization. Islamic law facilitated honest transactions, and Abbasid businessmen pooled their resources in group ventures. Improved transportation infrastructure and more sophisticated banking practices further contributed to this surge in commerce.

The Big History of Civilizations

Mecca during the holy pilgrimage of hajj

- Although territorial expansion of the Dar al-Islam continued under Abbasid leadership, it did so less because of official Abbasid policy and more as a result of campaigns carried out by regional Muslim forces.

- A significant yet not widely known battle was fought early in the Abbasid caliphate between Islamic and Tang Chinese forces in 751, deep in the heart of central Asia. The Chinese forces were eventually overwhelmed, marking the end of westward Tang expansion and opening up much of central Asia to Muslim penetration, leading to the further spread of Islam among the Turkic-speaking peoples of the region.

- The Dar al-Islam had a significant influence on the lives of women within its borders, and its customs affecting women also appear to have been influenced by some of the cultures it absorbed. As Muslims expanded their faith out of Arabia, they took control of regions of Afro-Eurasia that had long histories of patriarchy. These ancient cultural practices and social structures went on to profoundly influence the Islamic worldview.

- In spite of all its benefits, the prosperity of the Abbasids tested their administrative abilities. Over time, local authorities in North Africa, Egypt, and parts of Syria and central Asia took advantage of occasional weaknesses in central government to enhance their own power.

- Despite the cultural and economic vibrancy of the Abbasids, by the end of the 9th century, their administration was on the brink of political disintegration.

- An additional critical factor in the dissolution of the Abbasid caliphate might have been environmental. Climate evidence suggests that much of the Dar al-Islam experienced a period of significant cooling early in the 10th century, which led to a decline in agricultural production that the region took a long time to recover from.

- By about 900 C.E., the appearance of new regional powers, such as the Tahirids and Samanids, effectively ended any semblance of an all-powerful caliph in Baghdad.

- In the 10th century, Persian aristocrats took over the Abbasid "throne," and during the following century, power passed into the hands of the Seljuqs, a group of militarized Turkish nomads who had converted to Islam and now occupied much of the caliphate.

- But any hope that the golden age of Islam would be restored was destroyed in the 13th century by the Mongols, who in many ways changed the world forever.

SUGGESTED READING

Esposito, *Islam.*

Lombard, *The Golden Age of Islam.*

Wolfe, ed., *One Thousand Roads to Mecca.*

QUESTIONS TO CONSIDER

1. How was the Dar al-Islam able to expand at such a lightning-fast pace until it had taken control of huge regions of Afro-Eurasia?

2. Why would historians refer to the golden age of classical Islamic civilization as a "Lost Enlightenment"?

LEGACY OF THE MONGOLS

E arly in the 13th century, Mongol horsemen swept out of their homeland in the steppes to conquer the known world. By the time they had finished, the Mongol empire included all of China, Korea, central Asia, extensive regions of India and Russia, much of the Middle East, and a large chunk of eastern Europe. The Mongols were horrendously destructive, killing millions of humans and destroying many cities, but they also facilitated intensified levels of trade and exchange between east and west, patronized the finest artisans and craftsmen, and promoted religious tolerance. For these and other reasons, some historians credit the Mongols with helping to create the modern world.

THE MONGOLS

- The Mongols were militarized nomads, just one of many such confederations that had been interacting with agrarian sedentary communities since the 1st millennium B.C.E. Because of their steppe environment, which necessitated a nomadic life, Mongol politics were clan-based, with decisions generally made by councils of clan leaders. Individuals elected as khans, or great chiefs, had significant power, yet they were always regarded as "first among equals."

- The harsh steppe environment also demanded that all members of the community play a role in group survival, so there was little of the patriarchy that characterized contemporary sedentary societies.

- The Mongols held a distinct military advantage over the sedentary forces of their time, because of their mobility and superb skills as horse riders, their prowess with the composite bow and arrow, and their ability to survive in the field without need for supply trains.

- But once they had used these advantages to build their empire, the Mongols had to settle down and learn the languages, religions, and administrative techniques of the peoples they had conquered. It was in this second, lesser-known phase of their history—known as the *Pax Mongolica*, or Mongol Peace—that they created a connected cultural zone that unified much of Eurasia as never before.

THE MONGOL EMPIRE

- Mongol leader Chinggis Khan, who claimed a mandate from heaven to rule the world, was primarily responsible for creating the Mongol empire. The son of a minor Mongol chief, he was born in 1162 and named Temujin, or Man of Iron. When his father was killed by enemies, he spent years in exile on the steppes, gathering followers and using tribal war and diplomacy to patch together a new Mongol confederacy.

- His efforts were crowned in 1206, when he was recognized by the Mongol tribal council as Chinggis Khan, a title that can be interpreted as Great Ruler, or Strong Ruler.

- Chinggis commenced the creation of the Mongol empire by launching campaigns against the Uyghurs and Tanguts in central Asia and then against the Jin dynasty, which had been established by the Jurchen.

- The Jurchen had taken control of northern China in 1127, forcing the ethnic Han Song dynasty to the south. Mongol armies began raiding northern China in 1211 and by 1215 had captured the Jurchen capital near modern Beijing.

- Chinggis Khan next led Mongol forces west into Afghanistan and eastern Persia, regions that were under the control of the Khwarazm Turks. Mongol forces ravaged dozens of cities and killed hundreds of

Mongol leader Chinggis Khan was primarily responsible for creating the Mongol empire.

thousands of people in a show of devastating force and brutality that was felt in the region for centuries afterward.

■ Chinggis Khan died in 1227, having laid the foundations for empire. He had united the Mongols into a powerful force and established Mongol supremacy in northern China, central Asia and parts of Persia.

■ But Chinggis was a military ruler who never attempted to establish any form of civil administration for his empire. This meant that even as his sons and grandsons continued Mongol expansion, it also fell on them to take up the task of designing a more durable political structure. Just before his death, Chinggis divided the empire into four sections, or khanates, each to be administered by one of his sons or grandsons.

■ In 1229, the Mongol council of chiefs elected Chinggis's third son Ogedei as Great Khan, a position of leadership over the other Khans. Ogedei immediately launched campaigns in all directions: west into Afghanistan and Persia; northwest into Armenia, Georgia, and eastern Europe; south into China to renew the campaign against the Jin; and eastward into Korea until that entire peninsula came under Mongol control.

■ Only Ogedei's death may have prevented the conquest of western Europe. After his death in 1241, fighting broke out between the khans, and the four-khanate structure evolved into a very real division of the Mongol realm into four separate regional but allied empires whose relationships were often messy and tense.

■ Rulers known as the Great Khans now took control of China, always the wealthiest part of the empire. Descendants of another of Chinggis's sons, Chaghatai, took control of central Asia; Persia was ruled by a group of Mongols known as the Ilkhans. And Russia was dominated for the next two centuries by the Mongols known as the Golden Horde.

■ To the southeast, Chinggis's grandson Mongke led armies into Tibet and also maintained pressure on the Koryo dynasty in the Korean peninsula. In the heartland of Eurasia, Mongke's brother Hulegu destroyed the Muslim Abbasid caliphate that had ruled the Islamic world since 750, a monumental and shattering victory that brought to an end the classical age of Islam.

MONGOL RULE

- Mongol rule in China followed a different trajectory from that of the Ilkhans or the Golden Horde. Chinggis Khan's son Ogedei had renewed his father's attacks against the Jin dynasty, which finally fell in 1234, leaving the Mongols in control of northern China while the south was ruled by the Song.

- Ogedei's younger brother Tolui had four sons, and they were raised by their mother Beki to be skilled in the arts of warfare but also to be literate, well read, and tolerant of the various religions that were practiced within the Mongol khanates.

- As a daughter-in-law of Chinggis Khan and mother of four grown sons, Beki held enormous prestige in the Mongol world. She was an adept politician who used her status to ensure that her oldest son, Mongke, became Great Khan in 1251, a position he held for eight years until his death.

- Just before he died, Mongke led the first campaigns against the Song, but after his death, these campaigns were put on hold while civil war broke out among the Khans.

- One of Mongke's brothers was Hulegu, whose sacking of Baghdad brought to an end the Islamic Abbasid caliphate. Another was Qubilai Khan, perhaps the most famous Mongol after Chinggis, and a ruler who would have a major impact on Chinese history.

- Qubilai Khan succeeded Mongke and claimed the title of Grand Khan in 1260, but in this new, more divided Mongol polity, not all the hordes recognized his authority. Nevertheless, Qubilai and Beki proved to be effective administrators in northern China, supporting agriculture to build a reliable population of tax-paying farmers.

- In preparation for renewed campaigns against the Song, Beki and Qubilai used diplomacy to build alliances with Jin elites and also with several Song dynasty generals, alliances that would play a critical role in the total conquest of China.

- It took nine years to subdue the Song, whose capital city of Hangzhou finally fell to Qubilai Khan and his forces in 1276. A few years later, Qubilai Khan declared himself emperor of all China and constructed his capital where modern Beijing is today. The name he chose for his new dynasty was Yuan, meaning "the origins of the universe."

- Ruling a vast and complex state such as China was a new challenge for the Mongols. Qubilai and his successors tried to maintain political control, social stability, and tax revenue by creating a balance of power in government and by combining foreign and Chinese techniques of administration. The population of the Yuan dynasty was divided into four categories based on ethnicity: Mongols, diverse peoples, Han Chinese, and Southern Chinese.

- The emperor and court centered their administration on the capital and ruled the provinces through subordinate officials. To guard against the building of local power bases, provincial administrators needed the permission of imperial supervisors before any major decisions could be made.

- Qubilai Khan dismantled the Confucian exam system that had provided China with high-quality bureaucrats for 1,500 years and instead appointed Persian and central Asian Muslims to high administrative posts in Yuan government.

- But Yuan administration was not particularly efficient; both central and provincial government became so lackadaisical that even those Chinese

Han officials employed to work with the Mongols openly criticized the Yuan government for its ineptitude.

- Much of our knowledge of Yuan China comes from the famous Venetian traveler Marco Polo. In 1271, Marco set out on an epic journey across Asia, arriving three and a half years later at the court of Qubilai Khan.

- Marco Polo knew several languages and had acquired considerable political and geographical knowledge—skills that were so impressive to Qubilai Khan that he employed Marco as his advisor for the next 17 years.

- Marco eventually returned to Venice in 1295 after another epic journey but was caught up in a bitter war between Genoa and Venice and imprisoned for several years. While he was in prison, Marco dictated to his cellmate the famous account of his travels and his many years in China, known ever since as *The Travels of Marco Polo*.

- Even as Marco Polo was dictating his account in his jail cell, economic problems were beginning to beset the four khanates of the Mongol empire. After the death of Ilkhan Ghazan in 1304, the dynasty went into a steep decline blighted by factional disputes. When the last Mongol ruler of Persia died without an heir in 1335, the Ilkhanate collapsed, and local governors ruled Persia until the arrival of the Turks later in the 14th century.

Marco Polo
(c. 1254–1324)

- Similar financial problems beset the Yuan administration in China. Merchants lost confidence in the economy as prices rose sharply, and political infighting in the Yuan court led to virtual civil war between Mongol factions.

- An anti-Mongol rebellion broke out in the south led by a brilliant young Buddhist ruler named Hongwu. By 1368, Hongwu's forces had captured the Yuan capital and driven the Mongols back to the steppes. Hongwu then established the Ming dynasty, which would go on to successfully rule China and defend against any attempted foreign invasion for almost the next three centuries.

- Eventually, other parts of the former Mongol empire experienced similar outcomes. The Mongol domain, even once it had been subdivided into four khanates, was simply too extensive to be ruled by any semblance of the sort of organized administration that successful imperialists had employed in the past.

- This meant that the Mongols had to become evermore dependent on provincial governors, who used their positions to amass their own power and wealth, leading to the eventual erosion of Mongol control.

- From the perspective of big history, the Mongol experience suggests that there will always be a limit to the size of land-based empires, and the Mongols evidently exceeded it. The limit does not necessarily apply to maritime, noncontiguous empires, however, as the even larger British Empire would later prove.

THE IMPACT OF THE MONGOLS

- Although the Mongols are justifiably renowned for the slaughter and havoc wrought by their invasions, historians today tend to focus more on the stability and connections that they established through control of their vast empire.

The Big History of Civilizations

- By encouraging trade, they helped spread critically important Chinese innovations, such as gunpowder and printing, to Europe, with dramatic implications for subsequent world history.

- The Mongols also patronized art and architecture, facilitated the spread of new crops to China, and helped in the diffusion of Islamic scientific knowledge.

- And they gave Europeans a new awareness of the wider world, which acted as a powerful spur to European exploration, expansion, and ultimately colonization.

- The trans-Eurasian system they created laid the foundations for the future emergence of capitalism, genuine global connections, and the age of European hegemony.

- But the largest contiguous empire ever seen was fleeting and could not endure because of logistical problems and difficulties of imperial administration. Dominant for only about a century, the mighty Mongols soon slipped quietly from the great stage of world history and back to the steppes from whence they had come.

SUGGESTED READING

Jackson, *The Mongols and the West.*

Morgan, *The Mongols.*

Rossabi, *Khubilai Khan.*

QUESTIONS TO CONSIDER

1. How was Chinggis Khan able to turn a divided and inconsequential group of nomads into perhaps the most formidable military force the world has ever seen?

2. What ultimately was the impact of the Mongol era on world history? Was it positive, negative, or a mixture of both?

NORTH AMERICAN PEOPLES AND TRIBES

For most of the time humans have been on the planet, the world was effectively divided into four isolated world zones in which human communities evolved almost entirely separately from each other: Afro-Eurasia, the Americas, Australasia, and the Pacific. This lecture focuses on the Americas—specifically North American civilizations. What was happening in the Americas, and in North America in particular, while Sumerian, Egyptian, Persian, Indo-Aryan, Han Chinese, Roman, Islamic, and Mongolian civilizations were flourishing across Afro-Eurasia? Is American history utterly different from that of Afro-Eurasia, or will we find some similarities?

THE AMERICAS

- In the Americas, agriculture appeared from at least 6,000 years ago, leading to powerful chiefdoms, complex societies, and—by about 2,000 years ago—impressive agrarian civilizations.

- A comparison between the Americas and Afro-Eurasia also highlights some significant differences, the first of which is that the Americas were settled by humans tens of thousands of years later than Eurasia and hundreds of thousands of years later than Africa.

- Because of this, and also perhaps because of a difference in geographical orientation, agriculture appeared much later in the Americas, which meant that complex states and agrarian civilizations also developed much later.

■ Although humans might have arrived earlier, they had certainly reached the Americas by 15,000 years ago, traveling either down the West Coast in oceangoing canoes or on foot across the Beringia land bridge and then south between the great ice sheets.

■ These migrants came from East Asia and Siberia. They had survived for tens of thousands of years by exploiting coastal resources and by mammoth hunting, which meant that the technologies they had invented for survival in northeast Eurasia were not necessarily suitable for the environment of the New World.

■ The challenges presented by this new environment may have been exacerbated by the geographical orientation of the Americas. While Afro-Eurasia is essentially stretched out from east to west, the Americas are stretched out from north to south.

■ This meant that, for the first Americans traveling from the northern frozen tundra south through the plains, mountains, forests, and deserts of the Americas, the task of adapting to so many different environments was particularly challenging. In comparison, migrating east or west through Afro-Eurasia was considerably easier.

■ However, humans managed to migrate all the way from the very northern part of the Americas to the southern tip of Chile in only about 2,000 years. But once these newcomers had settled across this great diversity of environments, the exchanging of many technological ideas between them was of limited use, because the technologies were so well adapted to very particular environments.

■ The first Americans were confronted with species of plants and animals that humans had never seen before and that had never experienced human intervention before. Given these circumstances, and the fact that human population densities remained small for thousands of years, it is hardly surprising that agriculture developed much later in the Americas than it had in Afro-Eurasia, thousands of years later.

■ Because of successful hunting by the first Americans, many large animal domesticates had been driven to extinction. Many American plants were also much more difficult to domesticate, so it took a long time for potential farmers to figure out how to use them.

■ With all these impediments in mind—impediments that essentially kept human populations relatively small for thousands of years—it is no wonder that complex societies took a long time to appear in the Americas.

■ By around 1500 B.C.E., powerful chiefdoms had started to emerge in various regions of the Americas, such as the Olmec culture of Mesoamerica. But it was not for another 2,000 years that seriously large states appeared in Mesoamerica, such as the great city of Teotihuacán or the city-states of Mayan civilization.

■ Finally, by 1500 C.E., around the same time that European conquistadores came knocking at the door of the Americas, large-scale agrarian civilizations and empires had only just appeared in Mesoamerica and South America, created by the Aztecs and Inca.

■ Despite the many differences, however, the appearance of agrarian civilizations in the Americas also reveals some striking similarities with their counterparts in Afro-Eurasia, even though there was virtually no contact between these world zones until the early 16th century.

■ Early civilizations in both world zones were all based on agriculture, and they all featured an elaborate division of labor, with a huge range of specialist artisans, traders, and warriors. All agrarian civilizations, wherever they appeared, constructed monumental buildings; had wealthy and powerful rulers, large cities, taxation, record keeping, and impressive scientific understandings of the world; and engaged in seemingly endless warfare.

- Interestingly, however, no such large-scale structures appeared in North America, nor did civilizations or empires of the kind that arose in Afro-Eurasia, Central America, and South America.

- Instead, North America was populated by a wide variety of cultures that eventually occupied virtually every environmental niche across the vast continent and that were extraordinary in different ways.

NORTH AMERICAN CULTURES

- Across the vast North American continent, a remarkable variety of political, cultural, and social traditions emerged over the course of thousands of years—so varied that it is impossible to describe any single cultural model.

- Fishing and the gathering of marine resources remained the norm along the coasts, but inland, hunting of large animals, such as deer and bison, offered a sustainable lifeway. Both fishing and hunting peoples supplemented their diets by gathering berries, nuts, root vegetables, and wild grasses. But, as is the case with hunter-gatherer lifeways everywhere, limited food resources and the necessity for mobility resulted in small and diffused populations.

- However, in a few select regions of North America—regions that had just the right conditions in place—more complex societies and larger population densities did begin to appear, based on sedentary agricultural practices.

- These were communities that adopted agriculture and lived in semipermanent villages, but because environmental constraints made farming less productive, they continued to supplement it with hunting and gathering. This meant that, even though these communities made the transition to agriculture, they were unable to support populations large or dense enough to cross the threshold of complexity to become urbanized civilizations.

- East of the Mississippi River valley woodland, communities practiced horticulture, growing mostly corn and beans. Archaeologists can trace continuous cultural developments among the woodland peoples over thousands of years, including evolving skills in woodworking, cultivation, shelter construction, and toolmaking.

- Sometime between 600 and 800 C.E., the archaic spears of the Late Woodland period were replaced by the bow and arrow, and seminomadic lifeways were replaced by permanent villages and dependence on farming, although the people never lost their skills of forest and big-game herd management.

- This trend toward sedentism culminated in the emergence of large state-like structures, including the nation of the five Iroquois peoples (the Mohawk, Oneida, Onondaga, Cayuga, and Seneca) by around 1400.

- Forest-dwelling tribes certainly knew how to use the naturally provided fruits of the woodland, but they also became skilled in manipulating the forests to their advantage. Native peoples used fire extensively to clear land for planting corn. They also used fire as an aid to hunting.

- During the Woodland and later Mississippian eras, which date from roughly 800 C.E. to the early 16th century, native peoples of eastern North America also left their mark on the landscape by erecting impressive earthen mounds, which were sites for elaborate ceremonies and rituals and for burials.

- The woodland native peoples were very successful hunters and gatherers of the rich resources provided by their environment and supplemented their foraging by growing plants such as sunflowers and artichoke. Eventually, they began to establish larger semipermanent settlements.

- Once corn agriculture spread into the eastern woodlands after about 800 C.E., followed by the cultivation of beans and squash, much larger populations could be supported, and genuine chiefdoms appeared.

East of the Mississippi River valley woodland, communities practiced horticulture, growing mostly corn and beans.

- Those elites who established themselves in more favorable environmental niches had the resources necessary to control those based in less favorable environments, so that much of North America east of the Mississippi became an interconnected cultural and political complex held together by common ceremonial, cultural, and economic patterns.

- As these connections formed, it seems likely that mound building spread among the native eastern peoples. Perhaps the most impressive surviving collection of mounds is the complex at Cahokia, near St. Louis, Illinois. Cahokia flourished between 900 and 1250 C.E., when up to 40,000 people may have lived in the urban site.

- This was a huge population that was only sustainable because of several environmental advantages that Cahokia enjoyed. Key among these was that Cahokia lay amid river valleys that contained rich, fertile soil and plenty of water. It also functioned as something of a port, located conveniently close to the convergence of the Illinois, Missouri, and Mississippi Rivers. In the end, a serious earthquake probably destroyed and depopulated Cahokia.

- In the American Southwest, meanwhile, between roughly 2000 and 1000 B.C.E., Puebloan peoples learned to practice irrigation agriculture in their small fields, growing corn, beans, squash, and sunflowers.

- The environment of the Southwest was almost as harsh then as it is today, and even with the use of irrigation technology, it was not until the 7th century C.E. that Puebloan farmers were able to produce enough food to construct and sustain permanent villages of stone and adobe.

- Between about 600 and 1200 C.E., successful permanent farming communities flourished at more than 100 sites across modern New Mexico and Colorado, the most famous of which is Chaco Canyon.

- In this remote, arid, and desolate canyon, Puebloan peoples constructed several huge communal buildings—the so-called Great Houses—which were four stories high and contained thousands of different rooms. Anywhere from 2,000 to 10,000 people lived at Chaco, apparently a site of great spiritual power that functioned as a major ceremonial center.

- The mystery of Chaco's purpose and function is deepened by the fact that all the Great Houses were abandoned by 1300 C.E., perhaps in response to climate change—specifically drought. Eventually, farming became unsustainable across the region, and many Puebloan peoples were forced back to foraging, until by around 1500 C.E., the population of farmers across the Southwest had dropped by perhaps 70 percent.

- Far to the north of Chaco, and in a much more sustainable environment, foraging peoples such as the Chinook and Yakima established themselves on the West Coast of the modern United States and Canada, where the abundant resources enabled them to pursue successful hunting, gathering, and fishing lifeways for thousands of years.

- Cultural diffusion across the plains of North America ensured that technological innovations such as the bow and arrow spread widely among groups across the Great Plains.

- By the time European trappers made their way across the northern plains, socially ranked hierarchies had emerged in foraging communities such as the Nez Perce, Sioux, and Cherokee, often leading to increased conflict between them.

- In the frozen far north of the Americas, Paleo-Eskimo fishermen and hunters had adapted to a world of perpetual night during the long northern winter. They maintained superb fur clothing, canoes, and other sophisticated hunting and fishing equipment, all exquisitely adapted to this harsh environment, which allowed them to survive and prosper in regions where few other members of our species could endure.

CONTACT WITH OTHER PARTS OF THE WORLD

- Native peoples of North America cultivated corn and tobacco, but these crop species and others were not originally domesticated in North America. Rather, they were first domesticated in Mesoamerica and South America and then diffused into North America.

- Another example of contact between North American peoples and the outside world involves the great Scandinavian seafarers, the Vikings. After having established successful colonies in Iceland and Greenland, the hardy Viking longships didn't have to travel that much farther to cross the eastern Atlantic and make landfall on the coast of North America. Archaeologists have found evidence of a short-lived Viking colony that was established in Newfoundland around 1000 C.E., a site known as L'Anse aux Meadows.

SUGGESTED READING

Brotherson, *Book of the Fourth World*.

Gately, *Tobacco*.

Mann, *1491*.

QUESTIONS TO CONSIDER

1. Why is the sealing off of human populations in different isolated world zones an incredible advantage for big historians?

2. Why did none of the complex cultures that appeared over thousands of years in North America ever evolve into full-scale civilizations?

AGRARIAN CIVILIZATIONS OF MESOAMERICA

I n many ways, the evolution of complex societies in Central America followed similar patterns of historical development to what has unfolded in many other places around the globe. Yet the early civilizations of the region also developed in a unique and unlikely land with a rare combination of geological and climatic characteristics that played a significant role in shaping the way that those civilizations evolved.

MESOAMERICA

- Around 300 million years ago, as a product of the dynamic geological processes of earth, all the continents of our planet were fused together into a giant supercontinent called Pangaea. In this great conglomeration, North and South America were tightly connected with Africa and Eurasia.

- Beginning around 175 million years ago—that is, about 75 million years after the appearance of mammals on our planet—Pangaea began to tear itself apart in a series of violent tectonic rifts. In the Americas, the gigantic North and South American continents initially went their separate ways, but about three million years ago, they were reconnected by a long sinuous isthmus, essentially a land bridge, called Mesoamerica (or Middle America).

- At its narrowest point at the Isthmus of Panama, the tenuous connection between two of the great continents of our planet is a mere 40 miles wide, a distance that has been breached for more than a century by the Panama Canal. However, it is in the regions of Mesoamerica to the north of the isthmus, in what are today the nations of Mexico and Central America, that some of the most intriguing civilizations in world history appeared.

- Because of its geological history and features—most notably, its length—Mesoamerica is a region of great environmental diversity. It contains everything from warm tropical beaches to steamy rain forests to high snow-covered mountains, some of which are still active volcanoes.

- Mesoamerica is also a natural conduit for migration between the continents of North and South America, so the first migrants who arrived in the Americas about 15,000 years ago from what is today Siberia would have passed through the region on their way south.

- These migrants were foragers, and they would have found particularly rich resources throughout Mesoamerica. Archaeologists have discovered evidence of affluent foraging communities living along both the Gulf and Pacific Coasts of the isthmus, supporting themselves on abundant marine resources.

- Around 6,000 years ago, some of these communities began to make the transition to agriculture, domesticating corn, beans, and squash, each of which can be grown in close proximity to each other and supports the growth of the other two. Couple this with the fact that between them they provide all of the essential vitamins and nutrients needed for human survival, and all the necessary ingredients were present for the emergence and expansion of Mesoamerican civilizations.

- As we have seen in other regions of the world, increased agricultural resources and human populations eventually lead to increasing social complexity and the appearance of states. At that point, if the right conditions are in place, some of these states will evolve into full-scale agrarian civilizations, which is precisely what happened in Mesoamerica.

OLMEC SOCIETY

- By about 1400 B.C.E., a fascinating complex society known as the Olmec culture appeared in the lowlands of the Gulf region of modern Mexico, near the city of Veracruz. The Olmec thrived on the rich alluvial soils of the region and practiced slash-and-burn agriculture.

- Because of their success as farmers, the Olmecs developed a hierarchical society that fought wars and traded luxury goods with their neighbors and that also had the resources to construct monumental architecture in the form of pyramid tombs 100 feet high.

- We cannot classify the Olmec as a full-fledged, state-level civilization, nor can we answer the question of how best to understand the impact that their culture had on the later societies and civilizations of Mesoamerica. Some argue that their influence was profound while others believe their impact was more limited.

MONTE ALBAN

- As Olmec society faded in the mid-1ˢᵗ millennium B.C.E., another complex society emerged in the Oaxaca Valley, about 300 miles south of present-day Mexico City. The remains of its capital city are known as Monte Alban.

- This society, whose people are called the Zapotec, arose when a confederation of different communities formed and settled on top of a previously uninhabited mesa. With its base secure on the Monte Alban mesa, the society flourished, and by about 150 C.E., the population totaled perhaps 40,000 people, supported by sophisticated irrigation systems and governed by elites dwelling in elaborate residences.

- Monte Alban was occupied through around 850 C.E., although centuries before this, environmental problems had led to the migration of much of the population hundreds of miles to the north, which may have contributed to the formation of a new state centered on a great city that was later named Teotihuacán.

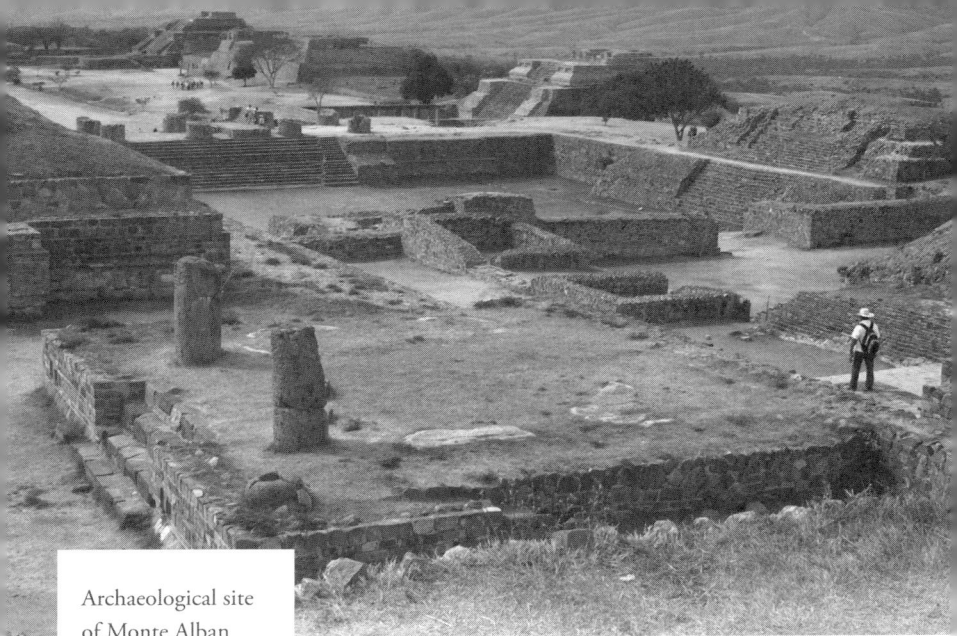

Archaeological site
of Monte Alban

TEOTIHUACÁN

- Teotihuacán is located in the Mexico Basin, where, on a plateau 7,000 feet above sea level, several large lakes are fed by water running down the surrounding mountains. Once farmers learned how to adapt their crops to its high altitude, agriculture flourished, and by 400 B.C.E., the plateau was supporting a population of perhaps 80,000 people living in half a dozen city-states.

- Teotihuacán was one of these city-states. By its peak in 500 C.E., it was supporting the astonishing population of more than 150,000 humans, making it by far the largest city seen in the Americas to that time and one of the six largest cities in the world in 500 C.E. But who the people of Teotihuacán were, and what language they spoke, is unknown.

- Teotihuacán wealth and success were based on the city's control of the trade of Pachuca obsidian, a hard volcanic glass that was almost the ancient equivalent of steel. Teotihuacán was able to coordinate the obsidian trade via exchange networks that stretched extensively across Mesoamerica, from Guatemala to the south to Oklahoma in the north.

- Teotihuacán flourished as a magnificent city for three centuries, complete with monumental architecture, palaces, marketplaces, and public plazas, all supported by a sophisticated irrigation system.

- The cause of Teotihuacán's collapse between 550 and 750 C.E. is also mysterious, but perhaps as a result of civil insurrection or invasion by outsiders, the city was burned and its core was abandoned.

MAYAN CIVILIZATION

- While Teotihuacán was flourishing in the Mexico Basin, farther south in the Yucatán Peninsula Mayan peoples were developing their own sophisticated agrarian civilization that would flourish through the end of the 1st millennium C.E.

- This was a tough environment for agriculture—a hot and humid climate with distinct wet and dry seasons, no large rivers, and low-quality soil—but early farmers persevered by draining swamps, terracing hillsides, and constructing water management systems.

- This worked so well that abundant harvests of corn, beans, squash, and peppers were produced, along with another plant destined to have a significant influence on the world: cacao, which produced chocolate beans. Like most ancient American cultures, the Maya also enjoyed the use of tobacco.

- By 750 C.E., Mayan farmers were supporting large populations; the city-state of Tikal, for example, located in present-day Guatemala, had about 50,000 inhabitants, with another 50,000 in the surrounding countryside.

- Mayan society was strictly hierarchical, with elites on the top and 90 percent of the population, mostly farmers, beneath them. Rulers communicated with the gods and the dead, constructed monumental architecture in the form of great pyramid-shaped temples, and served as military leaders.

■ The Maya developed an extraordinary writing system, which they used to record their administrative and astronomical records, genealogy, poetry, and history. They carved their writings into stone and also wrote on deerskin vellum to create books. Maya writing symbols were both pictographic and phonetic.

■ Before the writing system was deciphered in the 1990s, archaeologists had been inclined to view the Maya as a peaceful civilization. We now know, however, that their society was characterized by frequent warfare and human sacrifice.

■ The Maya developed a mathematical system that included the concept of zero, an idea that scholars on the Indian subcontinent had developed independently. The Maya used mathematics and careful observation to develop a phenomenal knowledge of the movements of the planets and applied this to develop a sophisticated understanding of time that they expressed through three different types of calendars.

■ The Maya never constituted a unified civilization. Like the early Sumerians or classical Greeks, Mayan society consisted of about 50 autonomous city-states, each with its own temples, public plazas, and ball courts. These city-states rose and fell continuously, some lasting less than a century and others lasting much longer. At its end, however, most of Mayan civilization collapsed very quickly.

■ Around 760 C.E., many Mayan cities in the southern Yucatán Peninsula were depopulated, although the northern city of Chichén Itzá continued to flourish for another 500 years, to about 1250 C.E.

■ It was probably a combination of erosion problems caused by deforestation, soil exhaustion caused by over-farming, natural disasters, and disease epidemics that led to Mayan demise. The fate of the

Maya demonstrates the inescapable nature of Malthusian cycles,
overpopulation, and the inability of agricultural innovation to keep
up, which leads to famine and disease. It's a reminder of the fragility
of all human agrarian communities and of our dependence on the
environment.

THE AZTEC EMPIRE

■ The regional collapses of Teotihuacán and Mayan civilization are
regarded by archaeologists as marking the end of the classic period of
Mesoamerican history. But the collapses ultimately paved the way for a

series of new states to appear, including the extraordinary Aztec empire in the 14th century.

■ The Aztecs were seminomadic people from the north who migrated into the region and eventually settled sometime around 1325 C.E. on a small, vacant island in Lake Texcoco in central Mexico. Surrounded by warring city-states, they built a city and honed their military skills by fighting as mercenaries in neighboring armies.

■ Eventually, they accumulated sufficient resources to take control of their region. Now calling their city Tenochtitlán, or the "place of the cactus fruit," they began to construct a very impressive civilization.

■ To deal with the agricultural challenges of their marshy region, they dredged fertile mud and plants from the bottom of the lake and built up small artificial plots of land in the water known as *chinampas*, which eventually ringed the island city of Tenochtitlán. On these *chinampas*, they grew several crops a year of corn, beans, squash, peppers, tomatoes, and domesticated grains.

■ In 1428, the Mexica formed a triple alliance with two other independent city-states around the lake, and this now-powerful alliance set out to conquer other neighboring peoples in pursuit of tribute.

■ In the century before Europeans appeared in the Americas, the Aztec military conquered hundreds of towns and cities until their empire controlled perhaps 10 million people, who paid tribute to the Aztecs in the form of food, textiles, blankets, jewelry, obsidian knives, and rubber balls.

■ Their wealth enabled them to turn Tenochtitlán into a magnificent capital, with a massive plaza surrounded by monumental buildings and causeways across the water to facilitate transport. Once their tributary empire was established, the Aztecs did not put in place any forms of provincial governance; fear of brutal reprisal is what kept the subject people in control.

- The Aztecs shared the ideologies and practices of their Mesoamerican predecessors, including ball games, ritual bloodletting and human sacrifice, and belief in cosmic cycles of creation and destruction, in which the Aztecs played a key role in maintaining order.

- The Aztec language is known as Nahuatl, and the Aztecs had a writing system to record their poems and histories in books. Nahuatl is still a living language spoken by hundreds of thousands people in Mexico.

- When the Spanish conquistadores first came to the Americas, they were astonished by the achievements of the Aztec and other early Central and South American peoples. Charmed as they may have been, the Spanish went on to subjugate the Aztecs, and they destroyed Tenochtitlán. They later built Mexico City on top of its remains.

SUGGESTED READING

Davies, *Human Sacrifice in History and Today*.

Smith, *The Aztecs*.

Webster, *The Fall of the Ancient Maya*.

QUESTIONS TO CONSIDER

1. Why did the Mayans never form a unified civilization, and why was warfare so endemic in their society?

2. In what ways was the Aztec empire similar to, and different from, the empires we have been considering in Afro-Eurasia?

CULTURE AND EMPIRE IN SOUTH AMERICA

D
espite their isolation from each other, Afro-Eurasia and the Americas shared many common experiences. In both zones, humans initially lived as foragers but then made the transition to agriculture so successfully that increased populations and resources led inevitably to the appearance of early states. In places where the conditions were just right—such as Tenochtitlán in central Mexico and the coasts and highlands of the Andes—some states evolved into fully developed agrarian civilizations. This lecture will focus on the development of South America specifically.

EARLY AGRARIAN ANDEAN SOCIETIES

- South America is a diverse continent with many different ecological zones, but it is dominated down the entire length of the western coast by the mighty Andes Mountains, which stretch for 4,500 miles from north to south, the longest mountain range on earth.

- This huge mountain barrier has a significant influence on the climate and environment of much of the continent. While many regions east of the Andes are wet and feature tropical rain forests, the west coast is a desert most of the time. The Atacama Desert, which stretches along the northern coast of Chile, is the driest nonpolar region on earth. Despite its hyperaridity, ancient human communities learned to live in the Atacama Desert.

- Aridity is not the only environmental problem the west coast faces; earthquakes caused by moving tectonic plates rock the region frequently. And the prevailing ocean current along the coast, the Humboldt Current, which usually runs south to north, reverses direction and flows north to south a few times a decade in response to an El Niño event, bringing torrential rains.

- In the heart of the Andes, along the mountains and thin coastal strip occupied by the modern nations of Peru and Bolivia, early foraging communities learned to survive by exploiting extensive marine resources.

- Eventually, perhaps from as early as 5000 B.C.E., these foragers made the transition to agriculture, learning to cultivate corn, beans, peanuts, and sweet potatoes as well as cotton, which grew in the wild in both Afro-Eurasia and the Americas and was used to make textiles.

- As these early agrarian societies became more complex, more sophisticated irrigation systems were constructed, along with some impressively large buildings. Several coastal Andean sites, such as the Peruvian site of Caral, show evidence of public architecture in the form of mounds and terraced temple platforms that date from as early as 3000 B.C.E. This is clear evidence of coordinated labor organization and therefore of hierarchical social structures.

- While these developments were occurring along the coast, agricultural communities were also appearing in the highlands, where they domesticated tobacco and potatoes, which, if eaten in sufficient quantities, can provide all the nutrition that humans need. They also domesticated guinea pigs for food and their pelts as well as two members of the camelid species: llamas for their meat and alpacas for their wool.

- Pottery first appeared in the Peruvian coastal and highland regions around 2000 B.C.E., a technological innovation that might have been associated with a shift away from a dependence on marine resources to a heavier reliance on agrarian production, and thus the need for better storage.

- Long-distance trade also played an important role in these early societies, with trade networks stretching up and down the coast of Peru and Ecuador. Trade routes also connected the coastal region to the highlands.

- But the question of whether there were any long-distance trade and exchange contacts between these early Andean societies and contemporary societies in Mesoamerica is a vexed one. Some sort of contact must have occurred, because the cultivation of corn and squashes gradually spread from Mesoamerica to the Andes, while gold, silver, and copper metallurgy as well as tobacco spread north into Mesoamerica.

- But these exchanges were limited by the challenging geography and environment that separated Central from South America, and also by the fact that megafaunal extinctions during the Paleolithic era meant that there were no real pack animals available. These limitations were destined to have profound historical ramifications.

THE RISE OF REGIONAL STATES

- The first clear archaeological evidence that one of these early agrarian Andean communities had evolved into a state is found at the site of Chavín de Huántar. Situated 3,000 feet up in the mountains, the town of Chavín emerged around 1000 B.C.E., flourished between 800 and 500, and had faded by 300 B.C.E.

- Chavín may have started as a ceremonial center before evolving into a small town-state, with flat-topped pyramid temples built around a central U-shaped plaza. One of the key reasons that explains why some villages evolved into towns all over the world was that they were regarded as having special sacred significance.

- As the site became more important, extensive building and expansion of the ceremonial core occurred, until Chavín was supporting a population of perhaps 3,000 people.

Chavín de Huántar
courtyard

- Chavín also functioned as a trading hub, and several Chavín artistic styles diffused widely throughout the region. After the demise of Chavín, several large town-states of up to 10,000 people emerged in the Andes, also with impressive public buildings constructed around ceremonial plazas, surrounded by residential districts.

- These town-states controlled regions stretching from the coast up through lowland valleys to the highlands. Each ecological niche contributed its own agrarian products to the state: Coastal populations provided fish, cotton, and sweet potatoes; lowland valley farmers provided corn, beans, and squash; and the highlanders offered potatoes, llama meat, and alpaca wool.

- This is a classic example of how, by utilizing the wide diversity of ecosystems within a state, communities are able to grow enough food to sustain growing populations and complex social structures.

- One of the most famous of these states is Nazca, renowned for the extensive linear and zoomorphic designs they constructed in the desert, some of them several miles long. The Nazca people lived along the dry southern coast of Peru and flourished between 100 and 800 C.E. Although we know something about their lifeways and religions, the purpose of their designs, known as the Nazca Lines, remains a mystery.

- Another important regional state that thrived in the 1st millennium was that of the Mochica, who flourished between 300 and 700 C.E. in the valley of the Moche and other rivers along a 250-mile stretch of coast.

- With no writing, the beliefs of the Mochicans remain difficult to determine, but they did leave behind a fascinating glimpse into their lifeways in the form of superb ceramics that depict almost all aspects of life in Moche times: farming, hunting, warfare, weaving, and sex.

- Moche populations were sustained by marine resources and successful highland farming. But given the nature of the environment, this was always tenuous, and in the end, a series of severe droughts between 562 and 594, followed by earthquakes and then torrential El Niño rains, destroyed the viability of the Mochica culture. The challenges of the environment simply proved too great for human resources to overcome, and the Moche state quickly crashed and disappeared.

- Toward the end of the 1st millennium C.E. new states established themselves in the highlands, such as the Wari, who ruled from a mountain city called Ayachuco, and the Tiwanaku, who ruled from their capital at Lake Titicaca.

- Living at a lower altitude, the Wari were able to grow corn. The Tiwanaku, at an altitude above 10,000 feet, were limited to a staple of potatoes and their domesticated herds of alpacas and llamas. Around 1050 C.E., the climate entered a dry spell that lasted for centuries; this led to economic stress that undermined faith in religion and government, and both states withered away.

Incan Civilization

- Two centuries later, a new group of people from the Lake Titicaca region settled at a town called Cuzco, at the very high altitude of 13,000 feet above sea level. These Inca people were just one of a dozen different ethnic groups living around Cuzco, and as population densities in the region increased, so did conflict over land. Eventually, the groups reached a settlement, which involved Inca chiefs marrying noble women of other groups to form coalitions.

- With their homeland secure, the Inca embarked on a series of expansionary campaigns that were begun in 1438 by the great Inca ruler Pachacuti and were completed by his grandson 25 years later. Pachacuti retired to Cuzco, where he designed the system of government the Incas would use to rule their empire and build Cuzco into a magnificent city fit to be an imperial capital.

- By the time the Inca expansion ended in the 1460s, their empire stretched for 2,500 miles down the western coasts and highlands of South America, from the modern city of Quito in Ecuador south to Santiago in Chile.

- This was by far the largest agrarian civilization established in the Americas, an empire that was divided into 80 administrative provinces and contained a population of about 10 million people. It was one of the most impressive agrarian civilizations in the world in the 15th century.

- A reminder of Incan civilization found high in the Andes today is the Inca masterwork Machu Picchu, which was most probably a vacation retreat for several generations of Inca rulers.

- At an altitude of 8,000 feet, Machu Picchu was lower and warmer than Cuzco, and it provided a royal haven that was never detected by the Spanish when they arrived early in the 16th century, bringing to an abrupt end the extraordinary Inca empire. Machu Picchu was therefore never besieged, but it appears to have been abandoned around the time of the Spanish invasion.

The Inca masterwork
Machu Picchu was most
probably a vacation retreat
for several generations of
Inca rulers.

AMAZONIAN COMMUNITIES

- The coasts and mountains of the Andean regions are not the only places in South America where complex states appeared. The work of archaeologists over the past few decades has also revealed chiefdom-level societies in parts of the Amazon basin.

- The Amazon River system is huge, providing about 20 percent of all the freshwater that flows into the world's oceans through a mouth that is 200 miles wide. The Amazon drains about 40 percent of the total area of South America, and the warm equatorial climate of the basin means that around 400 inches of rain falls every year.

- Only in the 1970s did archaeologists begin to examine Amazonia, and ever since, they have been engaged in a vigorous debate about the meaning of what they have found there.

- The story of humans in Amazonia remains somewhat vague, although there is no doubt that some parts were occupied by human farming communities long before the arrival of Europeans, with their deadly diseases that drove the inhabitants back to foraging.

- What we do know is that Amazon farmers were growing manioc, sweet potatoes, and squash, supplemented by fish and other river resources, from as early as 5000 B.C.E. By 2000 B.C.E., agrarian villages had been established, some of which evolved into complex societies.

- Between 1000 and 1500 C.E., the last half millennium before European contact, some Amazonian communities constructed earthen mounds and walls. These societies were structured as chiefdoms rather than states; power was consensual, and there was no attempt to collect coerced tributes.

- The establishment of these communities, which supported dense populations, is a testament to the creative skill of Amazonian farmers, given the notoriously poor soil of the region. In addition, some archaeologists believe that a significant percentage of the forests in Amazonia are actually ancient orchards of fruit and nut trees, which is a further testament to the creative genius of the former farmers of this harsh environment.

SUGGESTED READING

D'Altroy, *The Incas.*

Moseley, *The Incas and Their Ancestors.*

QUESTIONS TO CONSIDER

1. How were the Inca able to overcome significant environmental disadvantages and construct a vast empire?

2. What role did the environment play in limiting trade and exchange between the states and empires of the Americas, and what were the consequences of this for world history?

AFRICAN KINGDOMS AND TRADE

M any important developments in the history of civilization took place in Africa: the rise and longevity of Egyptian civilization, the Punic Wars, and the spread of Islam across North Africa to Morocco. These developments took place primarily in North Africa, but there were also tremendous developments underway in the regions to the south of the Sahara Desert that had significant effects on other parts of the world. This lecture will consider the trajectory of sub-Saharan African history, including the rise and fall of great kingdoms and the role that the environment played in influencing these processes.

AFRICAN SOCIETIES

- The Sahara dominates the northern third of the African continent, but the south is much more diverse, with everything from high alpine mountains to arid deserts, from dense tropical jungle to open grassy savanna plains.

- The savanna stretches across the continent in great belts, just south of the Sahara; around the mountains and lakes of East Africa; and across southern Africa to the Kalahari Desert. Between the northern and southern savanna belts lies a region of dense tropical rain forest sometimes called jungle.

- For the first 240,000 years of their occupation of sub-Saharan Africa, humans survived by foraging, but eventually some communities made the transition to farming, domesticating crops and animals that were well adapted to these various environments.

The Sahara Desert

- Particular cultural patterns emerged in these early agrarian communities that can still be found in many African societies today. The extended family, for example, became the foundation for larger social structures.

- These larger structures possessed all the features we have come to expect in agrarian civilizations: successful farming, large populations, rigid hierarchies, bureaucracies, long-distance exchanges, and hereditary rulers who combined sacred and secular power. Also in line with most other civilizations, African societies were mostly patrilineal.

- Reflecting the beliefs of their Paleolithic ancestors, native religions in sub-Saharan Africa were polytheistic. Rituals and sacrifices were carried out to keep the gods happy, but the arrival of Christianity and Islam had a dramatic impact on these beliefs and practices.

- The Muslim Arab invasions of North Africa after 632 C.E. added another religious layer, although North Africa proved much harder to conquer for Islamic forces than Persia or the Middle East. The Arabs were only able to overcome the combined forces of Byzantines and Libyans after a series of bloody battles. Possibly applying a Greek term, the Arabs came to refer to the Libyans as *Barbar*, or "Barbarians," and this is the origin of the term "Berbers."

- The impact of the Arab invasions further to the south was uneven. The near-ubiquitous demand for slaves, however, ensured connections between Africa's Mediterranean and sub-Saharan regions.

- This meant that, unlike in the north, the spread of Islam into the southern Sahara regions was not the result of conquest, but either by voluntary adoption of the religion or the deliberate conversion of rulers to facilitate the slave trade.

- Farming in Africa's early agrarian era was supplemented by fishing and foraging throughout the continent, even in the Sahara, which, during the Holocene, contained many lakes and rivers. But significant climate change, beginning around 3000 B.C.E., turned large sections of the Sahara into arid desert, which might have acted as a stimulus to the expansion of agriculture farther south.

- This change marks the end of the wet phase of the Holocene, and by 2000 B.C.E., much of North Africa had become as arid as it is today, emptying the Sahara of people except for the inhabitants of the few remaining oases.

- This had the effect of essentially creating two Africas—north and south—and inhibiting significant contact between them for the next two millennia.

SUB-SAHARAN AFRICA
- Bioarchaeologists have identified four independent centers of early farming south of the Sahara: the highlands of Ethiopia, central Sudan, and the savanna and forests of West Africa.

- Ethiopian highland farmers cultivated millet, sesame, and mustard; Sudanese farmers grew sorghum, millet, rice, peas, and nuts. In the West African savanna, oil palms, peas, and yams thrived, and in the forests, farmers grew bananas and coffee.

- A technological revolution occurred in the 7th century B.C.E. when iron metallurgy spread into sub-Saharan Africa. Ironworkers enjoyed high status, because they were thought to have magical powers. Their work increased agricultural productivity by replacing stone tools with metal ones, leading to population growth, craft specialization, more trade, and the evolution of more complex social and economic structures.

- The spread of iron-using farming societies transformed lifeways throughout much of central and southern Africa. Sedentary populations increased, society became more complex, and trade expanded to meet growing demand for iron and other products.

- In certain locations where the appropriate conditions were in place, towns with economies based on trade, farming, and manufacturing appeared. Some of them evolved into larger political structures.

- Such conditions were certainly in place by the start of the Common Era in Ethiopia, a source of valuable trade goods for thousands of years before the first kingdoms appeared there.

- By the Common Era, a state known as Aksum had emerged to dominate Red Sea trade. Aksum reached its peak in the 4th century C.E. under the ruler Ezana, who converted to Christianity. Centuries later, Syrian monks came to Aksum and also converted much of the rural population to Christianity.

- In 615, an Aksum king gave refuge to followers of Muhammad, who were being persecuted in Arabia, an event that marks the beginning of Islamic expansion into East Africa. By the 8th century, Islamic groups had taken over Aksum's position as a major trading center.

Ruins of Aksum
in Ethiopia

- Aksum rulers moved into the interior of Ethiopia and established a new Christian state there known as the Zagwe dynasty. In response to the Muslim capture of Jerusalem in 1187, a Zagwe emperor called Lalibela constructed 11 magnificent Christian churches in a town that came to bear the emperor's name.

WEST AFRICA

- Far to the west of Ethiopia, in the western savanna, the appearance of complex states along the Niger River was also closely associated with the expansion of trade, this time using trans-Saharan routes that led to the Mediterranean.

- The iron-working Nok culture was the first complex state to appear in what is Nigeria today. Nok culture covered a huge area of about 45,000 square miles, sustained by successful farming for about 700 years between 500 B.C.E. and 200 C.E.

- For the first two centuries, Nok farmers coexisted peacefully with the Berber nomads in the Sahara, but the appearance of walled settlements around 300 B.C.E. suggests increasing conflict between them. This culminated in the appearance of the seriously large town of Jenne-Jeno, which became an important center for trade, fishing, and agriculture.

- Founded in an exceptionally fertile area in the Niger Delta, Jenne, by 250 B.C.E., was a walled city 80 acres in area surrounded by a cluster of villages, each of which specialized in a particular craft. Jenne prospered because of its fertile location, but it was also the ideal place to control long-distance trade across the Sahara.

- Because of the obvious difficulty of the trans-Saharan routes, the first attempts by Mediterranean peoples to make contact with sub-Saharan Africa were by sea. An expedition was launched in the mid-5th century B.C.E. by the Carthaginians that sailed south down the Atlantic coast of Africa. The date at which sub-Saharan Africa was reconnected to the Mediterranean coast by trans-Saharan trade is less certain, but various pieces of evidence suggest this occurred during the early centuries C.E.

- With the collapse of the western Roman Empire, this trade declined, but it was revived again by Byzantine and Arab traders.

- Building on flourishing agriculture and trade, a new kingdom emerged just to the south of the Sahara in the Upper Niger region in the 4th century C.E. It was named after its legendary war chief, Ghana, and over the next four centuries became wealthy and powerful.

- The king of Ghana monopolized the gold trade. Salt was also an important export because of its taste and ability to preserve food and skins. Another valued commodity was slaves, often war captives or kidnapping victims from central Africa, who were in great demand among North African states. From there, they were exported all over the eastern Mediterranean.

- Thanks to all its commerce, Ghana became very wealthy. Yet within a decade, Ghana was badly weakened by attacks from the nomadic Berbers and lost its dominance of the gold, salt, and slave trade.

- The eventual successors to Ghana in the region were the Malinke people, who went on to create the enormous and successful Mali empire. They managed to regain control of the desert gold mines and trade from the Berbers. When gold replaced silver as the main currency of Europe in 1252, Mali became Europe's leading supplier, exporting several tons of gold annually.

- Mali reached its peak under Mansa Musa, a Muslim ruler who undertook the hajj to Mecca in 1324 and upon his return built beautiful mosques in the trading cities of his realm. This helped make the imported religion of Islam much better known in Mali, and it made Mali one of the most famous centers of Islamic learning anywhere in the Muslim world.

- Mansa Musa was renowned throughout Africa, Asia, and Europe because of the volume of Malian trade with the Mediterranean and Middle East, and because of how well organized the multicultural Mali state was.

- Eventually, the kingdom of Mali went into decline, crippled by infighting between factions and pressure from tributary states that demanded independence. By the late 15th century, the kingdom had fallen, yet Mansa Musa had ensured that Islam would continue to have a prominent place in West Africa, including up to the present day.

- The Songhai kingdom was one of the states that broke free of Mali's domination.

- It went on to replace Mali and establish the largest of all the empires of the western savanna, ruling from the great trading cities of Timbuktu and Jenne-Jeno. It was superbly administered, with a central bureaucracy and professional military forces.

- By the early 16th century, the mosque and madrasah at Timbuktu was recognized as one of the most important centers for Islamic scholarship in the Muslim world.

- The undoing of the Songhai was attacks by Moroccans from the north. This collapse of the last of the three great West African precolonial empires in the late 16th century brought to an end an extraordinary period in the history of sub-Saharan Africa, and indeed in the history of civilization more generally.

EAST AFRICA

- West Africa was not the only region where states prospered because of successful trade; along the East African coast, a number of successful trading states also emerged as part of Swahili civilization. Swahili was—and is—the language spoken along the east coast.

- The original Swahili farmed in the fertile soils of the region and fished in the many lagoons and rivers, but they also formed and expanded trading contacts with merchants from the Arabian Peninsula and Persian Gulf.

- The center of this trade was the port of Rhapta, which was governed by Arab merchants under the control of a kingdom in Yemen. As more Arab merchants settled along the Swahili coast, Indian Ocean trade thrived.

- Between 1000 and 1500, Swahili civilization thrived. Hundreds of city-states were established along the 1,800-mile coast from Mogadishu in the north to Sofala in the south, many with deep harbors and strong links to well-established land and maritime trade routes.

- These were highly competitive commercial states, which meant they never merged into a coherent empire, but they operated independently and peacefully until the arrival of the Portuguese in the 16th century.

- The key exports from major Swahili port cities were gold, ivory, and slaves. Trading expeditions even arrived from China. The Swahili coast was also well connected to the central and southern inland regions of the continent of Africa. Early agrarian communities in those regions consisted of scattered homesteads and villages, but during the 2nd millennium C.E., some of these also evolved into powerful states.

- Some of these states grew impressively large, such as Mapungubwe, Great Zimbabwe, and Kongo, which was one of the most powerful of Africa's precolonial states.

- By the time the Portuguese turned up late in the 15th century, Kongo was a well-organized state led by a king with a professional army. In 1665, the Portuguese killed the king and many of his courtiers, creating a power vacuum in the country that led eventually to Portuguese conquest of much of the region. This was the beginning of the end of African independence from foreign domination, a situation that would last into the 20th century.

SUGGESTED READING

Ehret, *An African Classical Age*.

Horton and Middleton, *The Swahili*.

Mbiti, *African Religions and Philosophy*.

McIntosh, *The Peoples of the Middle Niger*.

QUESTIONS TO CONSIDER

1. Is it appropriate to think of the vast African continent as essentially consisting of two very different environmental and cultural worlds?

2. Sub-Saharan Africa was home to many sophisticated and complex states. Why did none of these evolve into large-scale agrarian civilizations?

LIFEWAYS OF AUSTRALIA AND THE PACIFIC

T his lecture examines the communities of Australasia and the Pacific for the telltale signs of intensification and complexity: the increasing control of resources, larger and denser populations, and evolving social complexity. This will allow us to determine whether Australia and the Pacific were in essentially the same situation as Afro-Eurasia and the Americas: The right ingredients were present and the right processes had begun, but important differences in the timing of the processes in Australia and the Pacific meant that these nascent civilizations were never able to reach their full potential, because they were cut off at a critical moment by the arrival of Europeans.

AUSTRALIA

- At the time of British invasion in the early 19th century, Australia was home to about 1 million Aboriginal people. They were divided into hundreds of clan-based communities and spoke perhaps 250 different languages.

- The foundations of these communities and the cultures they constructed were laid down during the last ice age, when the Australian mainland was joined to the large islands of Tasmania in the south and New Guinea in the north, in a mega-island continent known as Sahul.

- Sahul was colonized by maritime peoples from Southeast Asia at least 50,000 years ago. Within 5,000 to 10,000 years of their arrival, all of the sustainable environments within Sahul were supporting humans. They had proven themselves remarkably adaptable to these new ecological niches and adept at making numerous innovations in response to ongoing climate change.

- The earliest solidly dateable evidence we have of humans in Sahul comes from the Ivane Valley in the highlands of Papua New Guinea, not far from the modern coastal city of Port Moresby, where radiocarbon dates of up to 49,000 years ago have been obtained on charcoal found with hunting-and-gathering stone tools. These Ice Age foragers lived in small clan-based communities and migrated with the seasons, connecting various resource-rich environments.

- By 10,000 years ago, agriculture had emerged independently in some highland communities of Papua New Guinea, where farmers had learned to domesticate yams and taro using swidden, or slash-and-burn, techniques.

- By 7,000 years ago, cultivation had intensified; farming communities were constructing artificial mounds and drainage channels in conjunction with ongoing swidden and the cultivation of grasslands.

- These constructions imply the appearance of hierarchies and new forms of leadership to facilitate larger-scale farming of taro, bananas, yams, sugarcane, and sweet potato. They also suggest increased human populations.

- These early agrarian villages never achieved the critical levels of population density necessary to evolve into towns and larger political structures. But Papua New Guinea's highland farming societies were considerably more complex than those of the island's coastal regions, where foraging remained the norm. Highlanders created more sophisticated art, rituals, and even forms of warfare.

- In Tasmania, at the far southern end of Sahul, rising sea levels after the last ice age eventually severed connections with the mainland, leaving Tasmania's population of perhaps 4,000 inhabitants isolated from other humans. As was the case with a number of Polynesian communities, archaeologists can trace a return to smaller and simpler lifeways in Tasmania.

- This shows us that technological innovation, or even the preservation of preexisting technologies, simply cannot be sustained in small isolated populations because the potential for collective learning is too limited and the struggle for mere survival is too pressing.

- Despite the incredibly ancient foundations of aboriginal communities, evidence suggests that, within the past 3,000 to 4,000 years, more complex social structures in Australian indigenous societies evolved quite rapidly.

- Distinctive types of stone tools were developed and spread across the continent. There was greater regional specialization of rock-art styles, the appearance of large-scale ceremonial gatherings involving hundreds of people, and the expansion of exchange systems.

- Significantly, where the right conditions, such as reliable rainfall, prevailed, particularly in communities along Australia's east, southeast, and southwest coasts, larger population densities appeared. There, we find evidence of economic and social intensification very similar to that which preceded the emergence of agriculture in other parts of the world.

- Archaeologists have found a significant increase in the number of inhabited sites during the two millennia prior to European conquest, a further indicator of substantial population increase. It may have been facilitated by the invention of new food acquisition technologies, such as fishhooks made from shells.

- Archaeologists have also discovered evidence in this period of numerous long-distance trade and exchange networks spanning hundreds and even thousands of miles across Australia.

- Evidence of social intensification is found in signs of large-scale gatherings that many groups participated in, which brought together hundreds of people for social, political, and religious reasons and included the performance of ceremonies such as initiation, gift exchange, and marriage. These gatherings, called corroborees, could only take place where there were sufficient resources to feed this many people, so they were organized when food was available.

- It wasn't just natural resources that sustained large communities; at Lake Condah in southeast Australia, Aboriginal people dammed off the lake's outlet to maintain water levels and eel stocks around 4,600 years ago, probably to help avert the negative impacts of a warming and drying climate.

Aboriginal art

- In Australia, just as in North America, evidence of these technological, cultural, and political developments can only leave us wondering how history might have played out differently had Australian aboriginals been left to pursue their historical trajectories without European interference.

THE PACIFIC

- As far as we know, the Pacific was the last world zone to be occupied by humans, an occupation that occurred in a series of colonizing processes that can be divided into two distinct phases.

- The first occurred late in the Paleolithic era, when the islands of the Philippines and parts of western Melanesia, including the Solomons, were settled 40,000 years ago. This occupation occurred not long after humans had also migrated into Australia, presumably using similar seagoing technologies.

- Then, the colonization of the Pacific stalled for many millennia, probably because crossing the vast distances of Remote Oceania that separated the islands of the Pacific required navigational and seafaring skills that simply had not yet been developed.

- It wasn't until the middle of the 2nd millennium B.C.E., more than 38,000 years later, that a new wave of migration took humans deeper into the vast Pacific zone. This migration was led by new seagoing peoples who appeared in Southeast Asia and who spoke languages belonging to the Austronesian language group that probably originated on the island of Taiwan.

- These migrations that began 3,500 years ago have left striking archaeological evidence: obsidian tools and sophisticated fishing technologies; evidence of domesticated dogs, chickens, and pigs; and Lapita pottery. The name given to the pottery is also the name used to describe the people who made it.

- Over the course of a millennium, the Lapita moved from Taiwan into the Philippines, and on to the islands of the Bismarck Archipelago. In the centuries that followed, new migrations took the Lapita deeper out into the Pacific: to the eastern Solomon Islands by 3,200 years ago; to Vanuatu, New Caledonia, and Fiji by 3,000 years ago; to western Polynesia and the central Pacific Islands of Tonga by 2,900 years ago; and by 2,700 years ago, to Samoa.

- Lapita peoples deliberately avoided settling in islands that were already densely populated, such as Papua New Guinea, presumably because they were looking for new lands that would be much easier to colonize. Although this meant sailing for thousands of miles across the open ocean, eventually they occupied a large number of islands spanning an area of more than 3,000 miles.

- Once settled in their new island homes, the Lapita constructed stilt villages over platform reefs and thrived on a combination of farming and the foraging of marine resources, such as fish, sharks, turtles, and shellfish.

- The Lapita had carried their agricultural domesticates with them in their canoes, introducing to Oceania animals, such as the pig, dog, chicken, and Pacific rat, and at least 15 plant species, including taro, yams, and bananas.

- Migrations over these enormous distances provide clear evidence of the kind of advanced navigation and sailing skills these seafaring colonists had attained. In fact, there is plenty of evidence of ongoing long-distance trade along what must have been regularly traveled, although incredibly extensive, maritime routes.

- Lapita exchange networks likely spanned an astonishing distance of more than 4,000 miles—a network almost of Silk Roads proportions. Exchange networks on this scale can only have been sustained by skilled community leaders who had learned to manage the complex sociopolitical relationships necessary to maintain kinship ties between distant communities.

- Like many early agrarian communities where forms of consensual power first emerged, it was the skill of these leaders, as much as any claim to superior lineage, that was probably the key definer of status and authority in Lapita communities.

- The Lapita were also responsible for crucial technological innovations without which voyages over such distances would not have been conceivable. One of the most important was the invention of the triangular sail, which allowed mariners to sail both with and into the prevailing southeasterly winds of the Pacific.

- Eventually, more and more of these maritime migrations took place, until most of the islands that make up the Pacific region of Polynesia had been settled in what must be regarded as the last great chapter in the human colonization of the globe.

- After living in Tonga and Samoa for 1,500 years, descendants of Lapita peoples began migrating to the north, west, and south across huge expanses of ocean to establish the more than 30 closely related Polynesian societies and languages we know today.

- Despite living on far-flung islands, Polynesians share common oral histories. They also share traditional stories and songs about their ancestral homeland of Hawaiki, which refers to Samoa and Tonga and the surrounding islands.

- Most Polynesian communities also share common sociopolitical structures, including hereditary chiefdoms with communities structured around the chief's extended household and common religious and agricultural practices.

- The voyages of Polynesian colonization covered such phenomenally long distances that they were probably one-way trips done in stages. The actual timing of this last dispersal is hotly debated by archaeologists, however. The most recent thinking is that these voyages began with the colonization of the Society Islands, beginning around 1,000 years ago.

- The islands of the Marquesas, Hawaii, and distant Rapa Nui were settled next, all at more or less the same time around 800 years ago. Finally, the two main islands of New Zealand were occupied around 700 years ago.

- Given the difficulty of reaching the islands of Polynesia and the near impossibility of return voyages, or of the establishment of exchange networks between them, the colonists of Polynesia were effectively isolated from each other and free to develop their own distinctive, though related, cultures.

- Like their Lapita forebears, Polynesian colonizers brought to their new island homes a range of plants and animals to help make them suitable for permanent occupation. Despite the ecological transformation that resulted, Polynesian colonization of the major island groups like New Zealand and Hawaii was undoubtedly successful, leading to increased populations and social complexity.

- But as in Tasmania, the communities of many islands that were initially colonized successfully followed a trajectory toward cultural simplification rather than complexity.

- An especially interesting example is isolated Rapa Nui, also known as Easter Island, where village communities based on successful farming grew large, wealthy, and organized enough to carve and erect the astonishing anthropomorphic stone statues for which the island is famous.

- Rapa Nui had enough cultivable land to sustain its peak population for a time. But eventually, partly because of deforestation caused by cutting down all the trees on the island to get the megaliths into place, the population—and the entire culture—collapsed, and the survivors were forced to revert to basic foraging for survival.

- The largest Polynesian communities, on Hawaii, Tonga, and Samoa, shared much with states all over the world: hierarchical and stratified social structures with supreme or paramount chiefs and priesthoods, monumental stone structures, and irrigation works. Their empires were territorial and militaristic.

- Small-scale chiefdoms may have contained just a few hundred people, but the complex paramount chiefdoms of Tonga, Samoa, and Hawaii included tens of thousands of people. Once again, all the preconditions for these states to evolve into full-scale agrarian civilizations were in place at the moment of European contact.

SUGGESTED READING

Hiscock, *Archaeology of Ancient Australia.*

Howe, *The Quest for Origins.*

Kirch, *On the Road of the Winds.*

QUESTIONS TO CONSIDER

1. Does a big history analysis of aboriginal communities in Australasia suggest that this world zone was subject to different developmental rules from those in Afro-Eurasia and the Americas or that these communities were on the same evolutionary path but had just not progressed as far because of their particular environmental conditions?

2. What lessons does the collapse of the Polynesian culture on the island of Rapa Nui have for humans living in the 21st century, as we wrestle with our own potentially devastating resource crisis and climate change problems?

THE ADVENT OF GLOBAL COMMERCE

F rom the collapse of Roman administration during the 5th century
C.E. until the establishment of the European Union in the second
half of the 20th century, western Europe remained a region of
divided states. Resisting all attempts to recombine, these states created
instead their own individual city, regional, and eventually national destinies
that drove the world across the next threshold of complexity and into
the modern era. Between roughly 500 and 1750 C.E., wealth, markets,
populations, and technologies steadily expanded in most regions of the
globe. And because European societies were preadapted to flourish in this
new environment, the position of Europe was transformed from historical
backwater into a new global hub.

THE POSTCLASSICAL MALTHUSIAN CYCLE

■ Throughout human history, cycles of innovation and population
increase stimulate the expansion of commerce, urbanization, and state
power. But populations always seem to grow too fast for innovation to
keep up, leading to overpopulation, disease, famine, war, and sudden
and often violent collapse. This pattern was noticed by 18th-century
economist and demographer Thomas Malthus and has come to be
known as a Malthusian cycle.

■ The period between roughly 500 and 1350 C.E., the postclassical
Malthusian cycle, was characterized by the expansion of traditional
agrarian civilizations into new regions of the planet and by an increase
in their wealth and power.

- Climate change might have played a role in this expansion. Climates were generally warmer between 800 and 1200 C.E. This meant more rainfall and increased harvests, particularly in once-marginal regions at the edges of the major civilizations, which previously had been too cold or too dry to sustain large populations.

- This Malthusian upsurge lasted into the mid-14th century, when it was checked by the rapid spread of plague and perhaps also by a return to cooler climates during what is known as the Little Ice Age, which lasted until about 1700.

- Certainly, up to 1200, population growth stimulated urbanization and increased farming in numerous marginal regions in eastern Europe and southern and western China. Cities multiplied and increased in size almost everywhere. It wasn't just climate change driving this expansion; human collective learning was also in evidence, at least partly in response to climate change.

- The expansion of imperial civilizations in Afro-Eurasia and the Americas increased state resources, which were used to support larger and better-equipped armies to facilitate even further growth.

- Exchange networks also expanded, leading to the colonization of regions far away from areas of dense settlement, such as in Polynesia or across Russia and the North Atlantic at the hands of the Vikings. Merchants seeking increased profits journeyed long distances, helping further expand commerce and connecting market economies all over Afro-Eurasia. Merchants also helped spread new crops, technologies, and ideas.

- As markets expanded, many peasants were able to leave their small farms to become wage earners instead, often moving into cities, which further intensified urbanization.

- During this postclassical Malthusian upswing, virtually every sector of society was affected. This expansion of commerce made all societies more "capitalistic," but this was even more the case among the smaller commercial states that flourished during this period, states whose income was no longer based on old-fashioned tribute taking, but on trade.

- In Europe, many of these city-states acquired the resources to begin the first wave of monumental building since the Romans; most of the great cathedrals of Europe were built during this period. Similar developments occurred in parts of Africa, such as the Malian city of Timbuktu.

- States and city-states also invested heavily in their militaries, particularly in conflict-riven Europe. Before long, the maritime states of Venice and Genoa were strong enough to take on and often defeat much larger agrarian civilizations, such as the Ottoman Empire.

- By the early 1300s, Malthusian signs of stagnation and overpopulation were appearing throughout Afro-Eurasia. Climates were also cooling, and famines became more common; the great European famines of 1315 to 1317 killed off 15 percent of Europe's population.

- Most devastating of all disasters was the Black Death, a plague that began in the 1330s and spread from east to west across Eurasia; it killed between a third and a half of the population in many cities and towns. The Black Death spread rapidly because of the expansion of exchange networks into regions with no immunities. But it left behind survivor populations with many shared immunities, and these would later prove to be of tremendous significance.

THE EARLY MODERN CYCLE

- With the huge population losses caused by the Black Death in many parts of Afro-Eurasia, cities shrank, farmlands were abandoned, and economies contracted. However, as had happened so many times in the past, growth soon resumed to kick-start a new Malthusian cycle that would last well into the 18th century.

- It was during this early modern cycle that humans became, for the first time, a truly global species. And it was the European states that prompted the transformation, by financially and militarily supporting expeditions of exploration and conquest to other regions of the world.

- Geography helps explains why these states' expansionist activities, which seemed relatively trivial at first, ended up having such momentous consequences, while the efforts of large empires fell short.

- Traditional empires, such as the Ming dynasty in China, were so large that they generated huge revenues simply by taxing the land, so they could afford to be unsupportive of commerce and merchants. But because European city-states were relatively small and very competitive, their rulers were more willing to support commercial activities that might generate a profit.

- They were only prepared to finance small-scale voyages into the Atlantic at first, but these generated just enough profit to encourage further exploration. Eventually, European mariners were able to sail across the Atlantic and also around the Cape of Good Hope into the Indian Ocean. They thus created, without really meaning to do so, the first genuinely global networks of exchange in human history.

- European merchants exploited these networks through the practice of arbitrage: buying goods cheaply in one place and selling them at a higher place somewhere else. Because of the geographical location of Europe and the Atlantic region, they were firmly located at the center of this newly interconnected world as trade expanded and networks intensified.

- During the 16th and 17th centuries, using brutal tactics, the Spanish and Portuguese created huge empires in the Americas, destroying the Aztec and Inca empires. In Brazil, they built new colonies where there had been no large states.

- The Europeans had a military edge over indigenous peoples through their use of horses and gunpowder technology. They also had a political edge because they felt free to conquer without moral constraint. But mostly they succeeded because of the deadly weapon they brought unintentionally in the form of diseases, against which peoples in the Americas had no immunity.

■ This was one of the key differences produced by Europe's early participation in Silk Roads trade; those Europeans who hadn't died of the diseases that traveled by that route had immunities that people in the New World lacked.

■ Merchants and entrepreneurs from other European countries, particularly Holland, France, and Britain, also built their own empires in the Caribbean and in North America, thus creating an entirely new zone of exchange, the Atlantic zone.

■ This zone linked the Americas into the global trading system and opened up new possibilities for arbitrage, possibilities driven particularly by Peruvian silver and economic growth in China. Chinese demand for silver and Spanish control of cheap supplies created the world's first global financial network.

■ The silver trade was only part of a larger process of global economic integration. In the Americas, plantations were established to exploit the resources there, beginning with sugar. The Portuguese established sugar plantations and worked them using African slave labor, and before long, the Dutch, British, and French had done something similar in the Caribbean. These plantations helped transform environments throughout the world.

■ Colonizers cleared native vegetation to create farms and moved species into environments they had never occupied before, helping humans gain increasing control over the resources of the planet. The African slave trade supplied the labor needed to do all of this, and eventually the plantation system was expanded to grow tobacco and cotton. As the demand for products and slaves intensified, the system became increasingly brutal.

■ Many other consequences followed the creation of the first global networks of exchange, such as the movement of crops, animals, and pathogens between world zones. These exchanges between the Old World and the New World became known as the Columbian exchange.

■ The effect of this reconnection of continents that had been separated by oceans for millennia was profoundly felt by populations all over the world zones, but with very different consequences. In Afro-Eurasia, the introduction of American crops increased farm yields, and as a consequence, populations and commerce grew.

■ But in the Americas, it was a disaster: Contact with Afro-Eurasian diseases, such as smallpox, measles, influenza, and typhus, led to catastrophic epidemics that depopulated large areas of the Americas— and eventually also Australasia and the Pacific region—which made it easier for European colonizers to import their own crops, people, state structures, and farming methods. These may have been the cruelest epidemics in human history.

■ The new global linkage also impacted the intellectual world of Europe, as new information from all around the globe flowed into European cities.

■ The discovery of new worlds, with new peoples, cultures, and religions never known before, led to growing skepticism about traditional forms of knowledge and attempts to assemble information more firmly based on empirical evidence and reason.

■ Both the skepticism generated by new knowledge and the conviction that knowledge should be sought in empiricism drove Europe toward the scientific revolution that exploded in the 17th century.

■ At the same time, as European societies grew wealthier from commerce and plunder, wars between them also intensified. These conflicts led to the development of new military technologies based on gunpowder, which had been invented by the Chinese centuries earlier. The power of these states grew as a result, even though they were still utterly dwarfed by enormous traditional agrarian civilizations, such as the Qing dynasty in China.

GLOBAL NETWORKS

- We used to think that the creation of the global networks of the 16th century was only made possible because of clever European innovations in navigation, shipbuilding, and military technology, but there were actually very few fundamental innovations in this period.

- Adaptation to local conditions was more important than revolutionary innovations in this period. European governments adapted bureaucratic practices that had been ongoing in the world's successful agrarian civilizations for millennia. Even business practices such as establishing new partnerships that led to the creation of the Dutch and British East India Companies were adaptations of much older Muslim mechanisms of doing business.

- But what was really new was the massive size and range of the activities of these new business partnerships, as well as their significant "private" military power. The British and Dutch East Indian Companies essentially established the template for all modern multinational companies. By 1700, the Dutch East India Company was the richest private company the world had ever seen, with more than 50,000 employees and a substantial private army and navy.

- In spite of these remarkable developments, many aspects of life in Europe and around the world remained unchanged as late as 1750. The speed of transportation and communication remained as slow as it had been for thousands of years. Most humans on the planet were still peasants, and much of the world was still living in rural settings.

- But all of this was about to change rapidly. Markets were beginning to deeply transform society and change how governments worked, and even how most people earned a living. These changes would become most apparent first in Europe, where the effects of the intensification of commercial, economic, and political activities around the world were most obvious.

- By 1800, everything was about commerce; it was all that merchants, bankers, and governments cared about. The foundations were laid for the imminent takeover of the entire world by capitalism.

- All the political, social, cultural, and economic conditions were thus in place at the end of the early modern cycle for the next revolution in human history to occur, which would be ignited by the burning of coal. The world was primed for the astonishing burst of genuine innovation known as the Industrial Revolution. And that revolution would usher in the age of modernity.

SUGGESTED READING

Goldstone, *Why Europe?*

Marks, *The Origins of the Modern World.*

Ringrose, *Expansion and Global Interaction.*

QUESTIONS TO CONSIDER

1. In what ways were the medium-sized commercial states of premodern Europe preadapted for capitalism, compared to the great agrarian civilizations?

2. How would world history have been different if Chinese Ming dynasty fleets had discovered the Americas a century before Columbus?

THE INDUSTRIAL REVOLUTION AND MODERNITY

T he Industrial Revolution that took off in Britain transformed the world, unlocking vast new sources of fossil energy that powered a dramatic increase in innovation. Mass production by machines in factories that were burning fossils swept away millennia of cottage industry and fundamentally changed political and social structures as a consequence. Industrialization allowed humans to cross the next threshold of complexity—a threshold that big historians call modernity—reshaping their societies for the first time since the introduction of agriculture 10,000 years earlier.

THE INDUSTRIAL REVOLUTION IN BRITAIN

- The question of why the Industrial Revolution began in Britain and not somewhere else has occupied historians for centuries, but the key factors seem to be the ready availability of money, cheap labor, raw materials, energy sources, and a precapitalist social structure. Other parts of the world had some of these characteristics, but not all of them, and elsewhere there were few incentives to encourage entrepreneurs.

- By the mid-18th century, Britain was also part of the new hub of global trade, which brought in raw materials such as cotton, sugar, and timber, produced with cheap slave labor, helping entrepreneurs amass huge amounts of capital.

- Britain also had good resources of coal, as well as coastlines and rivers that helped with trade and transportation of coal. And, as an island nation, Britain had natural defenses against invasion.

- Once it began, the Industrial Revolution quickly transformed Britain from an agrarian state into an industrial nation and from a tribute-taking society into a commercialized society, the first such transformation in history.

- It is hardly surprising that the first stage of the revolution was felt in the agricultural sector. Britain was still very much a traditional agrarian state in the 17th century, but it was primed for transformation: Aristocrats ran their farms for profit, and peasants worked for wages.

- The Enclosure Acts passed by Parliament had given landowners the right to increase their properties by buying land that had previously been accessible to small-scale farmers. Large profit-making farms soon appeared that encouraged innovation in crop rotation and the use of technology to sow and harvest.

- British agricultural production and efficiency soared, increasing output by 350 percent while reducing the labor force by 50 percent. Unwanted farm laborers moved to cities, creating a growing market for agricultural produce and consumer goods, as well as a cheap source of labor for hire.

- The next stage of the revolution coupled steam engines and textile production. The engines burned coal, solar energy trapped in ancient swamps laid down between 345 and 280 million years ago, during the Carboniferous period.

- Britain had depended on wood for most of its energy before industrialization, but by the 18th century, it had begun to run out of wood, so Britons turned to coal for heating and cooking.

- By the middle of the 19th century, textiles had become the largest business in Britain, employing half a million people out of 12 million

Developments in the coal-fired steam engine and iron production led to a dramatic expansion in railway and maritime transportation.

total. They had also destroyed the comparatively inefficient cotton industry in India with cheap British exports, the first sign of the huge shift in global power that was about to occur.

■ It wasn't long before the iron and steel industry was similarly transformed. Developments in the coal-fired steam engine and iron production led to a dramatic expansion in railway and maritime transportation. By the mid-19th century, almost 13,000 miles of rail tracks had been laid across Britain, and steamships were crossing the Atlantic Ocean.

- This was a veritable explosion of innovation. The British population and standard of living reached unprecedented levels, and London became the largest city on earth.

- This damp little island had led the world into the modern era. But more than that, Britain had established a model for industrialization that could be imitated by other nations in which similar preconditions existed, and in the second wave, Belgium, France, Prussia, and the United States all joined the club.

THE INDUSTRIAL REVOLUTION IN OTHER NATIONS

- The new nation of the United States of America had enormous advantages: huge expanses of land it had taken from native peoples, no traditional elites, no legal class distinctions, and isolation from Europe's wars. The young nation had a clean slate and could adopt technology quickly.

- Industrialization commenced in the textile industry in the 1820s, led by private entrepreneurs who had memorized British trade secrets. The U.S. government helped in the expansion of railroads by providing grants of land, but otherwise it was private companies using loans from European banks that financed the construction.

- The brutal U.S. Civil War between 1861 and 1865, which can accurately be called the world's first industrial war, led to a dramatic intensification of industrialization across the northern states as they arranged themselves to manufacture war material. Already, the political and military balance of global power was being reshaped.

- The next wave of industrialization occurred in Japan and Russia. In Japan in 1868, a partnership between the government and feudal aristocrats financed the modernization of the agricultural sector and the mechanization of silk production. Japan sought crucial natural resources, such as oil, through military expansion into Korea and Manchuria, defeating both Chinese and Russian forces in the process.

Through these policies, Japan industrialized at a faster rate than the West, and much faster than Russia.

■ Between 1861 and 1865, Tsar Alexander II freed about 47 million state-owned serfs and then pushed through a series of successful industrial reforms. By 1900, Russia had joined the ranks of the world's leading nations. A disastrous experience in the First World War led to revolution in 1917 that brought the Communist Party to power, which then had to figure out how to sustain industrialization in Russia.

■ Everywhere that industrialization occurred, the old structures of traditional civilizations were forced to give way to a new vision of the state: the nation. Starting in ancient times, states and systems of governance have evolved, from the first city-states of Sumeria, to the empire of Sargon, to the great agrarian civilizations of Afro-Eurasia and the Americas. The nation-state was the latest stage in this progression.

■ Each stage made more resources available to governments, allowing them to reach further into the private lives of citizens, as seen in the expanding powers of the military, for example.

■ In the nation-state, governments promoted nationalist ideologies to gain the support and loyalty of their citizens, emphasizing a common language and history to create a powerful new geopolitical ideology in place of the monarchic, dynastic, and imperial state models that preceded it.

■ The nation-state took much tighter control of the economy, increasing taxes to pay for services such as public education and infrastructure developments.

■ The modern state was a product of industrialization, and this had implications for the relationship between the state and the economy.

- Scottish philosopher Adam Smith argued that the state should limit excessive regulation and allow the economy to function as free of government intervention as possible. Although Smith did see a role for government in enforcing contracts, granting patents, and developing infrastructure, in *The Wealth of Nations*, he extolled the virtues of free enterprise.

- Adam Smith's ideas remain influential today, particularly in the United States, where the major parties in the U.S. are still divided over the degree that governments should regulate economic activity.

- But there is another, even deeper divide that we can associate with industrialization: the division of the world into two halves. Similar to the division ushered in by the agricultural revolution 10,000 years earlier, in which foraging persisted in some regions while in others sedentary farming and all its consequences became the norm, the Industrial Revolution allowed industrialized nations to become wealthy and powerful enough to impose their will on the nonindustrialized world.

Scottish philosopher Adam Smith argued that the state should limit excessive regulation and allow the economy to function as free of government intervention as possible.

- Britain, the first industrial power, created the largest noncontiguous empire the world had ever seen. Controlling such extensive territory required immense military might, which was possible because of the immense wealth industrialization generated.

- By the end of the 19th century, the gap between the world's richest and poorest countries, the developed and undeveloped worlds, was simply enormous. And this was something entirely new. In preindustrial periods, levels of wealth did not differ that much from region to region, although there were big differences between classes within societies.

- This change was felt most painfully in formerly wealthy states, such as China and India, who had dominated global economic output in 1750, but by 1900 had become two of the poorest countries in the world.

- Late in the 19th century an ugly scramble to acquire colonies in Africa broke out between European powers, eager to gain access to captive markets and raw materials. European nations simply carved up the continent between 1880 and 1900. African nations were powerless to resist European industrialized military power.

- The spread of Europeans in the United States also devastated native populations, forcing them onto reservations on marginal lands, and in Australia and New Zealand, European diseases wiped out hundreds of thousands of aboriginals and Maori.

CLIMATE AND SOCIAL CHANGES

- The European Industrial Revolution caused immense change in the world in just a few centuries. A simple decision to burn coal in the absence of wood can fairly be said to have led to industrialization, innovation, colonization, mass migration, the nation-state, and the justification of imperialism using racist ideology. Significantly, climate change might also have played a role in this process of world transformation, as it had done so often in the previous history of civilization.

- Records indicate that changes in ocean currents off the Pacific Coast of South America associated with El Niño events in the 1870s triggered severe and lengthy droughts in parts of India, Africa, Brazil, and China. Millions died and economies crashed as a result, leaving these regions ripe for colonial conquest.

- However, despite these disasters and devastating rebellions in China, global populations actually rose faster than ever before during the Industrial Revolution, from 610 million in 1700 to 1.6 billion in 1900.

- Despite all the changes associated with the Industrial Revolution, key social structures remained essentially unchanged from the structure that had emerged in the first city-states in Sumeria 5,000 years earlier: elites on top, a laboring class at the bottom, and a middle class that was achieving significant gains.

- Many used direct action to try to improve the conditions of the working class. In 1848, demonstrations, riots, and revolts in France, the Italian states, the Hapsburg empire, Switzerland, Spain, Denmark, and Britain were driven by poverty and the appalling conditions created by industrialization, but the military power of the state was too strong and monarchical authority was restored.

- Concerned governments in industrialized states used migration as a safety valve. Large numbers of impoverished Europeans migrated to the United States, Canada, Argentina, Brazil, Australia, and New Zealand, establishing neo-Europes around the globe.

- Governments also passed new political and social laws that gave their populations an increased democratic voice. Suffrage was extended, trade unions were legalized, and labor laws were passed to improve working conditions.

- Industrialization affected gender relations, too. Working-class girls and women in industrialized nations found jobs in factories or as domestic servants. Within the middle class, even though families acquired more resources, the role of the women returned to what it had been for most of human history: the homemaker. The fact that some middle-class women pushed back against this role laid the foundations for the suffragette movement that would erupt in the early 20th century.

SUGGESTED READING

Allen, *The British Industrial Revolution in Global Perspective*.

Bayly, *Birth of the Modern World*.

Headrick, *The Tools of Empire*.

Pomeranz, *The Great Divergence*.

QUESTIONS TO CONSIDER

1. What local and global advantages did Britain have in the 18th century that explain why the Industrial Revolution began there?

2. How did the Industrial Revolution create a global world of haves and have-nots?

THE TRANSFORMATIVE 20TH AND 21ST CENTURIES

This lecture examines the astonishing 20th and early 21st centuries, an instant on the scale of big history that nonetheless utterly transformed the human world in ways both positive and negative. Our species used more and more resources, and human impacts on the biosphere increased and threatened the very survival of many other species, bringing into question the very meaning of economic growth.

CAPITALISM VERSUS SOCIALISM

- By the year 1900, the world had been split in two. One part had reaped the benefits of a massive increase in resources made available by the Industrial Revolution; the other had experienced decline of its wealth and autonomy.

- Yet the situation was more complicated because within each region extremes of wealth and poverty also existed.

- In Britain, conditions in the major industrial cities in the 19th century had been so appalling that they helped fuel socialist ideologies. The socialists were determined to close the huge gap between capitalists and the working class, perhaps by Marxist revolution.

- Governments experimented with new ways of managing modern states and the tensions within them. Throughout the long era of agrarian civilizations, tribute-taking states had ruled through the use of force rather than the market.

- Modern governments had to take on an entirely new role as economic managers, because now the key to political and military power was sustained economic growth. This required a balancing act in administration between necessary government intervention to maintain infrastructure and law and order, but also nonintervention to help the market drive the capitalist economies.

- The experiments in government that took place during the 20th century were the first real innovations in how to administer a state since the great empires of the era of agrarian civilizations had appeared.

- Some modern governments limited their interference and let the markets drive growth, but others used more coercive techniques to manage society.

- Another challenge facing governments was the need to encourage participation and support of their policies from their citizens, which many sought through democracy, nationalism, and the provision of services.

- None of this stifled imperialist attitudes during the first half of the 20th century; the ancient habit of using military force for economic advantage was still alive and well and was still justified by social Darwinism.

- But brutal force was not just used to control less powerful parts of the world for commercial advantage; it was also used in bitter confrontations between the most powerful societies. In seeking to protect their access to raw resources and markets, modern states did not hesitate to use war to pursue their interests.

- This came to a head in the summer of 1914, when war broke out between the leading European nations. Because of the industrialization of weapons, this First World War was particularly bloody. The war generated such bitterness that the divisions that had caused it persisted after it was concluded. The anger this generated led to the appearance of fascist parties.

- Late in the 1920s, the global economic system came under tremendous strain as economies crashed in 1929 in the United States and Europe. This led to a global depression that lasted well into the 1930s.

- A second brutal world war erupted in Europe in 1939 and became globalized after Nazi Germany's army invaded Russia and the Japanese bombed a U.S. naval base in Hawaii. The climax of the Second World War was the use for the first time of an atomic bomb by the United States on two Japanese cities. At the war's end, the Soviet Union controlled much of eastern Europe, including half of Germany.

- Civil war erupted in China, the most populous country in the world, shortly after the Second World War ended. In 1949, the country's communist party took power.

- By 1950, the world was thoroughly divided into a capitalist bloc led by the United States and its allies, a communist bloc led by the Soviet Union and China, and a large number of nonaligned countries, many of them former colonies, that tried to maneuver between the two blocs.

- Governments in the capitalist and communist blocs had entirely different visions of how to move forward from the Second World War. Both understood that economic growth was the key to success in the modern world, but the Soviets believed their system of centralized control of the economy would best facilitate this, and the United States refocused on the power of markets and international trade to generate growth.

- The United States ended the war with its economic, political, and military power greatly enhanced, having endured none of the domestic

World War II soldiers

destruction or civilian loss of life suffered by most of the other combatants.

- By 1950, its economy accounted for more than one-quarter of global gross domestic product. The U.S. government believed that reigniting international trade and rebuilding the economies of other countries, including its former enemies, was the best way of sustaining growth for itself and the world as a whole.

- Before the war had even ended, a World Bank and an International Monetary Fund had been created to help establish a more stable capitalist financial order. A new world organization, the United Nations, was created in 1945.

- By the late 1950s, the economies of western Europe and Japan were booming, and the production of consumer goods created the sort of mass market that had already emerged in the United States.

- World trade took off more vigorously than ever before, and other East Asian nations followed the Japanese model. By 1989, the total share of global production coming from East Asia had risen to 25 percent.

- New economies were also established in the Muslim world, Africa, and South America, which held the promise of rapid economic growth, although in some, growth was sabotaged by the flow of profits into the hands of corrupt rulers or to pay massive international debts.

- As these commercial links expanded, it became increasingly difficult for European nations to justify colonialism, particularly as all the major imperialist powers had been weakened by war. Therefore, in the decades following the war, all remaining colonial powers gave up their empires and conceded independence to their former colonies—sometimes peacefully and other times after long and bloody wars.

- But because the colonial powers had done little to develop the economies, leadership, or education infrastructure of their colonies, the newly independent nations faced severe challenges and found themselves torn between following the capitalist or the socialist path.

- The Soviet Union was only too happy to lend economic, technical, and military support to allies in the former colonial world, and the results served to demonstrate that communism did indeed provide a viable alternative path to modernity.

- The U.S.S.R. rapidly caught up with the West in the decade following the Second World War. It boasted a superb modern educational system, a strong industrial sector, and nuclear weapons.

- Industrial growth was also rapid in China and parts of eastern Europe, and for a while it seemed possible that the communist system would raise the living standards of its citizens more rapidly and overtake the capitalist system.

- But during the 1970s, the communist system began to struggle, as it became obvious that its coercive methods of rule were not as capable of generating genuine innovation as free market economies. Eventually, the Soviet economy and the state itself came crashing down, and the communist experiment fizzled out in Europe.

- Regardless of their political ideologies and superstructures, governments around the world at the end of the 20th century demonstrated by their choices that capitalism provided the only viable means of maintaining prosperous societies over the long term.

GROWTH AND INNOVATION

- The sustained levels of growth achieved during the 20th century were staggering. In addition to the fact that there were many more humans on the planet by the end of the 20th century, people were also living much longer.

- The increase in human populations was supported by the generation of enormous new resources. Increased human numbers and life spans was also greatly facilitated by medical innovations in the 20th century, particularly the discovery of vaccines and antibiotics.

- Food production outpaced population growth in the 20th century. Increasing agricultural productivity was achieved by the application of industrial and scientific technologies to farming.

- Even as we live longer, we are also consuming more resources than at any other time in history. In the 20th century, humans consumed about double the resources that a person used two generations earlier.

- This was a further indication of the power of collective learning and innovation, which now spawned entirely new products, from plastics to the Internet. And because the competitive capitalist system forced greater efficiencies, these innovations became cheaper and more widely available.

- The revolution in the rapid movement of information has given an incredible boost to human collective learning. In 1837, Samuel Morse created the telegraph, and less than 40 years later, Alexander Graham Bell patented the first telephone. In 1899, Guglielmo Marconi used electric waves to send messages through the air, sending a radio message across the English Channel and, two years later, across the Atlantic.

- After the Second World War, humans had even figured out how to move pictures around the world through television, but it was the computer revolution of the late 20th century that has taken collective learning to an entirely new level again.

- In spite of their many horrors, the wars of the 20th century also produced, for good or ill, some remarkable innovations, including penicillin, radar, synthetic rubber, and the jet engine. Perhaps the most striking innovation was the increase in the power of our explosive devices, particularly after scientists unlocked the awesome power buried in atoms.

- These terrifying military innovations, coupled with an increasing willingness to bomb civilian populations in what had become total war, explain why more than 50 million people were probably killed in the Second World War alone.

- As tensions between the United States and the Soviet Union increased after the war, each began to stockpile nuclear weapons in a dangerous standoff that came to be known as the Cold War. Many began to question whether human creativity and achievement necessarily led to progress for civilization.

- The 20th century's innovations in food production, transport, communication, and warfare were coupled with a huge increase in human control of energy. It evolved from coal-fired steam power to the oil-driven internal combustion engine, which drove many of the century's gains.

It was the computer revolution of the late 20th century that has taken collective learning to an entirely new level.

- But late in the 20th century, it became apparent that it might be dangerous and shortsighted to rely exclusively on fossil fuels, so efforts were made to find alternatives, including the use of the energy within atoms for peaceful purposes.

- Other ways of generating energy, such as solar power and wind power, have also been developed, but none has been able to compete with our ongoing massive dependence on fossil fuels.

CONSUMER CAPITALISM
- Not all of the changes in human lifeways that originally looked like progress in the 20th century were beneficial. For example, subsistence farming largely disappeared as industrial agriculture took over the business of providing food, and unwanted peasant farmers were forced into squalid conditions in cities. However, eventually most cities became wealthier, and material standards of living rose as infrastructure improved and job opportunities multiplied.

- This increase in general wealth was driven by a new form of capitalism: consumer capitalism, whereby goods that had once seemed luxuries were now able to be produced cheaply enough for ordinary workers to purchase them. And as working-class living standards improved, the market for consumer goods expanded.

- Consumer capitalism also required an ethical revolution. Instead of encouraging restraint and thrift, the virtues of premodern societies, it celebrated consumption and extravagance, not just by elites, but within the population as a whole.

- Consumer capitalism also transformed the basic social unit of all human societies, the family. During the agrarian era, it made sense for parents to produce as many children as possible because children were an economically valuable resource who could be put to work. In the industrial age, having too many mouths to feed was an economic liability.

- Freed from the task of producing as many children for as long as possible, women found opportunities to play new roles in society. Women also finally gained voting rights in democracies after a long struggle.

SUGGESTED READING

Crosby, *Children of the Sun.*

Lovelock, *The Vanishing Face of Gaia.*

Ruddiman, *Plows, Plagues, and Petroleum.*

Zalasiewicz, et al, "Are We Now Living in the Anthropocene?"

QUESTIONS TO CONSIDER

1. How does a big history of the 20th century differ from other histories of the 20th century?

2. How did human impacts on the environment change intensity in the 20th century?

CIVILIZATION, THE BIOSPHERE, AND TOMORROW

T he civilizations that humanity has built, each atop the innovations and discoveries of the past, have enabled us to achieve remarkable things. But those achievements have come at a price. Our big history exploration of the past and the themes and patterns within it has left us uniquely positioned to seriously consider the future in a way that was previously unavailable to our species. In this lecture, you will apply what you know about our past to understand what may be our future.

NEGATIVE TRENDS

- Ever since humans made the transition to agriculture 10,000 years ago, populations have increased until they have inevitably outstripped the ability of innovation to feed, clothe, and house so many people, leading to famine, warfare, and decline.

- A pessimistic view of where we are right now in terms of a Malthusian cycle might suggest that we are heading for another widespread crisis, because the supply of fossil fuels that power our civilization seems certain to run out, eventually. Moreover, these same fuels are leading to a dramatic deterioration in the climate of the planet that sustains us.

- The impact of humans on the biosphere since the start of the modern era has been so profound that many geologists believe that the Holocene era has ended. They say we have entered a new era, the Anthropocene, a period in which humans are the most powerful shaping influence on the planet, making impacts that will be felt for perhaps tens of millions of years.

■ Many of these impacts are already apparent and will only intensify in the future: destruction of habitat, species extinction, acidification of oceans, worsening erosion, and increasing levels of carbon dioxide in the atmosphere that are leading to global temperatures not seen for millions of years.

■ Many voices are arguing that humans cannot continue with business as usual much longer and that the structure of an industrialized society based on the burning of fossil fuels is no longer sustainable if our species and millions of other species are going to have a future. Some scientists have concluded that human societies are on the brink of catastrophic decline.

■ One of the most startling Malthusian trends that occurred in the 20th century is the dramatic fourfold increase in human populations. In the 21st century, the rate of growth is actually declining, although we are still doubling the world's population about every 58 years. Yet the slowing of this growth is undoubtedly good news.

■ In many countries, including India, Japan, Russia, and Germany, populations are already shrinking because of falling birth rates; in others countries, such as Lesotho and Swaziland, populations are declining because of rising death rates.

■ By 2100, as a result of these trends, the location of the world's population will have shifted dramatically, with Europe's share declining to perhaps 6 percent and Africa's increasing to 25 percent. These changing percentages reminds us that it is not just the total number of humans on the planet that determines our environmental impact, but also the lifeways and levels of consumption that various populations enjoy.

- Of critical importance in this context is our consumption of fossil fuels, particularly oil. The most likely scenario is that oil will not completely run out; it will, however, require more complex and costly methods of extraction in the future, making it much more expensive than today.

- As with all commodities in a capitalist economy, the price of oil is determined by a combination of supply and demand, as well as by the policies of oil-producing countries and cartels. In the early 21st century, other countries, including the United States, using new extraction techniques, have been able to increase the supply of oil, driving the price of oil down to record lows.

- How much longer this can continue is a matter of speculation, but given that oil, and indeed all fossil fuels, are finite resources, we know that supplies will inevitably become much more limited in the future.

- The time is coming when all remaining fossil fuels will be too difficult to extract, and the longer humans wait to make the inevitable transition from fossil fuel to other forms of energy, the more chaotic and violent that transition will inevitably be.

- The other major problem with our dependence on fossil fuels is the effect it is having on the chemical constitution of earth's atmosphere and the impact this in turn has on climates around the globe.

- Scientists have been warning since the 1970s that human emissions of carbon dioxide into the atmosphere are creating a greenhouse effect, although many people—particularly many politicians—seem reluctant to accept this reality.

- The increase in the concentration of carbon dioxide and other gasses in the atmosphere has in fact created the greenhouse effect on the planet that scientists had predicted, trapping solar heat and leading to rapidly rising global temperatures.

- The effects of rising temperatures, as well as melting land ice, will be felt all over the planet. Erratic weather and devastating storms will become more common; crop yields will be reduced; tropical diseases will spread more quickly; the oceans will become increasingly acidic; ecosystems all over the planet will be dramatically changed; and there will be significant rises in global sea levels, leading to increased flooding and the almost inevitable abandonment of many of the planet's coastal cities.

- Global warming is surely the most serious environmental threat that human civilization has faced since the end of the last ice age, but it is just the top of a long list of problems. Notably, perhaps 50 percent of all species on earth face the threat of extinction in the 21st century.

- Our species is making demands on our planet's biosphere that are way beyond the capacity of the planet to sustain them. Essentially, we are devouring our own life support system by using the assets provided by ecosystems to pay for our unsustainable lifeways, and we are stealing these assets from future generations.

- The negative impacts unleashed in the modern era suggest that our species is currently facing its greatest challenge since we first appeared on the planet about 200,000 years ago. But humans have repeatedly proven themselves remarkably adaptable when facing challenges, using our unique ability of collective learning to solve problems of staggering proportions.

POSITIVE TRENDS

- The fact that human population growth is slowing is one of the more hopeful trends, even though it is happening inadvertently rather than as a result of consensus and deliberate action.

- Projections suggest that our species will peak at somewhere between 10 and 12 billion. But stabilizing the climate of our planet will be a much tougher task. Some sort of climate change is now unavoidable; the only

Global warming is surely the most serious environmental threat that human civilization has faced.

question is how much change our children and grandchildren will have to deal with in their lifetimes.

- Substitutes for fossil fuels, the chief culprits in greenhouse gas emissions, are starting to emerge—biofuels, wind turbines, solar energy, and thermal energy—but so far none of these can provide anything near our current energy requirements.

- The introduction by governments of more subsidies for these emerging alternative energies, while at the same time increasing taxes on gasoline and automobiles, might create strong incentives to help speed up the transition, but many do not have the political will to even consider this right now.

- We certainly have the technical knowledge to generate enormous amounts of energy using nuclear reactors, but we have yet to figure out how to store radioactive waste in the long term. And the security of nuclear plants and the materials they contain, particularly in an age of terrorism, remains a critical problem.

- A heartening sign is the increasing cooperation we have seen over recent decades between nations on dealing with environmental problems—an example of the transformative power of collective learning. Alternative sources of energy, or new methods of mitigating the effects of burning fossil fuels, might help humans limit the consequences of global warming.

- There is also much more careful monitoring of the impact of our species on the planet in modern times, as a variety of organizations track the dimensions of our environmental footprints on forests, freshwater, and marine ecosystems and propose strategies on how to reduce these impacts.

- Critical for the survival of species, including humans, is maintaining supplies of freshwater and healthy soils. So, we see a proliferation of water recycling systems and the creation of genetically modified crops that need less water, for example.

- Recent attempts to protect the oceans have led to the establishment of huge marine reserves and the reduction of toxic chemical runoff into the oceans. To slow the rate of species extinctions, many nations have created national parks, wilderness areas, and protected preserves.

- Great strides are also being made in many countries to reduce energy consumption and recycle waste materials. Many of our household appliances are now much more efficient than just a few years ago.

- Other positive trends include the global proliferation of more energy-efficient green buildings and the increase in the sustainability of many public sector industries, such as transport.

- Recycling is another positive development because this allows us to reduce the use of virgin raw materials and replace the "throwaway economy" that many people grew up in.

- The modern world is incredibly urbanized compared to all the earlier periods considered in this course. Today, roughly 50 percent of the world's population live in cities. Tokyo remains the largest city on the planet, with a population of almost 38 million. In total, 20 cities around the world have populations of more than 10 million people.

- These megacities have to deal with enormous problems of maintaining clean air, water and sewerage infrastructure, crime, traffic, and so on. However, even in these huge cities, we see great strides being made, such as huge improvements to public transport systems to cut back on private automobile use. Urban gardens are proliferating in cities, producing more and more food and decreasing our carbon footprint at the same time.

- These are all positive examples of the way our species is responding to the challenge of reducing consumption to preserve our environment and hopefully mitigating the impacts of global warming for current and future generations.

- The Industrial Revolution, sparked by the burning of coal, transformed our world in many ways, and these transformations dramatically intensified in the 20th century. In the 21st century, humans all over the planet have realized the dangers the Industrial Revolution unleashed and are doing whatever they can to preserve our ecosystems for other species, ourselves, and future generations.

Future Governance

- Humanity has experimented with numerous types of governance and administration throughout the history of civilization. In his 2006 book *The Great Turning: From Empire to Earth Community*, David Korten considers what future governments dedicated to preserving the environment through more sustainable practices might look like. As he sees it, our choice of governance will be a critical factor in determining whether or not we survive.

- David Korten contrasts empires with what he calls an earth community: a more egalitarian and democratic system of human relationships based on the idea of cooperation and partnership.

- Korten sees two possibilities for future governance: There will either be a great turning, in which humans demand stronger participatory democratic institutions and greater cooperation, or there will be a great unraveling, in which our environment collapses and human communities are plunged back into a period of violent conflict over dwindling resources.

- Such conflict, he argues, would lead to massive loss of human life, the breakdown of democracy and of the nation-state, political fragmentation, and the appearance of ruthless regional warlords.

- The choice is stark: Are we heading for a new age of violence and brutal dictatorship or one of harmony, deeper democracy at all levels, and a transformation in our attitudes toward each other and the planet?

- Surely there is reason to hope here, too, as we look back on decades of strong international cooperation through organizations such as the United Nations, which, despite its flaws, demonstrates what can be achieved through cooperative, genuinely global collective learning.

- It is not just global governments that are aware of the challenges facing us; there are also many nongovernmental organizations that are investing heavily in effective solutions. In addition, many wealthy philanthropists are increasingly directing their resources to climate, health, and social causes.

■ All of these developments, not to mention the way in which the Internet has utterly transformed and intensified our capacity for collective learning, are surely hopeful signs that through global cooperation we may avert a great unravelling. Yet nothing about the future is certain.

SUGGESTED READING

Brown, *Plan B 4.0*.

Diamond, *Collapse*.

Korten, *The Great Turning*.

Roston, *The Carbon Age*.

QUESTIONS TO CONSIDER

1. As we imagine the world 100 years from now, how optimistic should we feel about the ability of our species to make necessary changes in a managed way, before a crisis is upon us?

2. Is capitalism ecologically blind, or is it the best hope for saving the environment?

CIVILIZATIONS OF THE DISTANT FUTURE

I n this lecture, you will consider the distant future, starting with the next thousand years. Challenging as it may be to envision, the distant future is our hope: It's what we are fighting to preserve as we contend with the difficulties of today. Then, you will consider the incredibly far distant future, millions and billions of years from now. If any human societies should remain billions of years from now, there is actually a lot we can say about what our planet, our galaxy, and even the universe will be like in that time.

THOUSANDS OF YEARS IN THE FUTURE

- Thinking about what the world will be like 500 years—or 1,000 years, or 2,000 years—from now requires us to enter the imaginative realm of science fiction. We should not be surprised that science fiction writers have long been inspired by large-scale historical studies of the past to produce some of the best work in the genre.

- One historical study that has been among the most influential on science fiction authors is the multivolume *A Study of History* written by English historian Arnold Toynbee between 1934 and 1961.

- After comprehensively analyzing 22 different civilizations, Toynbee believed that he had detected a common life cycle that all civilizations had passed through. There was a period of initial growth; followed by a period of political crisis, which led to the establishment and maintenance of a large, coercive imperial state structure; and finally a period of disintegration.

■ This apparently inevitable disintegration was usually the result not of external problems, but of internal ones, such as, most commonly, a general loss of creativity through indolence and decadence.

■ Quite a few historians disagreed with many of Toynbee's conclusions, particularly his utopian claim that, unlike all previous civilizations, modern civilization would be saved by the emergence of "universal churches." Nevertheless, science fiction authors found his writing to be a particularly fruitful source of inspiration.

■ But it is not just science fiction authors who have thought hard about the future, and not all of these other writers have depicted it positively. Another group of writers has produced novels or works of nonfiction that might be described as "histories of the future," which seem to range from bleak dystopias to hopeful utopias.

■ In the first half of the 20th century, two great English writers, George Orwell and Aldous Huxley, wrote classic dystopias describing their own visions of a bleak and frightening future. Orwell's *1984* describes a totalitarian future in which global dictators use propaganda, torture, and violence to rule their people, and continuous war between empires is fought to maintain the power of a small privileged elite. In Huxley's *Brave New World*, humans are hatched like chickens and kept in a state of drug-induced happiness.

■ Still another dystopian future is the one articulated by Englishman James Lovelock, who is not a fiction writer but a scientist. He has argued that every species on earth should be considered part of a huge superorganism called Gaia. By working together, these species are able to maintain a habitable environment for all living organisms, but they can only do so if the surface of the earth remains within a critical range of temperatures and other parameters, thus ensuring the availability of liquid water.

- A complex feedback system between the atmosphere and the biosphere has managed to do this for billions of years, keeping the earth's surface and atmosphere at levels that are just right for all organisms to thrive—until now, that is.

- The human species is in the process of upsetting this ancient feedback system by hogging too many resources. According to Lovelock, one of two things will happen, both utterly dystopian: Like cancer, humans will indeed kill the Gaia organism of which they are a part, destroying themselves in the process; or Gaia will be forced to save itself by destroying the cancerous organism, either by global pandemics, famines, or simply waiting for humans to annihilate themselves by nuclear war.

- Not all histories of the future are this bleak, however. In 1985, British science writers Brian Stableford and John Langford published *The Third Millennium: A History of the World, AD 2000–3000*, which offers a much cheerier vision of a world ruled by a powerful United Nations and powered by cheap nuclear fusion energy.

- Other futurist accounts focus on innovations in technology that will lead to humans living longer, healthier lives; accessing free energy and resources; and using genetic engineering and nanotechnologies to eliminate most types of pain and other physical suffering. We might, according to such accounts, also engineer special bacteria to help us repair all the environmental damage we have caused.

- Other futurist thinkers imagine a slowdown in growth and consumption as humans realize that endless growth and consumerism are not the keys to happiness. There are far fewer humans living in these imagined futures, and they appear to have come to the revolutionary conclusion that they are content just to maintain a good life—they do not need to endlessly seek a better life.

MIGRATING INTO SPACE

- The history of humanity has largely been defined by extensive migrations. So, if the technology becomes available in the future, it is certainly conceivable that we will undertake voyages to remote locations.

- In fact, some of the technology we would need for such migrations is already available. Humanity has developed the means to mine minerals on asteroids, to build space stations on the moon or Mars, and to suspend expansive living and working quarters in space like much larger versions of the International Space Station.

- One model of such a floating station, called hoop world, involves enormous elongated cylinders hanging in space, slowly revolving to create a type of gravity and so that each of the three "continents" inside gets its share of night and day.

- Energy would be supplied by solar panels attached to the outer hull, converting sunlight into huge amounts of energy to meet all the needs of the inhabitants. By using solar energy, and creating vast indoor farms, such space communities have the potential to become the completely self-sufficient human communities of the future.

- The prototype for such massive hoop world communities will probably be smaller versions constructed as resorts to meet the needs of future space tourists. Even as companies such as SpaceX and Boeing are actively planning and building manned spacecraft, others, such as Bigelow Aerospace, are planning to build "space hotels" in orbit around the planet.

- Scientists involved in these projects think it possible that within just a few decades, such small space hotels will be in place, and tourists will be traveling to them and enjoying the effects of low gravity on a regular basis.

- Some entrepreneurs are even considering building retirement communities in space, where gravity is so low that people with infirmities would not need to use walkers or wheelchairs. And once that first step is taken—of people living permanently in space—then it is not such a big second step to imagining humans essentially colonizing space by building large, permanent space settlements.

- Far more complicated and ambitious are plans for terraforming other planets, such as Mars, essentially using artificial global warming to make them habitable for humans and their domesticated species.

- The terraforming of Mars seems like a modest proposal compared to our prospects of migrating beyond our solar system and into deep space, because the distances out there are unimaginably vast, and the technology does not yet exist to cross them, despite the best imagination of science fiction writers.

- Even if this technology were conceivable, migrations to even the closest stars in our galaxy would probably take humans hundreds or thousands of generations of travel through space.

- The nearest star to the earth (other than the sun) is Alpha Centauri, which is 4.3 light-years away; even at the average speed of a space shuttle (which is 17,600 miles per hour), it would take about 165,000 years to reach Alpha Centauri.

The terraforming of Mars would essentially involve using artificial global warming to make it habitable for humans and their domesticated species.

- Migrating colonists would need to live on their spacecraft for almost as long as humans have lived on earth. There would be no possibilities of resupply or repairs, and no guarantee that habitable planets would be found at the end of the journey. But much faster forms of travel might indeed be invented by future human engineers, so that perhaps in the distant future there will be colonies of humans living on distant planets.

- These human colonists will end up completely isolated from each other. The people of each colony would in all likelihood be able to breed only with one another, with no possibility of coming back to breed with the core human population.

- And this means that, like Darwin's finches on the Galapagos Islands, our species would slowly divide into numerous subspecies, just as we know there were various species of hominines coexisting on earth not so long ago. A person touring the various colonies at some distant time in the future would probably find startling differences in the characteristics of their respective inhabitants.

- Whether we ever send people to colonize distant planets in the future or just stay on earth, our species will certainly continue to evolve physically as we have done in our past. The direction such evolution takes, however, will be dependent on the state of our environment in the future.

MILLIONS OF YEARS IN THE FUTURE

- Either through Darwinian evolution or genetic manipulation, we will eventually reach a point where our species will be so different from what we are today that some imaginary time traveler from today's world would no longer be able to recognize our descendants as human. If anything like humanity still inhabits earth millions of years from today, we have a reasonably good idea what life on our planet will be like.

- Like evolution, plate tectonics never stops, and today we can measure with great accuracy the direction and speed of movement of all the major and micro tectonic plates, so we can make some pretty reasonable predictions about what earth will look like at various periods in the future.

- We know that the Atlantic Ocean will be much wider and the Pacific Ocean will be much narrower. Africa will have split along the great African Rift Valley, and Australia will end up squeezed between the coast of California on one side and China on the other in about 200 million years.

- We know that our sun will start to run out of fuel in about 5 billion years, and then it will start collapsing until it reaches temperatures hot enough to allow it to fuse helium, at which point it will expand massively to become a red giant. The sun will be so large that our planet will be ingested into it. Then, the sun will collapse one final time to form a white dwarf star, which will slowly cool over billions of years to become a dead black dwarf star floating aimlessly in space.

- Meanwhile, as our sun reaches its endgame, our Milky Way Galaxy will be colliding with our nearby neighbor, the Andromeda Galaxy. This will probably be a slow merge rather than a violent collision. Most stars in the two galaxies will not come close enough to crash into each other, but their gravitational pull will certainly mess up the neat orbits of many planetary systems and probably also transform the shape of both galaxies.

- No humans on earth will watch this extraordinary galactic event occur. But will the residents of millions of inhabited planets observe it? Might some of them even be distant descendants of humans who migrated from our tiny, now-nonexistent planet billions of years before?

- Our universe won't last forever, as far as we can determine. So, even if human or human-descended civilization somehow outlives our galaxy, it will have to come to an end someday.

- But that sad fact should remind us all of our incredible good fortune to be alive today in the springtime of the universe, when it is still bristling with energy and extraordinary potential, still full of stars and planets—and when civilization has advanced to such a point that we can probe the mysteries of the heavens all around us and perhaps take steps to extend our civilization's life into the future.

SUGGESTED READING

Miller, *A Canticle for Leibowitz.*

Spier, *Big History and the Future of Humanity.*

Stableford and Langford, *The Third Millennium.*

Wagar, *A Short History of the Future.*

QUESTIONS TO CONSIDER

1. Is it possible to draw together a single big history of the world? Is it desirable to do so?

2. What, if anything, can we say about the future on the scale of the next thousand years?

3. What is the ultimate future of humanity, planet earth and all life on it, our solar system, and the universe?

BIBLIOGRAPHY

Ali, Ahmed, trans. *Al Qur'an: A Contemporary Translation.* Princeton, NJ: Princeton University Press, 1984. A sensitive translation of the holy book of Islam.

Allen, Robert C. *The British Industrial Revolution in Global Perspective.* Cambridge and New York: Cambridge University Press, 2009. Superb study of the Industrial Revolution in Britain from a global perspective.

Anderson, B., and J. Zinsser. *A History of Their Own: Women in Europe from Prehistory to the Present.* New York: Harper and Row, 1988. A classic in women and gender history.

Andrea, A., and J. Overfield. *The Human Record: Sources of Global History—Vol. 1: To 1700.* 4th ed. Boston, MA: Wadsworth Publishing, 2008. Excellent collection of primary sources from the era of agrarian civilizations.

Anthony, David W. *The Horse, the Wheel, and Language: How Bronze-Age Riders from the Eurasian Steppes Shaped the Modern World.* Princeton, NJ: Princeton University Press, 2007. Fascinating study of the emergence of Indo-European speakers and their domestication of the horse.

Barber, Elizabeth Wayland. *Women's Work: The First 20,000 Years—Women, Cloth and Society in Early Times.* New York: W. W. Norton, 1994. A brilliant study of the relationship between weaving, textiles, and gender.

Bartlett, Robert. *The Making of Europe: Conquest, Colonization and Cultural Change, 950–1350.* Princeton, NJ: Princeton University Press, 1993. Important survey of this crucial 400-year period in European and global history.

Bayly, C. A. *Birth of the Modern World, 1780–1914: Global Connections and Comparisons*. Malden, MA: Blackwell, 2004. Masterful overview of the early modern period in global history up to the outbreak of the First World War.

Bellwood, P. *First Farmers: The Origins of Agricultural Societies*. Oxford: Blackwell, 2005. A comprehensive and comparative review of early agriculture and its effects.

Benjamin, Craig. "A Nation of Nomads? The Lifeway of the Yuezhi in the Gansu and Bactria." In *Toronto Studies in Central and Inner Asia*, vol. 7, edited by M. Gervers and G. Long, 93–122. Toronto: University of Toronto Press, 2005. A discussion of the complex relationship between early Chinese dynasties and the various nomadic confederations that dwelt along the borders.

———. "Hungry for Han Goods? Zhang Qian and the Origins of the Silk Roads." In *Toronto Studies in Central and Inner Asia*, vol. 8, edited by M. Gervers and G. Long, 3–30. Toronto: University of Toronto Press, 2007. This scholarly but readable paper explores the impact of the expedition of Han dynasty diplomat Zhang Qian.

———. "The Kushans." In *Berkshire Encyclopedia of World History*, vol. 3, edited by W. McNeill, J. Bentley, D. Christian, D. Levinson, H. Roupp, and J. Zinsser, 1090–1093. Great Barrington, MA: Berkshire Press, 2004. 2nd ed. 2010. Brief and readable account of the importance of the Kushans to world history.

———. "The Kushans in World History." *World History Bulletin* 25, no. 1 (Spring 2009, edited by H. M. Tarver): 30–32. A neat and readable overview of the importance of the Kushan empire to eastern civilization and world history.

———. "The Little Big History of Jericho." Chap. 17 in *Big History Anthology*, edited by B. Rodrigue, A. Koratyev, and L. Grinin. New Delhi: Primus Books, 2015. This essay uses the city of Jericho—which has been continually occupied for 14,000 years due to a range of favorable environmental factors—as a case study of the impact of the environment on human history.

Benjamin, C., ed. *The Cambridge World History: Volume 4—A World with States, Empires, and Networks, 1200 B.C.E.–900 C.E.* Cambridge: Cambridge University Press, 2015. A superb collection of 25 essays by leading scholars in their fields that traces the history of human societies over 2,000 years from a global, interregional, and regional perspective.

Benjamin, C., and S. Liu, eds. *Walls and Frontiers in Inner Asian History.* Silk Roads Studies Series. Vol. 6. Turnhout, Belgium: Brepols Publishers, 2002. A fascinating collection of papers and articles presented at the Australasian Society for Inner Asian Studies Conference in 2000.

Bentley, Jerry H. *Old World Encounters: Cross-Cultural Contacts and Exchanges in Pre-Modern Times.* New York: Oxford University Press, 1993. Important study of the spread of cultural and religious traditions before 1500 C.E.

Bentley, J., H. Zeigler, and H. Streets, with contributions by C. Benjamin. *Traditions and Encounters: A Global Perspective on the Past.* 6th ed. New York: McGraw-Hill, 2015. One of the finest world history textbooks currently available.

Berkey, Jonathan P. *The Formation of Islam: Religion and Society in the Near East, 600–1800.* Cambridge: Cambridge University Press, 2003. Views the development of Islamic society in the context of relationships between Muslims, Jews, and Christians.

Blundell, Sue. *Women in Ancient Greece.* Cambridge, MA: Harvard University Press, 1995. Important early study of women and their roles in ancient Greek society.

Boyce, Mary, ed. *Textual Sources for the Study of Zoroastrianism.* Totowa, NJ: Barnes & Noble Books, 1984. Important collection of annotated sources in English translation.

Bradley, Keith R. *Discovering the Roman Family: Studies in Roman Social History.* New York: Oxford University Press, 1991. An important analysis of Roman family life, with rich illustrations.

————. *Slavery and Society at Rome.* Cambridge: Cambridge University Press, 1994. A fascinating and readable essay on slavery in Roman society, with many individual case studies.

Brantingham, P. J., S. L. Kuhn, and K. W. Kerry. *The Early Upper Paleolithic beyond Western Europe.* Berkeley: University of California Press, 2004. An excellent survey of evidence for the Upper Paleolithic era from other regions of Afro-Eurasia.

Brosius, Maria. *The Persians: An Introduction.* London: Routledge, 2006. Brief and readable account of the three great Persian empires.

Brotherson, Gordon. *Book of the Fourth World: Reading the Native Americas through Their Literature.* Cambridge: Cambridge University Press, 1992. Thoughtful collection of early Native American literature.

Brown, Chip. "The King Herself." *National Geographic* (April 2009): 88–111. Fascinating article on the various female pharaohs of ancient Egypt.

Brown, Cynthia. *Big History: From the Big Bang to the Present.* New York: The New Press, 2007. A superb single-volume account of the big history of the cosmos, planet, life on earth, and humanity.

Brown, Lester R. *Plan B: Rescuing a Planet under Stress and a Civilization in Trouble.* New York: Norton, 2003. One of the first books to lay out the potential for ecological disaster, along with suggested plans to prevent or at least slow its impacts.

————. *Plan B 4.0: Mobilizing to Save Civilization.* New York and London: W. W. Norton, 2009. Contains very clear and practical strategies that the global community should be pursuing if it is serious about avoiding the looming ecological crisis.

Brown, Lester R., et al. *State of the World, 1999: A Worldwatch Institute Report on Progress toward a Sustainable Society.* London: Earthscan, 1999. The first in a series of annual reports on the state of the environment.

Brown, Peter. *The Making of Late Antiquity.* Cambridge, MA: Harvard University Press, 1978. Brilliant analysis of the cultural and religious history of the late Roman Empire that really brings the past to life.

———. *The Rise of Western Christendom: Triumph and Diversity, A.D. 200–1000.* 2nd ed. Oxford: Blackwell, 2003. A landmark analysis of early Christian history by an insightful scholar.

Bryce, Trevor. *The Kingdom of the Hittites.* New ed. Oxford: Oxford University Press, 2005. A scholarly account of the political and military history of the Hittites.

Burkert, Walter. *Babylon, Memphis, Persepolis: Eastern Contexts of Greek Culture.* Cambridge, MA: Harvard University Press, 2004. Explores a variety of Eurasian influences on Greek literature, philosophy, and science.

———. *Greek Religion.* Cambridge, MA: Harvard University Press, 1985. A classic in the field of understanding Greek religion.

Cameron, Averil. *The Mediterranean World in Late Antiquity, A.D. 395–600.* London: Routledge, 1993. A lively and well-informed synthesis of history and culture throughout the Mediterranean basin in late antiquity.

Casson, Lionel. *The Ancient Mariners: Seafarers and Sea Fighters of the Mediterranean in Ancient Times.* 2nd ed. Princeton, NJ: Princeton University Press, 1991. Uses the discoveries of underwater archaeologists to reconstruct the maritime history of the ancient Mediterranean.

Chang, Kwang-chih. *The Archaeology of Ancient China.* 4th ed. New Haven, CT: Yale University Press, 1986. Discussion of early archaeological discoveries of ancient Chinese civilization by a leading Chinese archaeologist.

Christian, David. *A History of Russia, Central Asia, and Mongolia: Vol. 1— Inner Eurasia from Prehistory to the Mongol Empire*. Oxford: Blackwell, 2004. Sweeping overview of the history of Inner Eurasia, with a strong focus on the role of the steppe nomads.

————. *Maps of Time: An Introduction to Big History*. Berkeley: University of California Press, 2004. The classic big history monograph, which considers human history in the context of planetary and cosmic history.

Christian, David, Cynthia Brown, and Craig Benjamin. *Big History: Between Nothing and Everything*. New York: McGraw-Hill, 2015. The first big history textbook written by three of the pioneers in the field.

Colaiaco, James. *Socrates against Athens*. New York: Routledge, 2001. Fascinating account of the relationship between Socrates and the Athenian state.

Cornford, F. M. *Before and after Socrates*. Cambridge: Cambridge University Press, 1965. Superb synthesis of classical Greek philosophy.

Crosby, Alfred W. *Children of the Sun: A History of Humanity's Unappeasable Appetite for Energy*. New York: Norton, 2006. An articulate and provocative analysis of why the 20th century should indeed be regarded as "something new under the sun."

————. *Ecological Imperialism: The Biological Expansion of Europe, 900– 1900*. Cambridge: Cambridge University Press, 1986. Evaluation of the ecological reasons for European expansion.

————. *The Columbian Exchange: Biological and Cultural Consequences of 1492*. Westport, CT: Greenwood Press, 1972. Landmark study of the biological consequences of European colonization of the Americas.

Crutzen, Paul. "The Geology of Mankind." *Nature* 415 (3 January 2002): 23. A clear argument in favor of renaming the current geological era the Anthropocene.

Cunliffe, Barry. *Greeks, Romans, and Barbarians: Spheres of Interaction.* New York: Methuen, 1988. Uses archaeological evidence to consider the impact of the Roman presence in Gaul, Britain, and Germany.

D'Altroy, Terence N. *The Incas.* Malden, MA: Blackwell, 2002. Succinct and comprehensive overview of Incan civilization.

Dandamaev, Muhammad A., and Vladimir G. Lukonin. *The Culture and Social Institutions of Ancient Iran.* Ed. by P. L. Kohl. Cambridge: Cambridge University Press, 1989. Uses the discoveries of Russian archaeologists to shed further light on the Achaemenid empire.

Davidson, Basil. *Lost Cities of Africa.* Rev. ed. Boston: Little, Brown and Co., 1970. Popular account with discussions of the ancient African cities of Kush and Meroe.

Davies, Nigel. *Human Sacrifice in History and Today.* New York: William Morrow, 1981. A readable world history of human sacrifice.

Davis, Mike. *Late Victorian Holocausts: El Niño Famines and the Making of the Third World.* London: Verso, 2001. A highly critical and insightful study of the way European colonial powers used naturally occurring climate events to enrich themselves while at the same time impoverishing the countries they had colonized.

Demand, Nancy. *A History of Ancient Greece in its Mediterranean Context.* New York: Sloan, 2013. Comprehensive overview of the history and culture of ancient Greece from the Neolithic to the Hellenistic era, with a particular focus on the broader Mediterranean environmental and cultural context in which it emerged.

di Cosmo, Nicola. *Ancient China and Its Enemies: The Rise of Nomadic Power in East Asian History.* Cambridge: Cambridge University Press, 2002. Superb study of the relationship between pastoral nomads and early Chinese agrarian societies.

Diamond, Jared. *Collapse: How Societies Choose to Fail or Succeed.* New York: Viking, 2005. Provocative and sobering study of the fate of numerous earlier societies that self-destructed through abusing their environments.

——. *Guns, Germs, and Steel: The Fates of Human Societies.* New York: W. W. Norton, 1997. A world history classic that places the adoption and early spread of agriculture in an environmental context.

Diehl, Richard A. *The Olmecs: America's First Civilization.* London: Thames & Hudson, 2004. A succinct introduction to Olmec society.

Ebrey, Patricia. *The Cambridge Illustrated History of China.* Cambridge: Cambridge University Press, 2000. This book contains a splendid collection of images, but it is the author's erudition and command of her subject that makes this one of the finest resources available on Chinese history and culture.

Ehrenberg, Margaret. *Women in Prehistory.* Norman and London: University of Oklahoma Press, 1989. Brings archaeological discoveries to bear on questions of sex and gender relations in prehistoric times.

Ehret, Christopher. *An African Classical Age: Eastern and Southern Africa in World History, 1000 BC to AD 400.* Charlottesville: University Press of Virginia, 2010. Excellent survey of 1,400 years of sub-Saharan cultural history.

——. *The Civilizations of Africa: A History to 1800.* Charlottesville: University Press of Virginia, 2001. An important work that views Africa in the context of world history.

Embree, Ainslie T., ed. *Sources of Indian Tradition.* 2 vols. 2nd ed. New York: Columbia University Press, 1988. Expansive collection of Indian primary sources translated into English.

Esposito, John. *Islam: The Straight Path.* 3rd ed. New York: Oxford University Press, 2005. Probably the best brief introduction to Islam available today.

Fernandez-Armesto, Felipe. *Civilizations: Culture, Ambition, and the Transformation of Nature.* New York: Free Press, 2001. A wide-ranging, superbly written discussion of the relationship between the earliest city-states and the environment.

————. *The World: A History.* Upper Saddle River, NJ: Pearson Prentice Hall, 2007. A ground-breaking single-volume history of the world.

Findley, Carter Vaughn. *The Turks in World History.* New York: Oxford University Press, 2005. A lucid account of the history of the Turkic peoples and their relationships with neighboring peoples.

Finkelstein, Israel, and Neil Asher Silberman. *The Bible Unearthed: Archaeology's New Vision of Ancient Israel and the Origin of Its Sacred Texts.* New York: Free Press, 2001. Compares the Hebrew scriptures concerning Israelite history with archaeological discoveries.

Finley, M. I. *Ancient Slavery and Modern Ideology.* Expanded ed. Princeton, NJ: Markus Wiener Publishers, 1998. Analyzes Greek and Roman slavery in the context of discussion about modern slavery.

Foltz, Richard C. *Spirituality in the Land of the Noble: How Iran Shaped the World's Religions.* London: Oneworld Publications, 2004. Excellent discussion of Zoroastrianism and its impact on world religions.

Foster, John L. *Ancient Egyptian Literature: An Anthology.* Austin: University of Texas Press, 2001. A useful and readable selection of literary works from ancient Egypt.

Franck, I. M., and D. M. Brownstone. *The Silk Roads: A History.* New York and Oxford: Oxford University Press, 1986. Sweeping and dynamic overview of the Silk Roads through world history.

Frye, Richard N. *The Heritage of Central Asia: From Antiquity to the Turkish Expansion.* Princeton, NJ: Markus Wiener Publishers, 1996. Terrific overview of the history of Iranian-speaking peoples in central Asia and Iran.

Garnsey, P. *Famine and Food Supply in the Greco-Roman World*. Cambridge: Cambridge University Press, 1988. Fascinating study of the often unreliable process of food acquisition in the ancient Mediterranean.

Gately, Iain. *Tobacco: The Story of How Tobacco Seduced the World*. New York: Grove Press, 2001. Lively account of the role of tobacco in world history.

Genet, Russell Merle. *Humanity: The Chimpanzees Who Would Be Ants*. Santa Margarita, CA: Collins Foundation Press, 2007. Compares the emergence of power and social relationships within human communities to social relationships between ants and chimpanzees.

George, Andrew, trans. *The Epic of Gilgamesh*. Rev ed. London: Penguin Classics, 2003. A fresh annotated translation of the most famous ancient Mesopotamian literary work.

Gillmor, Frances. *Flute of the Smoking Mirror: A Portrait of Nezahualcoyotl, Poet-King of the Aztecs*. Salt Lake City: University of Utah Press, 1983. First published 1949 by University of New Mexico Press. A collection with commentary of the work of this great Aztec poet.

Goldstone, Jack. *Why Europe? The Rise of the West in World History, 1500–1850*. Boston: McGraw-Hill, 2008. Fascinating analysis of the "rise of the West" and the often disastrous consequences of this for non-Western societies.

Gordon, C. D., ed. *The Age of Attila: Fifth-Century Byzantium and the Barbarians*. Ann Arbor: University of Michigan Press, 1972. Translations of primary sources on the society and history of nomadic and migratory peoples.

Grant, Frederick C., ed. *Hellenistic Religions: The Age of Syncretism*. Indianapolis: Bobbs-Merrill, 1953. Important collection of translated documents concerning the religious and philosophical beliefs of the Hellenistic era.

Guthrie, R. Dale. *The Nature of Paleolithic Art.* Chicago: University of Chicago Press, 2005. Examines Paleolithic art in the context of human physiology, sexuality, and preoccupations with food.

Halperin, Charles J. *Russia and the Golden Horde: The Mongol Impact on Medieval Russian History.* Bloomington: Indiana University Press, 1985. Thoughtful study of the Golden Horde and its influence on the development of Russian identity.

Hammond, N. G. L. *The Genius of Alexander the Great.* Chapel Hill: University of North Carolina Press, 1997. A classic work on Alexander of Macedon.

Harris, W. V., ed. *Rethinking the Mediterranean.* New York: Oxford Universiry Press, 2005. A collection of superb essays that explore regions bordering the Mediterranean in ancient times.

Hawass, Zahi. *Silent Images: Women in Pharaonic Egypt.* New York: Harry N. Abrams, Inc., 2000. Leading Egyptian archaeologist uses textual and archaeological evidence to try to understand the experience of women in ancient Egypt.

Headrick, Daniel R. *The Tools of Empire: Technology and European Imperialism in the Nineteenth Century.* New York: Oxford University Press, 1981. Important study of the relationship between technological evolution and imperialism in the 19th century.

————. *Technology: A World History.* Oxford: Oxford University Press, 2009. Masterful overview of the evolution of technology and its ongoing impact throughout world history.

Herrin, Judith. *Byzantium: The Surprising Life of a Medieval Empire.* Princeton, NJ: Princeton University Press, 2009. A thorough and insightful survey of Byzantine history.

Hiscock, Peter. *Archaeology of Ancient Australia*. London: Routledge, 2008. Thorough survey of the most important archaeological evidence for Australian aboriginal societies.

Hobsbawm, Eric. *Age of Extremes: The Short Twentieth Century, 1914–1991*. London: Little, Brown and Co., 1994. One of the classic studies of the 20th century from a master historian.

Hopkins, J. F. P., and N. Levtzion, eds. *Corpus of Early Arabic Sources for West African History*. Princeton, NJ: Markus Wiener Publishers, 2000. Translations of many of the most important primary-source accounts of West Africa by early Muslim merchants and geographers.

Horton, Mark, and John Middleton. *The Swahili: The Social Landscape of a Mercantile Society*. Oxford: Blackwell, 2000. Helpful account of Swahili culture using archaeological and written evidence.

Howe, K. R. *The Quest for Origins: Who First Discovered and Settled the Pacific Islands?* Honolulu: University of Hawai'i Press, 2003. A review of the multiple theories that have been offered to explain the great Polynesian migrations.

Huxley, Aldous. *Brave New World*. Harper & Brothers, 1932. Classic dystopian view of the future by one of the finest novelists of the 20th century.

Jackson, Peter. *The Mongols and the West, 1221–1410*. London: Routledge, 2005. Terrific review of military, diplomatic, commercial, and cultural relations between Mongol and European societies.

James, T. G. H. *Pharaoh's People: Scenes from Life in Imperial Egypt*. London: The Bodley Head, 1984. Draws on archaeological and literary scholarship in reconstructing daily life in ancient Egypt.

Johnson, A. W., and T. Earle. *The Evolution of Human Societies: From Foraging Group to Agrarian State*. 2nd ed. Stanford: Stanford University

Press, 2000. Comprehensive consideration of the transition from foraging to farming.

Kagan, Donald. *The Peloponnesian War.* New York: Viking, 2003. Outstanding account of this devastating war by its foremost contemporary scholar.

Kahn, Paul, ed. *The Secret History of the Mongols: The Origin of Chinggis Khan.* Adapted from the translation of F. W. Cleaves. San Francisco: North Point Press, 1984. A translation of the Mongols' history of the early stages of their own society.

Keightley, David N., ed. *The Origins of Chinese Civilization.* Berkeley: University of California Press, 1983. Classic collection of thoughtful articles on early Chinese society.

Kelekna, Pita. *The Horse in Human History.* Cambridge: Cambridge University Press, 2009. World history perspective on the role of the horse in human history.

Kelly, Christopher. *The Roman Empire: A Very Short Introduction.* New York: Oxford University Press, 2006. A concise but surprisingly comprehensive account of the empire and of its continuing influence on modern life in the form of Hollywood movies and contemporary political ideas.

Kemp, Barry J. *Ancient Egypt: Anatomy of a Civilization.* London and New York: Routledge, 1989. Comprehensive analysis of Egyptian culture and identity.

———. *Ancient Egypt: Anatomy of a Civilization.* 2nd ed. London and New York: Routledge, 2006. Superb overview of the great sweep of ancient Egyptian history.

Kenoyer, Jonathan Mark. *Ancient Cities of the Indus Valley Civilization.* Oxford: Oxford University Press, 1998. A well-illustrated investigation of archaeological evidence for the Indus cities.

Kenyon, K. *Digging Up Jericho*. London: Ernest Benn, 1957. A readable account of the unearthing of the long history of Jericho by the first major archaeologist to investigate the city.

Kirch, Patrick V. *On the Road of the Winds: An Archaeological History of the Pacific Islands before European Contact*. Berkeley: University of California Press, 2000. A valuable investigation of archaeological evidence for the peopling of the Pacific.

Kitch, P. V. *The Evolution of the Polynesian Chiefdoms*. Cambridge: Cambridge University Press, 1984. Scholarly political history of Polynesian societies.

Klein, Richard G. *The Dawn of Human Culture*. New York: Wiley, 2002. Considers the evolution of human consciousness in the context of evolutionary psychology.

Korten, David. *The Great Turning: From Empire to Earth Community*. San Francisco: Berrett-Koehler, 2006. Insightful argument in favor of a radical rethinking of the human relationship with the environment.

Lapidus, Ira M. *A History of Islamic Societies*. Cambridge: Cambridge University Press, 1988. Authoritative survey of Islamic history, concentrating on social and cultural issues.

Leick, Gwendolyn. *Mesopotamia: The Invention of the City*. London: Penguin, 2001. Focuses on the emergence and evolution of urban spaces in Mesopotamia.

Lewin, Roger. *Human Evolution: An Illustrated Introduction*. 5th ed. Malden, MA: Blackwell, 2005. A succinct and well-illustrated overview of the evolution of hominids and *Homo sapiens*.

Lewis, Mark Edward. *China's Cosmopolitan Empire: The Tang Dynasty*. Cambridge, MA: Belknap Press of Harvard University Press, 2009. Probably the best single volume available on China's mighty Tang dynasty.

———. *The Early Chinese Empires: Qin and Han.* Cambridge, MA: Belknap Press of Harvard University Press, 2007. Focuses on the long-term effects of dynastic rule established by the Qin and Han dynasties.

Lewis-Williams, D. *The Mind in the Cave: Consciousness and the Origin of Art.* London: Thames and Hudson, 2002. Thoughtful discussion of the intention behind the first art produced by our species.

Leys, Simon, trans. *The Analects of Confucius.* New York: W. W. Norton, 1997. Readable translation of the classic work of Confucianism.

Lichtenstadter, Ilse. *Introduction to Classical Arabic Literature.* New York: Schocken Books, 1974. A brief overview, accompanied by an extensive selection of texts in English translation.

Liu, Xinru. *The Silk Roads.* New York: Bedford/St. Martin's, 2010. Compelling narrative and interesting primary documents on the early history of the Silk Roads.

Loewe, Michael, and Edward L. Shaughnessy, eds. *The Cambridge History of Ancient China: From the Origins of Civilization to 221 B.C.* New York: Cambridge University Press, 1999. Contains 14 insightful essays by leading scholars of ancient China.

Lombard, M. *The Golden Age of Islam.* Princeton, NJ: Markus Wiener Publishers, 2004. Concentrates on the social and economic history of the glorious Abbasid period.

Lovelock, James. *The Vanishing Face of Gaia.* London: Penguin, 2010. The book in which Lovelock first made his argument in favor of thinking of the earth as a single, connected organism.

MacMullen, Ramsay. *Christianizing the Roman Empire.* New Haven, CT: Yale University Press, 1984. Scholarly study of the processes by which Christianity became established in the Roman empire.

————. *Romanization in the Time of Augustus*. New Haven, CT: Yale University Press, 2000. Considers the diffusion of a Roman lifestyle throughout the empire.

Mair, Victor H., Nancy S. Steinhardt, and Paul R. Goldin, eds. *Hawai`i Reader in Traditional Chinese Culture*. Honolulu: University of Hawai'i Press, 2005. Useful selection of primary sources in English translation.

Mallory, J. P. *In Search of the Indo-Europeans*. London: Thames & Hudson, 1991. Classic discussion of the possible origins and migrations of the Indo-Europeans.

Mallory, J. P., and Victor H. Mair. *The Tarim Mummies: Ancient China and the Mystery of the Earliest Peoples from the West*. London: Thames & Hudson, 2000. Careful and thoughtful analysis of the Indo-Europeans and their migration to western China.

Man, John. *Atlas of the Year 1000*. Cambridge, MA: Harvard University Press, 1999. Fascinating overview of a single year in a global context.

Mann, Charles C. *1491: New Revelations of the Americas before Columbus*. New York: Vintage Books, 2006. Superb summary of archaeological evidence for American societies on the eve of European arrival.

Marcus, Joyce. *Mesoamerican Writing Systems: Propaganda, Myth and History in Four Ancient Civilizations*. Princeton, NJ: Princeton University Press, 1992. A thoughtful survey of the evolution of writing systems in Mesoamerica.

Markale, Jean. *The Great Goddess: Reverence of the Divine Feminine from the Paleolithic to the Present*. Rochester, VT: Inner Traditions, 1999. Classic overview of the role of divine females from the first representations in the Paleolithic to the present.

Marks, Robert. *The Origins of the Modern World: A Global and Ecological Narrative from the Fifteenth to the Twenty-First Century*. 2nd ed. Lanham,

MD: Rowman and Littlefield, 2007. This is a superb and masterful world history overview of the key political developments over 600 years and their impact on the global environment.

Martin, Simon, and Nikolai Grube. *Chronicle of the Maya Kings and Queens: Deciphering the Dynasties of the Ancient Maya*. London: Thames & Hudson, 2000. Overview of Maya political history using both inscriptional and archaeological evidence.

Mascaró, Juan, trans. *The Upanishads*. London: Penguin Classics, 1965. Excellent English version of numerous Upanishads by a superb translator.

Mbiti, John S. *African Religions and Philosophy*. 2nd ed. London: Heinemann, 1990. Intelligent and systematic analysis of traditional African religions and cultures.

McAnany, Patricia A., and Norman Yoffee. *Questioning Collapse: Human Resilience, Ecological Vulnerability, and the Aftermath of Empire*. Cambridge: Cambridge University Press, 2010. A sustained analysis of the potential for ecological collapse but also of the ability of our species to perhaps avoid this.

McBrearty, Sally, and Alison S. Brooks. "The Revolution That Wasn't: A New Interpretation of the Origin of Modern Human Behavior." *Journal of Human Evolution* 39 (2000): 453–563. Two leading archaeologists of Paleolithic Africa argue cogently against the idea of the revolution of the Upper Paleolithic.

McCormick, Michael. *Origins of the European Economy: Communications and Commerce, A.D. 300–900*. Cambridge: Cambridge University Press, 2001. A comprehensive study focused on the role of early medieval Europe in the context of the Mediterranean economy.

McIntosh, Jane R. *A Peaceful Realm: The Rise and Fall of Indus Civilization*. New York: Westview, 2002. Readable and comprehensive account of evidence for the Indus civilization.

McIntosh, Roderick James. *The Peoples of the Middle Niger: The Island of Gold*. Oxford: Blackwell, 1998. Focuses on the connections between human cultures and the environment in West African history.

McNeill, William H. *The Shape of European History*. New York: Oxford University Press, 1974. A classic study of European history by one of the fathers of modern world history.

Miller, Walter M. *A Canticle for Leibowitz*. 1959. Reprint, New York: Bantam, 1997. Haunting and provocative science fiction story about the inevitability of human self-destruction.

Milner, George R., and W. H. Wills. "Complex Societies of North America." In *The Human Past: World Prehistory and the Development of Human Societies*, edited by Chris Scarre, 678–715. London: Thames & Hudson, 2013. Neat survey of major archaeological sites of North America.

Morgan, David. *The Mongols*. Oxford: Blackwell, 1986. Still the best short work available on the Mongols.

Moseley, Michael E. *The Incas and Their Ancestors: The Archaeology of Peru*. Rev. ed. London: Thames & Hudson, 2001. Excellent survey of the history of cultures and civilizations of the Andes.

Mote, Frederick W. *Intellectual Foundations of China*. 2nd ed. New York: Knopf, 1989. A classic account of the origins of Chinese philosophy, demonstrating a deep understanding of the intellectual underpinnings of Confucianism, Daoism, and Legalism.

Mueller, Richard A. *Physics for Future Presidents: The Science behind the Headlines*. New York and London: W. W. Norton, 2008. Helpful study for political leaders and general readers of the relationship between science and sensational news stories.

Nemet-Nejat, Karen Rhea. *Daily Life in Ancient Mesopotamia*. Westport, CT: Greenwood Press, 1998. A fascinating account of day-to-day life in the great urban centers of ancient Mesopotamia.

Niane, D. T., ed. *Sundiata: An Epic of Old Mali.* 2nd ed. Trans. by G. D. Pickett. London: Pearson, 2006. Translation of the oral legend of Sundiata, founder of the Mali empire.

Nissen, Hans J., and Peter Heine. *From Mesopotamia to Iraq: A Concise History.* Chicago: University of Chicago Press, 2009. An authoritative history of Mesopotamia in the context of the longer history of Iraq.

Orwell, George. *1984.* New York: Harcourt, Brace and Company, 1949. A classic dystopian novel about the future by this brilliant British intellectual.

Penna, Anthony N. *The Human Footprint: A Global Environmental History.* Oxford: Wiley-Blackwell, 2010. An ambitious book that charts the impact of human societies on the environment from the Paleolithic to the present.

Pomeranz, Kenneth. *The Great Divergence: Europe, China, and the Making of the Modern World Economy.* Princeton, NJ: Princeton University Press, 2000. A classic analysis of the different trajectories followed by China and the West in the 19th and 20th centuries.

Pomeranz, Kenneth, and Steven Topik. *The World That Trade Created: Society, Culture, and the World Economy, 1400 to the Present.* 2nd ed. Armonk, ME: Sharpe, 2006. A classic study on the role of expanding commerce in creating the modern world.

Pomeroy, Sarah B. *Goddesses, Whores, Wives, and Slaves: Women in Classical Antiquity.* New York: Schocken Books, 1975. Outstanding study of the status and role of women in classical Greece and Rome.

Possehl, Gregory. *The Indus Civilization.* Walnut Creek, CA: AltaMira Press, 2002. A fine summary of recent historical interpretations of the Indus civilization by a leading specialist.

Ratnagar, Shereen. *Trading Encounters: From the Euphrates to the Indus in the Bronze Age*. New Delhi: Oxford University Press, 2004. Uses archaeology to discuss commercial relations between the Indus and Mesopotamian civilizations.

Richards, John. *The Unending Frontier: An Environmental History of the Early Modern World*. Berkeley: University of California Press, 2003. A superb history of the world from an environmental perspective.

Richards, Julian D. *The Vikings: A Very Short Introduction*. Oxford: Oxford University Press, 2005. A concise but amazingly comprehensive and up-to-date view of the role of the Vikings in world history.

Ringrose, David. *Expansion and Global Interaction, 1200–1700*. New York: Longman, 2001. A thoughtful study of the development of a genuine global political economy during the early modern era.

Risso, Patricia. *Merchants and Faith: Muslim Commerce and Culture in the Indian Ocean*. Boulder, CO: Westview Press, 1995. A survey of the activities of Muslim merchants in the Indian Ocean basin from the 7th to the 19th century.

Ristvet, L. *In the Beginning: World History from Human Evolution to the First States*. New York: McGraw-Hill, 2007. A succinct and very readable overview of the earliest periods in human history.

Roaf, Michael. *Cultural Atlas of Mesopotamia and the Ancient Near East*. New York: Facts on File, 1990. Richly illustrated volume with thoughtful essays on various aspects of Mesopotamian history.

Robinson, Francis, ed. *The Cambridge Illustrated History of the Islamic World*. Cambridge: Cambridge University Press, 1996. A beautifully illustrated introduction to Islam and the Muslim world.

Roehrig, Catharine H., Renée Dreyfus, and Cathleen A. Keller, eds. *Hatshepsut: From Queen to Pharaoh*. New York: The Metropolitan Museum of Art, 2005. Superbly illustrated study of the reign of the New Kingdom's famous female pharaoh.

Rossabi, Morris. *Khubilai Khan: His Life and Times.* Berkeley: University of California Press, 1988. Scholarly but eminently readable study of the founder and great ruler of the Mongol Yuan dynasty in China.

Roston, Eric. *The Carbon Age: How Life's Core Element Has Become Civilization's Greatest Threat.* New York: Walker & Co., 2008. Excellent study of the long relationship between human societies and fossil fuels.

Ruddiman, William. *Plows, Plagues, and Petroleum: How Humans Took Control of Climate.* Princeton, NJ: Princeton University Press, 2005. An extraordinary deep history overview of the relationship between humans and the environment from the earliest periods of human history to the present.

Sachs, Jeffrey D. *Common Wealth: Economics for a Crowded Planet.* New York: Penguin, 2008. New thinking about economics in an age of massive human population growth and environmental stress.

Scarre, C., ed. *The Human Past: World Prehistory and the Development of Human Societies.* London: Thames & Hudson, 2005. A very helpful collection of chapters by leading specialists on the Paleolithic and Neolithic eras of human history.

Schick, Kathy D., and Nicholas Toth. *Making Silent Stones Speak: Human Evolution and the Dawn of Technology.* New York: Simon and Schuster, 1993. Leading specialists offer this fascinating examination of Paleolithic stone tools.

Schirokauer, Conrad, et al. *A Brief History of Chinese and Japanese Civilizations.* 3rd ed. New York: Wadsworth Publishing, 2006. Written by a team of experts, this is a sweeping overview of the history of Chinese and Japanese culture, with a particular emphasis on art, religion, philosophy, and literature.

Schmandt-Besserat, Denise. *How Writing Came About: Handbook to Life in Ancient Mesopotamia*. Austin, TX: University of Texas Press, 1996. Thoughtful and comprehensive account of the evolution of cuneiform writing in ancient Mesopotamia.

Sherwin-White, Susan, and Amélie Kuhrt. *From Samarkhand to Sardis: A New Approach to the Seleucid Empire*. Berkeley: University of California Press, 1993. Detailed consideration of the political and economic history of the Hellenistic Seleucid empire.

Shipley, Graham. *The Greek World after Alexander*. London: Routledge, 2000. Excellent and sweeping work in the field that has become a standard reference work.

Smith, B. *The Emergence of Agriculture*. New York: Scientific American Library, 1995. An early but still relevant discussion of why some groups of humans made the transition to agriculture.

Smith, Michael E. *The Aztecs*. 2nd ed. Malden, MA: Blackwell, 2003. Terrific history of Aztec history and culture.

Sourvinou-Inwood, Christiane. *Athenian Myths and Festivals*. Oxford: Oxford University Press, 2011. Authoritative discussion of the key festivals in the Athenian calendar and their relationship with Greek myths.

Spier, Fred. *Big History and the Future of Humanity*. Chichester, West Sussex, England: Wiley-Blackwell, 2010. A superb account of the big history narrative, with a particular emphasis on the future.

Stableford, Brian, and David Langford. *The Third Millennium: A History of the World, AD 2000–3000*. London: Sidgwick and Jackson, 1985. Science writers consider potential technological developments in the future.

Staccioli, Romolo Augusto. *The Roads of the Romans*. Los Angeles: J. Paul Getty Museum, 2003. A well-illustrated volume that surveys the entire Roman road system.

Stearns, Peter. *Globalization in World History*. London and New York: Routledge, 2010. One of the most prolific contemporary world historians traces the process of globalization by examining major changes in global interactions since 1000 C.E.

Stearns, Peter, et al. *Documents in World History, Vol 1*. 4th ed. Upper Saddle River, NJ: Prentice Hall, 2006. An excellent collection of primary sources from the ancient world.

Strayer, R. *Ways of the World: A Global History*. New York: Bedford/St. Martin's, 2009. A superb single-volume history of the world.

Thapar, Romila. *Early India: From the Origins to A.D. 1300*. Berkeley: University of California Press, 2003. Sweeping overview of ancient Indian history by one of the leading specialists in the field.

Thorp, Robert L. *China in the Early Bronze Age: Shang Civilization*. Philadelphia: University of Pennsylvania Press, 2006. Uses archaeological studies to investigate the history of the Shang dynasty.

Toner, J. *Popular Culture in Ancient Rome*. Cambridge, MA: Polity, 2009. A short and readable account of popular culture and attitudes in ancient Rome.

Tucker, Jonathan. *The Silk Road: Art and History*. London: Philip Wilson Publishers, 2003. Lavishly illustrated volume exploring the history and geography of the Silk Roads.

van de Mieroop, Marc. *A History of the Ancient Near East, ca. 3000–323 B.C.* Oxford: Blackwell, 2004. A concise and readable history of the civilizations of the Mesopotamian region over 3,000 years.

Vansina, Jan. *Paths in the Rainforests: Toward a History of Political Tradition in Equatorial Africa*. Madison: University of Wisconsin Press, 1990. Masterful overview of the early history of sub-Saharan Africa.

Wade, Nicholas. *Before the Dawn: Recovering the Lost History of Our Ancestors.* New York: Penguin, 2006. Sweeping study of human physical and psychological evolution.

Wagar, Warren. *A Short History of the Future.* 3rd ed. Chicago: University of Chicago Press, 1999. A thoughtful consideration of the future.

Waldron, Arthur. *The Great Wall of China: From History to Myth.* Cambridge: Cambridge University Press, 1989. Sweeping overview of the history of the Great Wall from the Qin dynasty to the present.

Watson, Burton, trans. *Records of the Grand Historian.* Rev. ed. 2 vols. New York: Columbia University Press, 1993. A classic translation of Sima Qian's great work, the *Shiji,* certainly the most important narrative source for ancient Chinese history.

Webster, David. *The Fall of the Ancient Maya: Solving the Mystery of the Maya Collapse.* London: Thames & Hudson, 2002. Scholarly but readable consideration of the causes of the collapse of Maya society.

Weisner-Hanks, M. *Gender in History: New Perspectives on the Past.* Oxford: Blackwell, 2001. A fascinating study of the role of gender in world history by one of the leading proponents of the field.

Welsby, Derek A. *The Kingdom of Kush: The Napatan and Meroitic Empires.* London: British Museum Press, 1996. Draws on both written and archaeological sources in tracing the development of ancient Nubia and its often stormy relationship with Egypt.

Whitfield, Susan. *Life along the Silk Road.* Berkeley, 1999. Focuses on the experiences of 10 individuals who lived or traveled along the Silk Roads.

Whittow, Mark. *The Making of Byzantium, 600–1025.* Berkeley: University of California Press, 1996. This excellent study focuses on relations between Byzantium and neighboring societies.

Wolf, Eric. *Europe and the People without History*. Berkeley, CA: University of California Press, 1982. A superb anthropological study of the origins and evolution of the many peoples that would eventually constitute European civilization.

Wolfe, Michael, ed. *One Thousand Roads to Mecca: Ten Centuries of Travelers Writing about the Muslim Pilgrimage*. New York: Grove Press, 1997. Presents selections from 23 accounts describing travelers' experiences undertaking the hajj.

Wolpert, Stanley. *A New History of India*. 7th ed. New York: Oxford University Press, 2004. A concise and readable survey of the complete history of India.

Wood, Francis. *The Silk Road: Two Thousand Years in the Heart of Asia*. Berkeley: University of California Press, 2002. A brilliantly illustrated volume discussing the history of the Silk Roads from antiquity to the 20th century.

Wright, G. A. "Social Differentiation in the Early Natufian." In *Social Archaeology: Beyond Subsistence and Dating*, edited by C. L. Bergman, et al., 201–230. New York: Academic Press, 1978. Discusses archaeological evidence for the emergence of social hierarchies at many Natufian sites.

Zalasiewicz, Jan, et al. "Are We Now Living in the Anthropocene?" *Geological Society of America* 18, no. 2 (Feb. 2009): 4–8. A short paper in which the author follows up on Paul Crutzen's arguments for renaming our era the Anthropocene.

IMAGE CREDITS

Page 162: © thelefty/iStock/Thinkstock.

Page 171: © DVB60/iStock/Thinkstock.

Page 178: © Crisfotolux/iStock/Thinkstock.

Page 182: © JSSIII/iStock/Thinkstock.

Page 189: © RNMitra/iStock/Thinkstock.

Page 199: © Leonid Andronov/iStock/Thinkstock.

Page 205: © SonerCdem/iStock/Thinkstock.

Page 209: © zaihan/iStock/Thinkstock.

Page 213: © heckepics/iStock/Thinkstock.

Page 217: © bwzenith/iStock/Thinkstock.

Page 225: © venturecx/iStock/Thinkstock.

Page 232: © fotoember/iStock/Thinkstock.

Page 235: © f9photos/iStock/Thinkstock.

Page 241: © DC_Colombia/iStock/Thinkstock.

Page 244: © aronaze/iStock/Thinkstock.

Page 248: © Oleg Seleznev/iStock/Thinkstock.

Page 251: © Siempreverde22/iStock/Thinkstock.

Page 259: © SheraleeS/iStock/Thinkstock.

Page 275: © Thomas_Marchhart/iStock/Thinkstock.

Page 278: © robvs/iStock/Thinkstock.

Page 285: © Ivan Cholakov/iStock/Thinkstock.

Page 289: © fergregory/iStock/Thinkstock.

Page 295: © draco-zlat/iStock/Thinkstock.

Page 304: © Sergydv/iStock/Thinkstock.